Thoughts & Feelings:

The Art of Cognitive Stress Intervention

By Matthew McKay, Ph.D.

Martha Davis, Ph.D.

Patrick Fanning

Grateful acknowledgement is
made to Norman Cavior, Ph.D.,
our teacher, and the one
who first introduced us to
cognitive behavioral techniques.
His editorial work has been
an essential component
of this book.

We are also grateful to
Kirk Johnson for his
intelligent and insightful
editing of the text.

First printing August 1981, 3,000 copies
Second printing December 1981, 10,000 copies
Third printing February 1983, 10,000 copies
Fourth printing December 1984, 10,000 copies
Fifth printing July 1987, 10,000 copies
Sixth printing November 1989, 3,000 copies
Seventh printing November 1990, 3,000 copies
Eighth printing August 1991, 5,000 copies

Contents

How to Use This Book

These Cognitive Stress Intervention techniques are presented in workbook format so that, with the possible exception of Paradoxical Intention, you can practice them without the assistance of a therapist or instructor.

Be sure to read chapters one and two first. They are the foundation of the book. After you have read the first two chapters, you will know enough about how thoughts and feelings create your stress syndrome to decide which techniques will be most beneficial for you.

This book is particularly useful if you work with people who are in stress. Therapists, doctors, nurses, teachers, or supervisors will find many of these techniques not only of use in their personal lives, but also of help to their clients, patients, students, or employees.

The full benefits of Cognitive Stress Interventions can only be realized after regular practice for some time. Intellectual understanding of most techniques is of little value without first hand experience. Therefore, if you plan to use stress interventions in a professional setting to help others, first try the techniques yourself.

The length of time required each day to practice a particular stress intervention will vary. You should spend some time doing the exercises daily. If doing exercises daily seems too difficult, schedule one or two holidays a week—but don't just let them happen. Regular practice will enable you to use stress intervention skills any time you need to, without referring to written materials. Practice will also develop new patterns of thought and behavior that will gradually become automatic.

When learning these techniques, choose a quiet place where you will not be disturbed. Explain to others around you what you are doing and ask them to help you by leaving you alone without distractions. Friends, relatives and others are usually quite understanding once you explain what you are doing.

If you have poor self-discipline or are not highly motivated, make a contract with another person as described in the last chapter. That way you can report your experiences and receive encouragement.

If your stress syndrome involves physical symptoms such as stomach problems, high blood pressure, or frequent headaches, get a checkup before practicing Cognitive Stress Intervention. If you experience any prolonged physical ill effects once you start, consult your physician.

Chapter 1

Stress Syndromes and Symptoms

This book is about emotional pain and how to stop it. It is about interventions that short-circuit stress. A stress syndrome is defined here as a combination of three elements: your environment, your negative thoughts, and your physical responses. These interact in specific ways to make you feel anxious, angry, or depressed.

Almost anyone feeling emotional pain will try tracing back to its cause. Usually the environment is blamed. The lists of negative and positive events seem to determine emotional climate. You can often go back to "what happened" or "how it started." But this is a delusion and language helps create the delusion. Consider statements such as "It scared me stiff...He makes me see red...I've got the Monday morning blahs." The implication is that your feelings directly result from environmental stimuli. The truth is that events in the world are only the first step in your stress syndrome. You also need thoughts which label and interpret those events, and a physical response which you interpret as a particular emotion.

Stress brings distress. The events, your thoughts, and your body's arousal constitute a stress syndrome. The result is distress: a painful emotion. If you label an event as dangerous, if you interpret your body's reaction as fear, then you will *feel* afraid. Examine the experience of falling in love. Falling in love can be painful, but the pain doesn't result directly from an intense and novel event. It occurs when you say to yourself, "What if I'm left" or "What if it doesn't work out, what if I get trapped?" When these statements also accompany increased physical tension, which you interpret as anxiety, you are likely to feel anxious.

There are two basic formulas for a stress syndrome:

1. Environmental stimulus → physiological arousal → negative thoughts = painful emotions

2. Environmental stimulus → negative thoughts → physiological arousal = painful emotions

Stress Formula One

In Formula One, an environmental stimulus (flat tire) leads to physiological arousal (tension and exertion changing flat), followed by a negative interpretation of the arousal ("I must be angry"), and finally a painful emotion (anger). The painful emotion depends on your label for any arousal felt inside your body.

Stress Formula One was introduced by Stanley Schachter's *Attribution Theory*. In 1962 Schachter and Singer conducted a classic experiment that has greatly influenced how psychologists view emotions. They administered adrenalin injections to a subject who was told that the drug was Suproxin, a new vitamin compound. The subject was then placed in a waiting room for 15 to 20 minutes. A stooge, supposedly just Suproxin injected, was brought in to pass the waiting time with the subject. A short while after the adrenalin injection the subject experienced typical nervous system arousal: hand tremors, heart pounding, and rapid breathing. As the adrenalin took effect the stooge began behaving in one of two ways. He either became progressively more angry or he became increasingly euphoric and playful. During this period the subject was watched through a two-way mirror and his behavior was observed and systematically recorded. It was found that those subjects who had waited with the angry stooge became angry, and those who waited with the euphoric stooge became euphoric. Schachter also discovered that subjects with a saline placebo had no emotional reaction, no matter how the stooge functioned. And subjects who were warned in advance that Suproxin sometimes had side effects of trembling and heart pounding had no emotional reaction, regardless of the stooge's behavior.

Schachter made the following conclusions from his experiment:

1. Emotion is not merely a physiological event, a chemical reaction in the body which automatically creates feelings. Physiological arousal, by itself, cannot produce emotions.

2. A state of physiological arousal for which you have no immediate explanation makes you want to evaluate and understand it. This causes you to actively search your environment for an appropriate explanation or "label" for the arousal. Choice of labels will determine the emotional response.

Emotion is therefore created by your evaluations of internal and external events. Subjects in the study attributed their arousal to either anger or euphoria depending on what appeared to be appropriate, i.e. the emotional reaction of the stooge. If the stooge was angry they interpreted the adrenalin reaction as anger and thereafter expressed and reported feeling angry.

To take a simple example, a man hit on the head with a coconut may, when he gets up from the ground, feel irritated that he has to endure a lump and a headache. He may look up, observe that the grove is ripe with coconuts, and develop

Negative Feedback Loop

In the stress syndrome a negative feedback loop is created between mind and body. Each influences and reacts to the other in an escalating pattern of arousal. Here's how it works: In Stress Formula One, your body tenses and you think, "I must be getting anxious." Your body then reacts to the belief that you are anxious by becoming more aroused. You notice your heart rate increasing and think, "I'm going to freak out." This results in more physiological arousal, plus increasingly dire assessments and predictions about your experience. As this dialogue between mind and body unfolds, you begin, in fact, to feel afraid.

The feedback loop in Stress Formula Two has a similar pattern. You interpret an event as dangerous by saying to yourself, "I'm in trouble now, I could get hurt." Your body reacts to this thought with a typical alarm response: heart pounding, tightened gut, sweating. You interpret the arousal as further evidence for alarm. You think, "Oh God, this is awful." Your body gets the message that there is increased danger. And so it goes, a steady escalation until you feel thoroughly frightened.

To break a negative feedback loop you have to change your thoughts, your physical responses, or you must alter the situation which triggered an alarm reaction.

Cognitive Stress Intervention

Cognitive Stress Intervention is the art of using your head. Each of the exercises in this book is a method of self instruction that can help you change how you respond to the world.

In the beginning a stress syndrome was defined as a combination of three elements: your environment, your negative thoughts, and your physical responses. You can short-circuit stress by intervening and changing any one of these elements. Some of the techniques are specifically designed to change how you behave so you can effectively alter your environment. Several of the chapters will teach you self instructions to change how you think. You will learn how to restructure old thought patterns that chronically breed anxiety, anger, and depression. Some chapters focus on ways of telling your body to relax. You can learn to short-circuit stress by calming your alarm response and loosening tight muscles.

Wherever you intervene in the stress syndrome you are acting to break the negative feedback loop. Negative thoughts and physical arousal can no longer escalate into painful emotions. And you have taken a major step toward changing your emotional life.

Symptoms Checklist

The major objective of this book is to help you achieve symptom relief using Cognitive Stress Intervention. So that you can determine exactly which symptoms you want to work on, complete the following checklist. This checklist will tell you a great deal about how you respond to stress. Depending on the nature of your unique stress syndromes, some techniques will be more helpful to you than others.

After you have used this book to master the Cognitive Stress Intervention techniques that work best for you, return to this checklist and use it to measure your symptom relief.

Rate your stress syndrome-related symptoms below for the degree of discomfort they cause you, using this 10-point scale:

Slight Discomfort			Moderate Discomfort				Extreme Discomfort		
1	2	3	4	5	6	7	8	9	10

Symptom (Disregard those you don't experience)	Degree of Discomfort (1-10) Now	Degree of Discomfort (1-10) after Mastering Cognitive Stress Intervention
Anxiety in specific situations		
tests.	_____	_____
deadlines.	_____	_____
interviews.	_____	_____
other _____	_____	_____
Anxiety in personal relationships		
spouse.	_____	_____
parents	_____	_____
children.	_____	_____
other _____	_____	_____
Anxiety, general—regardless of the situation or the people involved.	_____	_____

Symptom	Degree of Discomfort (1-10) Now	Degree of Discomfort (1-10) after Mastering Cognitive Stress Intervention
Depression	_____	_____
Hopelessness	_____	_____
Powerlessness	_____	_____
Poor self-esteem	_____	_____
Hostility	_____	_____
Anger	_____	_____
Irritability	_____	_____
Resentment	_____	_____
Phobias — specify object or situation:		
_____	_____	_____
_____	_____	_____
Obsessions, unwanted thoughts	_____	_____
Muscular tension	_____	_____
Procrastination	_____	_____
Overeating	_____	_____
Smoking	_____	_____
Problem drinking	_____	_____
Gambling	_____	_____
Overspending	_____	_____
Physical pain/illness	_____	_____
Compulsions	_____	_____
Insomnia	_____	_____
Sleeping difficulties	_____	_____
Unwanted sexual fantasies	_____	_____
Unwanted sexual behavior	_____	_____
Perfectionism	_____	_____
Ineffective problem solving	_____	_____

(A note about guilt: Guilt has not been included in the symptom checklist because it is a hybrid emotion. Guilt is usually a combination of anxiety and anger. You are afraid you'll be rejected for your actions, or that you'll lose esteem in your own eyes. You also may feel angry with the person who "makes you feel guilty.")

Symptom Effectiveness Chart

Having identified the symptoms related to your stress syndromes, you can now choose the one or two symptoms that bother you most and select the techniques that you will use to relieve them. Since everyone is unique, it is impossible to dictate which Cognitive Stress Intervention technique will work best for you. However, this chart will give you a general idea of what to try first and where to go from there.

Chapter headings for each technique are across the top and typical symptoms

	Combating Distorted Thinking	Covert Assertion	Problem Solving	Systematic Desensitization	Stress Inoculation
Anxiety in specific situations (tests, deadlines, interviews, etc.)		X	x	X	X
Anxiety in your personal relationships (spouse, parents, children, etc.)	X	x	X	x	X
Anxiety, general (regardless of the situation or the people involved)	X				x
Depression, hopelessness, powerlessness, poor self-esteem	X	X	X		
Hostility, anger, irritability, resentment	X	x	x		X
Phobias		x		X	x
Obsessions, unwanted thoughts		X			
Muscular tension				X	
Procrastination			x		
Habits (overeating, smoking, problem drinking, gambling, overspending)					
Physical pain / illness					
Compulsions					
Insomnia, sleeping difficulties		X			
Unwanted sexual fantasies or behavior					
Perfectionism	X	x			
Ineffective problem solving			X		

are listed down the side. You may have only one or several of these symptoms. The most effective techniques for a particular symptom are marked with a boldface X, while other helpful techniques for that same symptom are indicated by a lighter x.

Important: Physical symptoms may have purely physiological causes. You should have a medical doctor eliminate the possibility of such physical problems before you proceed on the assumption that your symptoms are completely stress-related.

Before you move to the chapter on the technique that most interests you, read chapter two. Practice in uncovering your automatic thoughts is a prerequisite to the successful application of nearly all the techniques in this book.

Covert Desensitization	Visualization	Covert Reinforcement	Covert Modeling	Values Clarification	Paradoxical Intention	Orgasmic Reconditioning
		X	X	x		
			x	X		
				x		
		x	x	x		
			x	x		
		X	x			
	x					
		X	X	x		
X						
	x					
x						
x						X
			X	x		

Further Reading

Beck, A. **Depression: Clinical, Experimental, and Theoretical Aspects.** New York: Hoeber, 1967.

London, H. and Nisbett, R. **Thought and Feeling.** Chicago: Aldine Publishing, 1974.

Schachter, S. and Singer, J. E. "Cognitive, Social and Physiological Determinants of Emotional State." **Psychological Review.** 69, 1962, 379-99.

Valins, S. "Cognitive Effects of False Heart Rate Feedback." **Journal of Personality and Social Psychology.** 4, 1966, 400-8.

Valins, S. and Ray, A. A. "Effects of Cognitive Desensitization on Avoidance Behavior." **Journal of Personality and Social Psychology.** 7, 1967, 345-50.

Chapter 2

Uncovering Your Automatic Thoughts

In a crowded theater a woman suddenly stands up, slaps the face of the man next to her, and hurries down the aisle to an exit door. Each person watching the event reacts in his own, idiosyncratic way. One woman is frightened, a teenager is angry, a middle-aged man becomes depressed, a social worker feels a pleasurable excitement. Why did the same event trigger very different emotions throughout the audience? The answer can be found by examining the thoughts of each observer.

The fearful woman thought, "He's going to go after her when they get home, and then she's really going to get it." She imagined the details of a brutal beating and recalled times when she had been physically abused. The angry teenager thought, "He just wanted a kiss and she humiliated him. That poor guy, she must really be a bitch." The middle-aged man who reacted with sadness thought, "Now he's lost her and he'll never get her back." He could see his ex-wife's face set in angry lines. The social worker felt a delicious pleasure as she thought, "Serves him right. What a strong woman—I wish some timid women I know had seen that."

In every case the observer's emotion was a consequence of his or her thoughts. The event was interpreted, judged, and labeled in such a way that a particular emotional response was inevitable. You are constantly describing the world to yourself, giving each event or experience some label. You make interpretations of what you see and hear, you judge events as good or bad, painful or pleasurable, you predict whether they will bring danger or relative safety.

These labels and judgments are fashioned from the unending dialogue you have with yourself, and color all your experience with private meanings. The dialogue has been compared to a waterfall of thoughts cascading down the back of your mind. The thoughts are constant and rarely noticed, but they are powerful enough to create your most intense emotions. The internal dialogue has been called "self talk" by Rational Emotive therapist Albert Ellis, and "automatic thoughts" by cognitive theorist Aaron Beck. Beck prefers the term automatic thoughts "because it more accurately describes the way thoughts are experienced. The person perceives these thoughts as though they are by reflex—without any prior reflection or reasoning; and they impress him as plausible and valid." (Beck, 1976, p. 237)

Most people talk to others very differently from the way they talk to themselves. To others they usually describe events in their lives as a rational sequence of cause and effect. But they may at the same time talk to themselves with a horrifying or self-depreciating venom. One executive explained aloud, "Shortly after losing my job, I found myself getting increasingly depressed." What nobody else heard were the thoughts that unemployment triggered: "I'll never be able to provide for my family again...Nobody would hire me...I'm a failure...Can't make it." No matter how unrealistic these overgeneralizations may be, the executive believed them at the moment he said them to himself.

Automatic thoughts usually have the following characteristics:

1. **They are specific, discrete messages.** A young man who fears rejection tells himself, "She doesn't want you. You look silly." A woman who fears death simply says the word "hearse." A stock broker says "gone" to himself to generate depression about a financial loss.

2. **Automatic thoughts often appear in shorthand,** composed of just a few essential words or a brief visual image. A woman who was afraid of heights had a half-second image of the floor tilting and felt herself sliding down toward the window. This momentary fantasy triggered acute anxiety whenever she ascended above three floors. The shorthand is often phrased in telegraphic style: "lonely...getting sick...can't stand it...cancer...no good." One word or a short phrase functions as a label for a group of painful memories, fears, or self reproaches. Sometimes the automatic thought is a brief reconstruction of some event in the past. A depressed woman kept seeing the stairway in Macy's where her husband had first announced his plan to leave her. The image of the stairway was enough to unleash all the feelings associated with that loss.

3. **Automatic thoughts, no matter how irrational, are almost always believed.** A man who reacted with rage to the death of his best friend was able to think for a time that the death was deliberately done to punish him. These thoughts have the same believable quality as direct sense impressions. The same truth value is attached to automatic thoughts as to your perceptions of the external world. If you see a man getting into a Porsche and have the thought, "He's rich, he doesn't care for anyone but himself," the judgment is as real to you as your visual impression of the man climbing into the car. Automatic thoughts are plausible because they are hardly noticed, let alone questioned or challenged. They simply don't get tested, nor are their implications and conclusions submitted to logical analysis.

4. **Automatic thoughts are experienced as spontaneous.** They just pop into the mind—insidious, sometimes undermining labels or judgments that seem true.

5. **Automatic thoughts are often couched in terms of should, ought, or must.** A recent widow thought, "You have to go it alone, you can't burden your friends." Each time the thought popped into her mind she felt a wave of hopelessness. People torture themselves with "shoulds" such as, "I should be happy...I should be more energetic, creative, responsible, loving, generous." Each ironclad "should" precipitates a sense of guilt or loss of self-esteem.

6. **Automatic thoughts tend to "awfulize."** These thoughts predict catastrophe, see danger in everything, and always expect the worst. A stomach ache is a symptom of cancer, the look of distraction in a lover's face is the first sign of withdrawal. Awfulizers are the major source of anxiety.

7. **Automatic thoughts are relatively idiosyncratic.** In the initial example, where a woman slapped her companion and left the theater, everyone had a different response. Each response was based on a unique way of viewing the stimulus situation and resulted in a different strong emotion.

8. **Automatic thoughts are hard to turn off.** Because they are reflexive and plausible, automatic thoughts weave unnoticed through the fabric of your internal dialogue. They seem to come and go with a will of their own. They also tend to act as cues for each other. Everyone has had the experience of one depressing thought triggering a long chain of associated depressing thoughts.

9. **Automatic thoughts are learned.** Since childhood people have been telling you what to think. You have been conditioned by family, friends, and the media to interpret events a certain way.

Tunnel Vision

Chronic anger, anxiety, or depression result from a focus on one particular group of automatic thoughts, and the exclusion of all contrary thoughts. People who are anxious are preoccupied with the anticipation of danger. They create spectres of future pain. Depressed individuals obsess about losses they have already sustained. Chronically angry people are preoccupied with the unacceptable and malicious behavior of others.

Each preoccupation creates a kind of tunnel vision in which you think only one kind of thought and notice only one aspect of your environment. The result is one predominant and usually quite painful emotion. Beck has used the term *selective abstraction* in his examination of tunnel vision. Selective abstraction means looking at one set of cues in your environment to the exclusion of all others. Tunnel vision is the foundation of most neurosis.

To achieve tunnel vision you should do the following:

- Never notice your automatic thoughts.
- Unquestioningly believe your automatic thoughts.
- If anxious, keep your focus on danger.
- If depressed, devalue yourself and think of loss.
- If angry, focus on injustice and the wrongness of others.

Listening to Your Automatic Thoughts

Hearing your automatic thoughts is the first step in gaining control of unpleasant emotions. Most of your internal dialogue is innocuous. The automatic thoughts which cause harm, however, can be identified because they almost always precede a continuing painful emotion.

To identify the automatic thoughts which are causing continued painful feelings, try to recall the thoughts you had just prior to the start of the emotion and those that go along with the sustained emotion. You can think of it as listening in on an intercom. The intercom is always on, even while you are conversing with others and going about your life. You are functioning in the world and you are also talking to yourself at the same time. Listen in on the intercom of your internal dialogue, and hear what you are telling yourself. The automatic thoughts are assigning private, idiosyncratic meanings to many external events. They are making judgments and interpretations of your experience.

The automatic thoughts are often lightning fast and very difficult to catch. They flash on as a brief mental image, or are telegraphed in a single word. Here are two methods for coping with the swiftness of your thoughts:

1. Reconstruct a problem situation, going over and over it in your imagination until the painful emotion begins to emerge. What are you thinking as the emotion comes up? Regard your thoughts as a slow motion film. Look at your internal dialogue, frame by frame. Notice the millisecond it takes to say, "I can't stand it" or the half-second image of a terrifying event. Notice how you are internally describing and interpreting the actions of others: "She's bored...He's putting me down."

2. Stretch out the shorthand statement into the original sentence from which it was extracted. "Feeling sick" is really "I'm feeling sick and I know I'm going to get worse...I can't stand it." "Crazy" means "I feel like I'm losing control, and that must mean I'm going crazy ..my friends will reject me." Hearing the shorthand isn't enough. It is necessary to listen to the entire syllogism in order to understand the distorted logic from which your painful emotions bloom.

Thoughts Diary

To appreciate the power or your automatic thoughts and the part they play in your emotional life, make your own thoughts diary. Make a notation each time you experience an unpleasant emotion. Include everything you tell yourself to keep the emotion going. A bookkeeper kept the following diary on a very busy Friday.

Time	Emotion	Situation	Automatic thoughts	How true now	How true at bedtime
9:15	anger	Stuck on freeway	Late . . . Boss angry . . . last one in . . . have to rush all day.	90%	40%
10:30	anxiety	Given additional work	I'll be here all night . . . can't stand it . . . Jenny'll be mad if I'm late.	100%	30%
11:50	anxiety	Computer breaks down	I'll never get it done now . . . Oh God . . . I should work faster or he'll get angry.	100%	55%
12:30	anxiety	Have to work through lunch	My stomach is really going to hurt . . . I can't stand this.	80%	20%
4:00	anger	More work comes in	Why don't these jerks get enough help . . . this is too much for one person.	100%	60%
5:00	anxiety	Working late, have to call wife	She's going to really blow up.	100%	0%
7:45	depression	Driving home	This is my whole life . . . there's no way out of this.	100%	35%
9:00	depression	Watching TV with kids	They never talk to me . . . they hardly know me . . . they don't care.	75%	15%
10:45	depression	Wife goes to sleep early	She really is mad . . . she's disgusted with me.	80%	40%

Just before going to sleep, the bookkeeper went over his thoughts diary. He filled in the percentages of how true each automatic thought felt now, hours later. He noticed that the thoughts always seemed believable when they first came up, but later felt much less true. After several days of keeping the diary, he felt increasing distrust for his automatic thoughts. They seemed terribly distorted when he reflected on them late at night. Moreover, he noticed that his painful emotions always seemed to be associated with these same distorted judgments and perceptions.

Use your thoughts diary for one week, making an entry only when you feel a painful emotion. It is very important to assess the veracity of your automatic thoughts both at the times they occur and later, when the emotional storm has passed. You will take a major step toward reducing stress in your life when you begin to distrust your automatic thoughts and begin questioning and disputing them as they pop up. The next chapter on combating distorted thinking will give you specific tools for disputing automatic thoughts. At this point it is important for you to recognize that thoughts create and sustain emotions. To reduce the frequency of painful emotions, you will first need to listen to what you think, then ask how true it is. What you think will ultimately create what you feel.

Further Reading

Beck, A. T. **Cognitive Therapy and Emotional Disorders.** New York: New American Library, 1979.

Ellis, A. **A New Guide to Rational Living.** North Hollywood, California: Wilshire Books, 1975.

Chapter 3
Combating Distorted Thinking

A man walks up to a drugstore counter and asks for a pack of Camels. The clerk says they're out. The man concludes that the clerk had the cigarettes, but just wanted to get rid of him because he didn't like his looks. This "logic" seems obviously irrational and paranoid.

But consider the case of the woman whose husband comes home with a cloudy look on his face. She immediately concludes that he is angry because she was too tired to make love the previous night. She expects to be hurt now by some sort of retaliation and responds quickly by becoming peevish and defensive. This "logic" makes perfect sense to her and she does not question her conclusion until she learns that her husband had a minor auto accident on the way home.

The syllogism she used goes like this: "(1) My husband often gets upset when I disappoint him; (2) My husband looks upset; (3) Therefore I must have disappointed him." The problem with this logic lies in her assumptions that her husband's moods must all relate to her and that she is the prime cause of his ups and downs. This style of distorted thinking is called *Personalization*, the tendency to relate all the objects and events around you to yourself. It creates a great deal of pain because the victim consistently misinterprets what he or she sees and then acts on that misinterpretation.

This chapter will list and examine fifteen distorted thinking styles and give you practice identifying them. You will become alert to cues indicating the presence of distorted thinking in yourself and develop ways of combating it.

Much of human pain is unnecessary. It comes from faulty conclusions you have made about the world. It is your interpretations, what you say to yourself about your experience, that create anxiety, anger, and depression. If you decide that someone's sour look means rejection, when in fact the poor soul has heartburn, you are creating your own climate—and it is destined to be a sad or stormy one.

The two theorists who have contributed most to combating distorted thinking styles are Albert Ellis and Aaron Beck. In his 1961 book, *A Guide to Rational Living*, Ellis argues that emotions have little to do with actual events. In between the event and the emotion is realistic or unrealistic "self talk." The emotion actually comes from what you say to yourself (your interpretation of the event) and not from the event itself. He uses an ABC model to describe how it works:

A Facts and events

> A paperboy tosses the morning news on a customer's wet lawn. The customer runs out his front door and shouts down the block for him to be more careful.

B Paperboy's self talk

> "This is bad...he might report me...they'll take my route away...I'm really screwing up...that guy's a real jerk...he hates kids."

C Emotions

> Anxiety and anger

The event itself did not cause the emotions. It was when the paperboy decided he was in danger, when he decided that he was "screwing up" and that his customer was a "jerk" that anxiety and anger were generated. If the paperboy later decides that everyone makes mistakes and no harm will come of it, his emotional response will be entirely changed.

Aaron Beck is a leading theorist in the treatment of depression. In his 1967 book, *Depression: Clinical, Experimental, and Theoretical Aspects,* he describes how distorted thinking styles set off and exacerbate the downward spiral of depression. By correcting such thinking styles as overgeneralization and polarization the depressed person can begin climbing out of the pit. As his interpretations of the events around him change, so do his mood and attitude toward the future.

Symptom Effectiveness

The Cognitive Therapy advocated by Beck and Ellis has proven effective in reducing the frequency and intensity of interpersonal and general anxiety, depression, chronic anger, and compulsive perfectionism.

Time for Mastery

An assessment of your distorted thinking styles takes several days, as you observe your thinking in a variety of stress situations. The *habit* of combating the distortions will take from two weeks to several months to become automatic.

15 Styles of Distorted Thinking

1. Filtering

This distortion is characeried by a sort of tunnel vision—looking at only one element of a situation to the exclusion of everything else. A single detail is picked out and the whole event or situation is colored by this detail. A draftsman who was uncomfortable with criticism was praised for the quality of his recent detail drawings and asked if he could get the next job out a little quicker. He went home depressed, having decided that his employer thought he was dawdling. He selected only one component of the conversation to respond to. He simply didn't hear the praise in his fear of possible deficiency.

Each person has his own particular tunnel to look through. Some are hypersensitive to anything suggesting loss, and blind to any indication of gain. For others, the slightest possibility of danger sticks out like a barb in a scene that is otherwise warm with contentment. Depressed people select elements suggesting loss from their environment, those prone to anxiety select danger, and those who frequently feel angry select evidence of injustice.

The process of remembering can also be very selective. From your entire history and stock of experience, you may habitually remember only certain kinds of events. As a result, you may review your past and re-experience memories that characteristically leave you angry, anxious, or depressed.

By the very process of filtering you magnify and "awfulize" your thoughts. When you pull negative things out of context, isolated from all the good experiences around you, you make make them larger and more awful than they really are. The end result is that all your fears, losses, and irritations become exaggerated in importance because they fill your awareness to the exclusion of everything else. Key words for this kind of filtering are "terrible...awful...disgusting...horrendous," and so on. A key phrase is "I can't stand it."

2. Polarized Thinking

The hallmark of this distortion is an insistence on dichotomous choices: You tend to perceive everything at the extremes, with very little room for a middle ground. People and things are good or bad, wonderful or horrible. This creates a black and white world, and because you miss all the nuances of gray, your reactions to events swing from one emotional extreme to another. The greatest danger in polarized thinking is its impact on how you judge yourself. If you aren't perfect or brilliant, then you must be a failure or an imbecile. There is no room for mistakes or mediocrity. A charter bus driver told himself he was a real loser when he took the wrong freeway exit and had to drive several miles out of his way. One mistake and he was incompetent and worthless. A single parent with three children was determined to be strong and "in charge." The moment she felt tired or slightly anxious, she began thinking of herself as weak, felt disgusted with herself, and criticized herself in conversations with friends.

3. Overgeneralization

In this distortion you make a broad, generalized conclusion based on a single incident or piece of evidence. One slipped stitch means "I'll never learn how to sew." A rejection on the dance floor means "Nobody would ever want to dance with me." If you got sick on a train once, never take a train again. If you got dizzy on a sixth floor balcony, never go out there again. If you felt anxious the last time your husband took a business trip, you'll be a wreck every time he leaves town. One bad experience means that whenever you're in a similar situation you will repeat the bad experience.

This distortion inevitably leads to a more and more restricted life. Overgeneralizations are often couched in the form of absolute statements, as if there were some immutable law that governs and limits your chances for happiness. You are overgeneralizing when you absolutely conclude that "*Nobody* loves me...I'll *never* be able to trust anyone again...I will *always* be sad...I could *never* get a better job...*No one* would stay my friend if they really knew me." Your conclusion is based on one or two pieces of evidence and carefully ignores everything you know about yourself to the contrary. Cue words that indicate you may be overgeneralizing are all, every, none, never, always, everybody, and nobody.

4. Mind Reading

When you mind read you make snap judgments about others: "He's just acting that way because he's jealous...she's with you for your money...he's afraid to show he cares." There's no evidence, but it just *seems* right. In most instances, mind readers make assumptions about how other people are feeling and what motivates them. For example, you may conclude, "He visited her three times last week because he was (a) in love, (b) angry at his old girlfriend and knew she'd find out, (c) depressed and on the rebound, (d) afraid of being alone again." You can take your choice, but acting on any of these arbitrary conclusions may be disastrous.

As a mind reader, you also make assumptions about how people are reacting to things around them, particularly how they are reacting to you. "This close he sees how unattractive I am... she thinks I'm really immature...they're getting ready to fire me." These assumptions are usually untested. They are born of intuition, hunches, vague misgivings, or one or two past experiences, but they are nevertheless believed.

Mind reading depends on a process called projection. You imagine that people feel the same way you do and react to things the same way you do. Therefore, you don't watch or listen closely enough to notice that they are actually different. If you get angry when someone is late, you imagine everyone acts that way. If you feel excruciatingly sensitive to rejection, you expect most people to feel the same. If you are very judgmental about particular habits and traits you assume others share your belief. Mind readers jump to conclusions that are true for them without checking whether they are true for the other person.

5. Catastrophizing

If you catastrophize, a small leak in the sailboat means it will surely sink. A contractor who gets underbid concludes he'll never get another job. A headache suggests that brain cancer is looming. Catastrophic thoughts often start with the words "what if." You read a newspaper article describing a tragedy or hear gossip about some disaster befalling an acquaintance. As a result you start wondering if it will happen to you. "What if I break my leg skiing. . .What if they hijack my plane. . .What if I get sick and have to go on disability. . .What if my son starts taking drugs?" The list is endless. There are no limits to a really fertile catastrophic imagination.

6. Personalization

The chapter began with an example of personalization. It is the tendency to relate everything around you to yourself. A somewhat depressed mother blames herself when she sees any sadness in her children. A recently married man thinks that every time his wife talks about tiredness she means she is tired of him. A man whose wife complains about rising prices hears the complaints as attacks on his abilities as a breadwinner.

A major aspect of personalization is the habit of continually comparing yourself to other people: "He plays piano so much better than I do. . .I'm not smart enough to go with this crowd. . .She knows herself a lot better than I do. . .He feels things so deeply while I'm dead inside. . .I'm the slowest person in the office. . .He's dumb (and I'm smart). . .I'm better looking. . .They listen to her but not to me." The opportunities for comparison never end. The underlying assumption is that your worth is questionable. You are therefore continually forced to test your value as a person by measuring yourself against others. If you come out better, you have a moment's relief. If you come up short, you feel diminished.

The basic thinking error in personalization is that you interpret each experience, each conversation, each look as a clue to your worth and value.

7. Control Fallacies

There are two ways you can distort your sense of power and control. You can see yourself as helpless and externally controlled, or as omnipotent and responsible for everyone around you.

Feeling externally controlled keeps you stuck. You don't believe you can really affect the basic shape of your life, let alone make any difference in the world. Everywhere you look you see evidence of human helplessness. Someone or something else is responsible for your pain, your loss, and your failure. They did it *to* you. You find it difficult to strive for solutions because they probably wouldn't work anyway. An extreme example of this fallacy is the person who walks through skid row wearing three diamond rings and a $500 watch. He feels helpless and resentful when he gets mugged. He can't imagine how he had anything to do with it. He was the passive victim. The truth of the matter is that we are constantly making decisions, and that every decision affects our lives. In some way, we are responsible for nearly everything that happens to us.

The opposite of the fallacy of external control is the fallacy of omnipotent control. If you experience this distortion, you feel responsible for everything and everybody. You carry the world on your shoulders. Everyone at work depends on you. Your friends depend on you. You are responsible for many people's happiness and any neglect on your part may leave them lonely, rejected, lost, or frightened. You have to right all wrongs, fill every need, and balm each hurt. And if you don't, you feel guilty. Omnipotence depends on three elements: a sensitivity to the needs of people around you, an exaggerated belief in your power to fill those needs and the expectation that you, and not they, are responsible for filling those needs.

8. Fallacy of Fairness

This distorted thinking style hinges on the application of legal and contractual rules to the vagaries of interpersonal relations. The trouble is that two people seldom agree on what fairness is, and there is no court or final arbiter to help them. Fairness is a subjective assessment of how much of what one expected, needed, or hoped for has been provided by the other person. Fairness is so conveniently defined, so temptingly self-serving, that each person gets locked into his or her own point of view. The result is a sense of living in the trenches and a feeling of ever-growing resentment.

The fallacy of fairness is often expressed in conditional assumptions: "If he loved me, he'd do the dishes. . .if he loved me, he'd help me to orgasm. . .if this was a real marriage, she'd hike with me and learn to like it. . .if he cared at all, he'd come home right after work. . .if they valued my work here, they'd get me a nicer desk."

It is tempting to make assumptions about how things would change if people were only fair or *really* valued you. But the other person hardly ever sees it that way and you end up causing yourself a lot of pain.

9. Emotional Reasoning

At the root of this distortion is the belief that what you feel must be true. If you *feel* like a loser, then you must *be* a loser. If you feel guilty, then you must have done something wrong.   If you feel ugly, then you must be ugly. If you feel angry, someone must have taken advantage of you.

All the negative things you *feel* about yourself and others must be true because they feel true.   The problem with emotional reasoning is that emotions by themselves have no validity.   They are products of what you think.   If you have distorted thoughts and beliefs your emotions will reflect those distortions.   Always believing your emotions is like believing everything you see in print.

10. Fallacy of Change

The only person you can really control or have much hope of changing is yourself.   The fallacy of change, however, assumes that other people will change to suit you if you just pressure them enough.   Your attention and energy are therefore focused on others because your hope for happiness lies in getting them to meet your needs.   Strategies for changing others include blaming, demanding, withholding, and trading.   The usual result is that the other person feels attacked or pushed around and doesn't change at all.

The underlying assumption of this thinking style is that your happiness depends on the actions of others.   In fact, your happiness depends on the many thousands of large and small decisions you make during your life.

11. Global Labeling

Your supermarket stocks rotten food at ripoff prices. A person who refused to give you a lift home is a total jerk. A quiet guy on a date is labeled a dull clam. Republicans are a bunch of money-hungry corporation toadies. Your boss is a gutless imbecile.

Each of these labels may contain a grain of truth. Yet it generalizes one or two qualities into a global judgment.   The label ignores all contrary evidence, making your view of the world stereotyped and one-dimensional.

12. Blaming

There's such relief in knowing who's to blame.   If you are suffering, someone must be responsible.   You're lonely, hurt, or frightened and someone provoked those feelings.   A man got angry because his wife suggested he build the fence he'd been meaning to put up. She ought to have known how tired he was—she was being totally insensitive.   The problem was that he expected her to be clairvoyant, to read his mind, when it was his responsibility to inform her of his fatigue and say no.

Blaming often involves making someone else responsible for choices and decisions that are actually your own responsibility. A woman blamed the butcher for selling hamburger that was always full of fat. But it was really her problem: she could have paid more for leaner meat, or gone to a different butcher. In blame systems, somebody is always doing it to you and you have no responsibility to assert your needs, say no, or go elsewhere for what you want.

Some people focus blame exclusively on themselves. They beat themselves up constantly for being incompetent, insensitive, stupid, too emotional, etc. They are always ready to be wrong. One woman felt she had spoiled her husband's entire evening when she caused a fifteen minute delay in getting to a party. Later when the party broke up early she decided that she had bored everybody.

13. Shoulds

In this distortion, you operate from a list of inflexible rules about how you and other people should act. The rules are right and indisputable. Any deviation from your particular values or standards is bad. As a result, you are often in the position of judging and finding fault. People irritate you. They don't act right and they don't think right. They have unacceptable traits, habits, and opinions that make them hard to tolerate. They should *know* the rules and they should follow them. One woman felt that her husband *should* want to take her on Sunday drives. A man who loved his wife *ought* to take her to the country and then out to eat in a nice place. The fact that he didn't want to go meant that he "only thought about himself."

Cue words indicating the presence of this distortion are should, ought, or must. In fact, Albert Ellis has dubbed this thinking style "musterbation."

Not only are other people being judged, but you are also making yourself suffer with shoulds. You feel compelled to do something, or be a certain way, but never bother to ask objectively if it really makes sense. The famous psychiatrist Karen Horney called this the "tyranny of shoulds."

Here is a list of some of the most common and unreasonable shoulds:

- I should be the epitome of generosity, consideration, dignity, courage, unselfishness.
- I should be the perfect lover, friend, parent, teacher, student, spouse.
- I should be able to endure any hardship with equanimity.
- I should be able to find a quick solution to every problem.
- I should never feel hurt, I should always be happy and serene.
- I should know, understand, and foresee everything.
- I should always be spontaneous and at the same time I should always control my feelings.
- I should never feel certain emotions, such as anger or jealousy.
- I should love my children equally.
- I should never make mistakes.
- My emotions should be constant—once I feel love I should always feel love.
- I should be totally self-reliant.
- I should assert myself and at the same time I should never hurt anybody else.
- I should never be tired or get sick.
- I should always be at peak efficiency.

14. Being Right

In this distortion you are usually on the defensive. You must continually prove that your viewpoint is correct, your assumptions about the world accurate, and all your actions correct. You aren't interested in the possible veracity of a differing opinion, only in defending your own. Every decision you make is right, every task you perform is done competently. You never make mistakes.

Your opinions rarely change because you have difficulty hearing new information. If the facts don't fit what you already believe you ignore them.

An auto mechanic got in the habit of stopping at the bar for three or four drinks on the way home. Frequently he got in after seven, and his wife never knew when to have dinner ready. When she confronted him he got angry and said that a man has a right to relax. She had it soft while he was pulling off cylinder heads all day. The mechanic had to be right and couldn't comprehend his wife's viewpoint.

Having to be right makes you very hard of hearing. It also makes you lonely because being right seems more important than an honest, caring relationship.

15. Heaven's Reward Fallacy

In this framework for viewing the world you always do the "right thing" in hope of a reward. You sacrifice and slave, and all the while imagine that you are collecting brownie points that you can cash in some day.

A housewife cooked elaborate meals for her family and did endless baking and sewing. She drove her children to all their afterschool activities. The house was immaculate. She carried on for years, all the while waiting for some kind of special reward or appreciation. It never came. And she became increasingly hostile and bitter. The problem was that while she was doing the "right thing" she was physically and emotionally bankrupting herself. She had become a crab and no one wanted to be around her.

Acknowledgement: Several of these distortions are drawn from the work of other cognitive therapists. From Aaron Beck come Filtering (selective abstraction), Polarized Thinking, Overgeneralization, Personalization, and Mind Reading (arbitrary inference). From David Burns' work comes the concept of Emotional Reasoning.

Instructions

As you read through the distortions you will notice that you have favorite ones. Others you will rarely if ever indulge in. Your high-frequency distortions are the ones you need to sensitize yourself to so that your inner alarm sounds whenever they come up.

Before going on, read and familiarize yourself with the chart summarizing these 15 styles of distorted thinking. In the next section you will get some practice identifying them.

Summary

15 Styles of Distorted Thinking

1. **Filtering:** You take the negative details and magnify them while filtering out all positive aspects of a situation.

2. **Polarized Thinking:** Things are black or white, good or bad. You have to be perfect or you're a failure. There is no middle ground.

3. **Overgeneralization:** You come to a general conclusion based on a single incident or piece of evidence.   If something bad happens once you expect it to happen over and over again.

4. **Mind Reading:** Without their saying so, you know what people are feeling and why they act the way they do. In particular, you are able to divine how people are feeling toward you.

5. **Catastrophizing:** You expect disaster. You notice or hear about a problem and start "what if's:" What if tragedy strikes? What if it happens to you?"

6. **Personalization:** Thinking that everything people do or say is some kind of reaction to you. You also compare yourself to others, trying to determine who's smarter, better looking, etc.

7. **Control Fallacies:** If you feel externally controlled, you see yourself as helpless, a victim of fate. The fallacy of internal control has you responsible for the pain and happiness of everyone around you.

8. **Fallacy of Fairness:** You feel resentful because you think you know what's fair but other people won't agree with you.

9. **Blaming:** You hold other people responsible for your pain, or take the other tack and blame yourself for every problem or reversal.

10. **Shoulds:** You have a list of ironclad rules about how you and other people should act. People who break the rules anger you and you feel guilty if you violate the rules.

11. **Emotional Reasoning:** You believe that what you feel must be true—automatically. If you *feel* stupid and boring, then you must *be* stupid and boring.

12. **Fallacy of Change:** You expect that other people will change to suit you if you just pressure or cajole them enough. You need to   change people because your hopes for happiness seem to depend entirely   on them.

13. **Global Labeling:** You generalize one or two qualities into a negative global judgment.

14. **Being Right:** You are continually on trial to prove that your opinions and actions are correct. Being wrong is unthinkable and you will go to any length to demonstrate your rightness.

15. **Heaven's Reward Fallacy:** You expect all your sacrifice and self-denial to pay off, as if there were someone keeping score. You feel bitter when the reward doesn't come.

The following exercises are designed to help you notice and identify distorted thinking. The first is a matching test. Draw a line between the sentence in the first column and the distortion which it exemplifies in the second column.

1. Ever since Lisa I've never trusted a redhead.	Filtering
2. Quite a few people here seem smarter than I am.	Polarized thinking
3. If you'd be more sexually open, we'd have a much happier marriage.	Overgeneralization
4. I worked and raised these kids and look what thanks I get.	Mind reading
5. You're either for me or against me.	Catastrophizing
6. I could have enjoyed the picnic except the chicken was burnt.	Personalization
7. I feel depressed, life must be pointless.	Control fallacies
8. You can't fight the system.	Fallacy of fairness
9. It's your fault we're always in the hole each month.	Blaming
10. He was a loser from the first day he showed up here.	Shoulds
11. It isn't fair that you go out and have fun while I'm stuck doing homework.	Emotional reasoning
12. He's always smiling, but I know he doesn't like me.	Fallacy of change
13. I don't care what you think, I'd do it exactly the same way again.	Global labeling
14. We haven't seen each other for two days and I think the relationship is falling apart.	Being right
15. You should never ask people personal questions.	Heaven's reward fallacy

In the next exercise, circle the distortion which is exemplified by each example. There may be more than one right answer.

1. The washing machine shorts out. A housewife, who has twins in diapers, says to herself, "This always happens. I can't stand it, the whole day's ruined."

   a. Overgeneralization   c. Being right   e. Filtering
   b. Emotional reasoning   d. Control fallacies

2. "He looked up from across the table and said, 'That's interesting.' I knew he was dying for breakfast to be over so he could get away from me."

   a. Blaming   c. Shoulds   e. Fallacy of fairness
   b. Polarized thinking   d. Mind reading

3. "We can't let him do it. There's no fool like an old fool."

   a. Personalization   c. Fallacy of change   e. Heaven's reward fallacy
   b. Global labeling   d. Emotional reasoning

4. "So what if you told me to sell my shares before the market collapsed. So it's taking a dive. I've survived before and I'll survive again. I feel confident, so I know everything will be all right."

   a. Fallacy of fairness   c. Control fallacies   e. Emotional reasoning
   b. Mind reading   d. Being right

5. A man was trying to get his girlfriend to be warmer and more supportive. He got irritated every night when she didn't ask him how his day was or failed to give him immediate attention. He blamed her for the fights, and told her she should move to Alaska because "they like ice up there."

   a. Shoulds   c. Overgeneralization   e. Blaming
   b. Fallacy of change   d. Catastrophizing

The following exercise requires a little more work on your part. Read the statement and circle the applicable distortions in the list following the statement. Next to the distortion write in the phrase that contains it.

1. "Jim's so easily upset, you just can't talk to him. He blows up at everything. If only he had a decent job, instead of being just a swingshift night watchman. His paycheck comes to next to nothing, so whose fault is it that we can't fix this crummy house up? It isn't fair to make me live in conditions like this."

Distortions   **Phrase containing the distortion**

Filtering
Polarized thinking
Overgeneralization
Mind reading
Catastrophizing
Pesonalization
Control fallacies
Fallacy of fairness
Blaming
Shoulds
Emotional reasoning
Fallacy of change
Global labeling
Being right
Heaven's reward fallacy

2. "One time she came up to me and said, 'This nursing station looks like a cyclone just hit it. Better straighten out the mess before the shift is over.' Well, I said, 'This was a mess when I got here. They left it for me so I guess I can leave it for somebody else.' I mean, who cares if a few charts are lying out. Anybody who looked could find the one they wanted. I think she wants to fire me and she's just looking for an excuse."

Distortions   **Phrase containing the distortion**

Filtering
Polarized thinking
Overgeneralization
Mind reading
Catastrophizing
Personalization
Control fallacies
Fallacy of fairness
Blaming
Shoulds
Emotional reasoning

Fallacy of change
Global labeling
Being right
Heaven's reward fallacy

Answer key:

1. Overgeneralization: "Blows up at everything."
Fallacy of fairness: "It isn't fair to make me live . . . like this."
Blaming: "So whose fault is it we can't fix this hovel."
2. Mind reading: "I think she wants to fire me."
Being right: "Who cares . . . anybody who looked could find them."

Now try some really tough ones.   After you read each story circle each
distortion you find. Write in the phrase from the story reflecting that distortion.

1. "A lot of the time I feel nervous when I'm out with Ed. I keep thinking how
smart he is, how sophisticated, and I'm just a hayseed by comparison. He
cocks his head and looks at me and I know he's thinking how dumb I am.
He's really sweet and we have a good time talking. But when he cocks his
head I feel like I'll be dumped. One time he kind of wrinkled up his face
when I said something a little critical about his jacket. Now I'm afraid to say
anything for fear of hurting him.

"Usually I think Ed is completely wonderful. But last week he made
me take the bus to his house instead of picking me up. I suddenly felt he
didn't give a damn, that he was just another jerk. That was a passing thing,
and now he's wonderful again. My only problem is this business of being
nervous when he cocks his head."

Distortions   **Phrase containing the distortion**
Filtering
Polarized thinking
Overgeneralization
Mind reading
Catastrophizing
Personalization
Control fallacies
Fallacy of fairness
Blaming
Shoulds
Emotional reasoning
Fallacy of change
Global labeling
Being right
Heaven's reward fallacy

2. "There are three ways to make a magazine go: work, work, and more work. If you have to go 16 hours a day to get it out, that's what you should do. These kids today want to go home at 5:00. If they don't want to work, I say get rid of them. Profits get slimmer every year because of total laziness. I can't do a damn thing. It's the way they're raised, the way the whole damn country is falling apart. In five years it'll drive me under, and I can't do a damn thing about it. There are just two kinds of editors: the ones who get the job done, and the nine-to-fivers. It's the nine-to-fivers who will put me under."

Distortions	Phrase containing the distortion
Filtering	
Polarized thinking	
Overgeneralization	
Mind reading	
Catastrophizing	
Personalization	
Control fallacies	
Fallacy of fairness	
Blaming	
Shoulds	
Emotional reasoning	
Fallacy of change	
Global labeling	
Being right	
Heaven's reward fallacy	

3. "I've got some sick neighbors right now I'm doing for. And a husband who's driving me nuts. I'm running in all day with soup for them and doing little chores. My husband's retired and I know he just sits and feels lonely while I'm gone. I try to pay as much attention to him as I can, but it seems like everybody depends on me and calls me up because I'm obliging. Sometimes I think the whole town would fall apart if we moved away.

"Emmy's got a little cough, but I think it's emphysema, being around John smoking all those years. He shouldn't have smoked in the house. It wasn't fair to her.

"My husband ought to stop sitting in the yard and get something done, then he wouldn't miss me all the time. The more I get after him, the more he sits.

"I just can't let a sick person down, no matter what. I just can't. A person ought to take care of her neighbors. It's a hard job, but I know they'll take care of me someday."

Distortions	Phrase containing the distortion
Filtering	
Polarized thinking	
Overgeneralization	
Mind reading	
Catastrophizing	
Personalization	
Control fallacies	
Fallacy of fairness	
Blaming	
Shoulds	
Emotional reasoning	
Fallacy of change	
Global labeling	
Being right	
Heaven's reward fallacy	

4. "I keep thinking what if the earthquake came now, while we're having drinks on the 50th floor. What if the glass broke and we all fell out. I even think I can feel it shaking a little. Skyscrapers are ugly, put up by those money-barons who couldn't care less if they fell down. Nobody has much to say while we're drinking. I think I make everybody nervous because I'm so nervous. You have to trust your feelings in something like this. If you feel afraid to go up in a skyscraper, then there must be something dangerous about it."

Distortion	Phrase containing the distortion
Filtering	
Polarized thinking	
Overgeneralization	
Mind reading	
Catastrophizing	
Personalization	
Control fallacies	
Fallacy of fairness	
Blaming	
Shoulds	
Emotional reasoning	
Fallacy of change	
Global labeling	
Being right	
Heaven's reward fallacy	

5. "She won't talk to me. She just keeps reading the blue books from her Ed Psych class. You call this a life? I tell her, stop being a slug, let's go out. You call this living? I say be merry for tomorrow we die, but she keeps taking her work home. Sometimes she's on me to turn the television down,

but I can't sit two inches from the set trying to hear Bogie whisper, 'play it again.' "

Distortions	Phrase containing the distortion
Filtering	
Polarized thinking	
Overgeneralization	
Mind reading	
Catastrophizing	
Personalization	
Control fallacies	
Fallacy of fairness	
Blaming	
Shoulds	
Emotional reasoning	
Fallacy of change	
Global labeling	
Being right	
Heaven's reward fallacy	

Answer key:

1. Polarized thinking: "'Wonderful' . . . just another jerk.'"
Overgeneralization: "'His face wrinkled up . . . Now I'm afraid . . . of hurting him.'"
Mind reading: "I know he's thinking how dumb I am."
Catastrophizing: "'I'll be dumped.'"
Personalization: "I'm just a hayseed by comparison."

2. Filtering: Laziness obsession
Polarized thinking: "'There are just two kinds of editors.'"
Overgeneralization: "'The whole damn country is falling apart.'"
Catastrophizing: "'In five years it will drive me under.'"
Control fallacies: "'It'll drive me under . . . I can't do a damn thing about it.'"
Blaming: "'The nine-to-fivers will put me under.'"
Shoulds: "'16 hours a day . . . that's what you should do.'"
Global labeling: "Lazy nine-to-fivers."

3. Mind reading: "'He just sits and feels lonely.'"
Catastrophizing: "I think it's emphysema."
Control fallacies: "'Town would fall apart if we moved away.'"
Fallacy of fairness: "'It wasn't fair to her.'"
Shoulds: "'A person ought to take care of her neighbors.'"
"'My husband ought to stop sitting.'"
Fallacy of change: "'The more I get after him, the more he sits.'"
Heaven's reward fallacy: "'They'll take care of me someday.'"

4. Filtering: Earthquake obsession. "I can feel it shaking."
Catastrophizing: "'What if the earthquake came now.'"
Personalization: "I think I make everybody nervous."
Emotional reasoning: "'If you feel afraid . . . then there must be something dangerous about it.'"
Global labeling: "'Money barons who couldn't care less.'"

5. Polarized thinking: "'Stop being a slug . . . be merry.'"
Blaming: "'You call this a life?'"
Shoulds: "'Be merry.'"
Fallacy of change: "'I tell her, stop being a slug, let's go out.'"
Global labeling: "'Slug.'"
Being right: "'I can't sit two inches from the set.'"

Don't be surprised if you missed many of the distortions. They are often very hard to pick out. The important thing is to begin noticing the distortions that you use most often.

The Two Signs of Distorted Thinking

The best tipoff that you are using a distorted thinking style is the presence of painful emotions. You feel nervous, depressed, or chronically angry. You feel disgusted with yourself. You play certain worries over and over like a broken record.

You may notice that psychological pain fluctuates, feeling worse at certain times during the day than at other times. Use the Thoughts Diary in chapter two to identify the situations which classically increase your distress and the habitual thoughts which accompany these situations.

Ongoing conflicts with friends and family can also be a cue that you are using one or more of the distorted styles. Notice what you say to yourself about the other person. Notice how you describe and justify your side of the conflict.

Combating Distortions

When you become aware of a painful emotion or conflict in a relationship, it is time to focus on what you are thinking. Faulty logic is at the root of many thinking errors and a great deal of human pain. A logical syllogism has three parts:

Major premise   (rule)
Minor premise   (special case)
Conclusion

Example:

All men are mortal   (Major premise)
Socrates is a man   (Minor premise)
Socrates is mortal   (Conclusion)

An error made in either the major or minor premise often results in a false conclusion. Human beings operate on all sorts of hidden beliefs which become rules (major premises) in faulty syllogisms. Some typical rules are:

Any criticism means I'm stupid.
All criticism is meant to hurt.
All mistakes are intolerable.
If I get rejected, I'll be destroyed.
People can't be trusted.

The difficulty with these rules is that they are sweeping generalizations that fail to include any alternative experience or interpretation. Because the rule (major premise) is false, the conclusion will often be false. A few examples:

All criticism is meant to hurt.   (Rule, major premise)
My boss just criticized me.   (Special case, minor premise)
He was trying to hurt me.

If I get rejected, I'll be destroyed.
She just got angry and walked out.
This is horrible, I'm destroyed.

There's something wrong with people who aren't married by 30.
I'm unmarried at 30.
There is something very wrong with me.

Each of these painful conclusions is based on a rule that is fallacious. Most people believe one or more cherished rules like these. They result in misinterpretations, poor decision making, lowered self-esteem, and stressful emotions. To uncover a rule, ask yourself, "What do I believe to be true about situations like this? When_____happens, what does that usually mean?" Once you identify a rule you can observe how you apply it to specific situations in order to formulate your assumptions. Look for the exceptions to your rule.

To begin combating your distortions, you should go back to a time when you were experiencing a painful emotion or were in the middle of some interpersonal conflict. The following four-step procedure will help you identify what you felt and thought in that situation. It will also assist you in uncovering your distortions and restructuring how you look at things. The four steps are:

1. Naming your emotion

2. Describing the situation or event

3. Identifying your distortions

4. Eliminating your distortions

The homework sheet that follows will help you structure this work. A separate sheet should be used to examine each painful emotion or interpersonal conflict.

Homework Sheet

1. Name emotion:

2. Describe the situation or event

    a. Write a detailed description of the situation or event about which you are upset. Write as if you were telling a close friend.

    b. Write what you thought about during the situation or event.

3. Carefully read what you have written and circle the distortions that apply.

Filtering	Personalization	Emotional reasoning
Polarized thinking	Control fallacies	Fallacy of change
Overgeneralization	Fallacy of fairness	Global labeling
Mind reading	Blaming	Being right
Catastrophizing	Shoulds	Heaven's reward fallacy

4. For each distortion you uncovered: list the distortion in column A, in column B write the phrase or sentence you used which included the distortion, in column C rewrite the phrase or sentence without the distortion.

A	B	C

Often people have difficulty rewriting their statements without including the distortions. The distortions are so automatic they seem to make a lot of sense. If you need help eliminating your distortions, turn to the Rational Comebacks section at the end of this chapter. It is important that you believe what you put in column C. What you write in substitution for your old distortions will work only if it makes sense to you—only if it seems true.

The Three Column Technique

After you become proficient at combating your distortions, you can abbreviate the process by eliminating steps 1, 2, and 3. Then modify step 4 by doing the following: If you have been saying something to yourself that is triggering anxiety, depression, or anger, write that statement down in column A. Name the distortion involved in column B. Finally, in column C rewrite the statement without the distortion. The three columns should look like this:

A	B	C
Original statement	Distortion	Rewritten statement without distortion

Examples

Sandra was a member of a babysitting co-op. She was frequently called to take care of another member's hyperactive three year old. The child had to be supervised constantly and sometimes broke things in her house. She began to dread the prospect of babysitting this particular little boy and felt angry when called upon to do so. She used her homework sheet as follows to begin coping with the problem:

1. **Name emotion:** anxious, angry

2. **Describe the situation or event**

   a. I think she calls me up all the time because I'm the only one who will look after that kid. He screams and shrieks around the house, throws and breaks things. He's a terror because she lets him get away with it, and then can't stand it herself and tries to dump the problem on me. That's what she's doing, just dumping the problem on me. Every time I see that kid, it ruins my day. I'm always expecting something to break. I keep waiting for her to call, and when she does I'm furious. You're not supposed to refuse a co-op member if you've got the time, so I'm stuck.

   b. During the situation I think I can't stand this, what's he going to do next?

3. Carefully read what you have written and circle the distortions that apply.

Filtering
Mind reading
Control fallacies
Blaming

4. Rewrite the distortions.

A	B	C
Filtering	"It ruins my day . . . expecting something to break . . . keep waiting for her to call . . . I can't stand this."	"It will ruin my day only if I let it. I don't have to magnify this, it's only for a little while and I can tolerate him that long. I'll have a quiet morning before he comes."
Mindreading	"She calls me up because I'm the only one who will look after her kid . . . she's dumping her problem on me."	"I don't know why she calls me all the time, but I plan to ask her."
Control fallacies	"So I'm stuck."	"This is happening to me because I let it. This is a special problem that the co-op needs a special policy to handle."
Blaming	"He's a terror because she lets him get away with it."	"He terrorized me because I've been putting up with the situation without trying to change it."

Eventually Sandra phoned the woman to ask why she seemed to be doing a disproportionate share of the babysitting. They agreed on a maximum number of hours per month. On occasions when the child was left with her, Sandra experimented with different approaches to control his problem behavior. She gave herself some quiet time to prepare for the child's arrival and told herself that she could tolerate a few hours with a hyperactive boy. She was no longer blaming, making assumptions about the motivations of others, or feeling quite so helpless. She had shifted from obsessing about pain to a focus on coping strategies.

A second example is the case of the petrified pawnbroker. There had been a spate of neighborhood robberies by a particularly brutal gunman who always wore a denim vest. The pawnbroker became increasingly anxious and was soon experiencing nausea and sweats at the sight of any sort of denim jacket. He confronted his problem in the following way:

1. **Name emotion:** fear

2. **Describe the situation or event**

   a. I keep waiting for him to come in. I'm just waiting and there's nothing I can do about it. He's going to hit my place sooner or later. Then he's going to pistol-whip me like he did one of the others. My wife says take a vacation. But I say you either face a situation or you run away from it like a coward. I'll stay right here, behind the counter. I've got help, but the only way to run a shop is to stand here, right behind the counter with them.

   b. I keep looking for the denim vest and thinking about him hitting me with the gun.

3. **Carefully read what you have written and circle the distortions that apply.**
   Polarized thinking
   Catastrophizing
   Control Fallacies
   Shoulds

4. **Rewrite the distortions**

A	B	C
Polarized thinking	"Either face a situation or run away like a coward."	"It doesn't make sense to think in black and white. I don't have to judge my actions as either cowardly or brave."
Catastrophizing	"I keep waiting for him to come in . . . he's going to hit my place . . . he's going to pistol-whip me."	"The odds are one in ten he'll hit this shop, and the odds are pretty small that I'll be hurt if I cooperate."
Control fallacies	"There's nothing I can do about it."	"I can do something about this anxiety if I want to. I can get an attack dog, I can install a silent alarm, I can spend less time out at the counter, I can take some time off."
Shoulds	"The only way to run a shop is to stand right here behind the counter . . . you can't run away."	"Very few things in life are absolutely necessary. I don't have to be behind the counter all the time. I could come out from the back room just to do appraisals."

The pawnbroker's anxiety was reduced when he stopped catastrophizing and started focusing on realistic odds. He had forced himself into a corner with value judgments about his own cowardice and with "shoulds" about his role as a shopowner. After doing his homework he realized that he had more control of his fear than he'd previously thought. There was something he could do about it once he became willing to change his old distorted ways of thinking.

Rational Comebacks

Listed below are rational correlatives to the fifteen distorted thinking styles. It isn't necessary to read through the list from beginning to end. Use it as a reference when you are having problems with a particular distortion. The key comeback statements for each distortion are listed on the right in boldface.

1. Filtering

Shift focus
No need to magnify

You have been stuck in a mental groove, focusing on things from your environment that typically tend to frighten, sadden, or anger you. To conquer filtering you will have to deliberately shift focus. You can shift focus in two ways: First, place your attention on coping strategies to deal with the problem rather than obsessing about the problem itself. Second, categorize your primary mental theme as: Loss, Injustice, or _____ (fill in your own theme). If your theme is loss, focus instead on what you do have that is of value. If your theme is danger, focus on things in your environment that represent comfort and safety. If your theme is injustice (including stupidity, incompetence, etc.), shift your attention to what people do that *does* meet with your approval.

When you are filtering you usually end up magnifying your problems. To combat magnifying, stop using words like terrible, awful, disgusting, horrendous, etc. In particular, banish the phrase "I can't stand it." You *can* stand it, because history shows that human beings can survive almost any psychological blow and can endure incredible physical pain. You can get used to and cope with almost anything. Try saying to yourself phrases such as "No need to magnify" and "I can cope."

2. Polarized Thinking

No black and white judgments
Think in percentages

The key to overcoming polarized thinking is to stop making black or white judgments. People are not either happy or sad, loving or rejecting, brave or cowardly, smart or stupid. They fall somewhere along a continuum. They are a little bit of each. Human beings are just too complex to be reduced to dichotomous judgments. If you have to make these kinds of ratings, think in terms of percentages: "About 30% of me is scared to death, and 70% is holding on and coping. . .about 60% of the time he seems terribly preoccupied with himself, but there's the 40% when he can be really generous. . .5% of the time I'm an ignoramous, the rest of the time I do all right."

3. Overgeneralization

Quantify
Evidence for conclusions?
There are no absolutes

Overgeneralization is simply the tendency to exaggerate, the propensity to take a button and sew a vest on it. You can fight this tendency by quantifying instead of using words like huge, awful, massive, miniscule, etc. Moreover, you can examine how much evidence you really have for your conclusion. If the conclusion is based on one or two cases, a single mistake, or one small symptom, then throw it out till you have more convincing proof. Use this variant of the three column technique:

Evidence for my conclusion	Evidence against my conclusion	Alternative conclusion

If you overgeneralize you think in absolutes. You should therefore avoid statements and assumptions that require the use of words such as every, all, always, none, never, everybody, and nobody. Thoughts and statements that include these words ignore the exceptions and shades of gray. To become more flexible, use instead words such as may, sometimes, and often. Be particularly sensitive to absolute predictions about the future such as, "No one will ever love me." They are extremely dangerous because they can become self-fulfilling prophecies.

4. Mind Reading

Check it out
Evidence for conclusion?

Mind reading is the tendency to make inferences about how people feel and think. In the long run, you are probably better off making no inferences about people at all. Either believe what they tell you or hold no belief at all until some conclusive evidence comes your way. Treat all of your notions about people as hypotheses to be tested and checked out by asking them. If you lack direct information from the person involved, but have other evidence, evaluate your conclusion using the three column technique above.

5. Catastrophizing

Realistic odds

Catastrophizing is the royal road to anxiety. As soon as you catch yourself, make an honest assessment of the situation in terms of odds or percent of probability. Are the chances one in 100,000 (.001%)? One in a thousand (.1%)? One in twenty (5%)? Looking at odds helps you realistically evaluate whatever is frightening you.

6. Personalization

Check it out
Evidence for conclusion?
Why risk comparisons?

If your tendency is to personalize, force yourself to *prove* what the boss's frown has to do with you. Check it out. If you can't ask the person, use the three column technique shown above to test your conclusions. Make no conclusions unless you are satisfied that you have reasonable evidence and proof. It is also important to abandon the habit of comparing yourself—negatively or positively—with other people. Comparisons are an exciting form of gambling. Sometimes you win and really outshine someone else. But when you lose, you set yourself up for a blow to your self-esteem and maybe the beginning of a long, deep depression. Your worth doesn't depend on being better than others, so why start the comparison gamble?

7. Control Fallacies

Aside from natural disasters, you are responsible for what happens in your world. You make it happen. If you are unhappy there are specific choices you have made, and continue to make, that have the byproduct of unhappiness. You usually achieve in life whatever your top priority is. For example, if security is more important than anything else, you may have it at the expense of passion and excitement. You may long for excitement, but security was the higher priority. Ask yourself, "What choices have I made that resulted in this situation? What decisions can I make now to change it?"

The omnipotence fallacy is the opposite side of the coin from the external control fallacy. Instead of everyone else being responsible for your problems, you are responsible for everyone else's problems. If someone is in pain, it's your responsibility to do something about it. The fault is with you if you don't take up the burdens of others. The key to overcoming the omnipotence fallacy is to recognize that each one is responsible for himself. We are all captains of our own ships, making the decisions that steer our lives. If someone is in pain, he or she has the ultimate responsibility to overcome or accept it. There is a difference between generosity and the slavish adherence to a conviction that you have to help everybody. Also remember, part of respecting others includes letting them live their own lives, suffer their own pains, and solve their own problems.

8. Fallacy of Fairness

Outside of a court of law, the concept of fairness is too dangerous to use. The word fair is a nice disguise for personal preferences and wants. What you want is *fair*, what the other person wants is bogus. Be honest with yourself and the other person. Say what you want or prefer without dressing it up in the fallacy of fairness.

9. Blaming

I make it happen
Each one is responsible

It is your responsibility to assert your needs, say no, or go elsewhere. The other person is not responsible for knowing or helping you meet your needs. No one else can really be at fault if you, a responsible adult, are distressed or unhappy. Focus on the choices you have made that created this situation. Examine what options you have now for coping with it.

There is a difference between taking responsibility and turning the blame on yourself. Taking responsibility means accepting the consequences of your own choices. Blaming yourself means attacking your own self-esteem and labeling yourself bad if you make a mistake. Taking responsibility doesn't imply that you are also responsible for what happens to others. Blaming yourself for another person's problems is a form of self-aggrandizement. It means you think you are having more impact on their lives than they are.

10. Shoulds

Flexible rules
Flexible values

Re-examine and question any personal rules or expectations that include the words *should, ought,* or *must.* Flexible rules and expectations don't use these words because there are always exceptions and special circumstances. Think of at least three exceptions to your rule, and then imagine all the exceptions there must be that you can't think of.

You may get irritated when people don't act according to your values. But your personal values are just that—personal. They may work for you but, as missionaries have discovered all over the world, they don't always work for others. People just aren't all the same.

The key is to focus on each person's uniqueness, his or her particular needs, limitations, fears, and pleasures. Because it is impossible to know all of these complex interrelations even with intimates, you can't be certain whether your values apply to another. You are entitled to an opinion, but allow for the possibility of being wrong. Also, allow for other people to find different things important.

11. Emotional Reasoning

Feelings can lie

What you feel is entirely dependent on what you think. If you have distorted thoughts, your feelings won't have validity. Your feelings can lie to you. In fact, if you're feeling depressed or anxious all the time, it's almost certain they are lying to you. There is nothing sacred or automatically true about what you feel. If you *feel* unattractive or *feel* foolish and embarrassed, you tend to believe yourself ugly or a fool. But stop a minute. Maybe it isn't true and you are suffering for nothing. Be skeptical about your feelings and examine them as you would a used car.

12. Fallacy of Change   I make it happen

When you try to push people to change, you are asking them to be different so you can be happy. The assumption is that your happiness is in some way dependent on them and on how they behave. Your happiness depends on you, on each of the decisions you make. You have to decide whether to leave or stay, work as a baker or an electrician, say yes or no. Each person makes it happen for himself or herself. It's dangerous to ask someone else to make it happen for you because people resist when they are pressured to change. If they do change they often resent the person who made them change.

13. Global Labeling   Be specific

Global labels are usually false because they focus on only a single characteristic or behavior but imply that it's the whole picture. Rather than applying global labels, you can limit your observations to a specific case. Ask yourself if a case is always true, or only true now, or only true some of the time.

14. Being Right   Active listening

If you've always got to be right, you don't listen. You can't afford to. Listening might lead you to conclude that you are wrong sometimes. The key to overcoming being right is active listening. As an active listener you participate in communication by repeating what you think you've heard in order to make sure you really understand what's been said to you. This checking out process helps two people who disagree to appreciate each other's point of view. A proportionately greater amount of time is spent trying to understand the other person than in devising your own rebuttals and attacks. Remember that other people believe what they are saying as strongly as you believe in your convictions, and that there is not always one right answer. Focus on what you can learn from the other person's opinion.

15. Heaven's Reward Fallacy   The reward is now

This distorted thinking style accepts pain and unhappiness because those who do good are rewarded in the end. But if doing good means you are doing things you don't want to do and sacrificing things you resent giving up, then you are likely to reap no reward at all. You'll become so bitter and unhappy that people will steer clear of you.

In reality, the reward is now. Your relationships, your progress toward your goals, and the care you give to people you love should be intrinsically rewarding. Most days, your emotional bank balance should be in the black. If you are drained, running in the red ink for days or weeks at a time, something is wrong. You need to arrange your activities to provide some here-and-now reward, dropping or sharing the activities that chronically drain you. Heaven is a long way off and you can get very tired waiting.

It is part of your responsibility to those you care about *not* to do things that will lead you to feel resentful. Remember that you wouldn't want others doing things for you that they didn't want to do.

Special Considerations

When writing the description of a situation on your homework sheet, you may develop "writer's cramp." You may become so concerned about whether you use the distorted thinking styles that you write very little or heavily edit what you write. In either case, you will not get the full benefit of the exercise. You will not be able to experience or change distortions unless you write freely, just as you would describe the situation to yourself or to someone you trust. Write a lot and write the first thing that comes to mind. You can worry about the presence or absence of distortions later.

Further Reading

Beck, A. T. **Cognitive Therapy and Emotional Disorders.** New York: New American Library, 1979.

Beck, A. T. **Depression: Clinical, Experimental and Theoretical Aspects.** New York: Hoeber, 1967.

Burns, D. D. **Feeling Good.** New York: William Morrow, 1980.

Ellis, A. **Growth Through Reason.** Palo Alto, California: Science and Behavior Books, 1971.

Ellis, A. and Harper, R. **A Guide to Rational Living.** North Hollywood, California: Wilshire Books, 1961.

Foreyt, J. P. and Rathjen, D. P., eds. **Cognitive Behavior Therapy: Research and Application.** New York: Plenum Press, 1978.

Chapter 4

Covert Assertion

Covert Assertion helps you end emotional distress through the development of two separate skills: thought interruption and thought substitution. At the first hint of a habitual thought that you know leads to unpleasant emotions you interrupt the thought by subvocalizing the word "stop" or by using some other interrupting technique. Then you fill the void left by the interrupted thought with previously prepared positive thoughts that are more realistic, assertive, and constructive. Acquiring these skills enables you to cope successfully with thoughts that used to lead to high levels of anxiety, depression, or anger.

Thought interruption was first explored in Bain's 1928 book *Thought Control in Everyday Life*. In the late 1950's Joseph Wolpe and other behaviorists adapted Bain's methods for treating obsessive and phobic thoughts. The technique of substituting covert assertions for the interrupted thoughts was developed primarily by Meichenbaum, who called his system "Stress Innoculation Training."

Thought interruption acts as a "punishment" or distracting tactic, lessening the chance of the same thought coming up again and creating space in your train of thought for the positive assertion. Negative emotions are cut off before they can arise. Instead, a positive feedback loop is created in which the positive assertions give rise to a more comfortable emotion, which provides reinforcement for making further positive assertions.

Time for Mastery

Effective mastery of Covert Assertion can be attained if it is practiced conscientiously throughout the day for three days to one week.

Symptom Effectiveness

Covert Assertion has been used effectively to treat obsessive memories, fears of sexual inadequacy, frightening impulses, depression, thoughts of loss and failure, chronic anger, perfectionism, insomnia, hypochondriasis, and phobias such as fear of the dark, being alone, insects, automobiles, going crazy, or someone lurking in the house.

This technique works well if you suffer from multiple phobias or a constellation of related, general fears. This is in contrast to Systematic Desensitization, which is indicated when dealing with a single phobia or a particular fear. Also, Covert Assertion works best when the constellation of fears or obsessions is primarily cognitive rather than acted out. For example, it is a good technique to use for combating the tendency to repeatedly count things in your mind or to ruminate constantly on past disappointments. But it would not be as effective in dealing with compulsive, ritualistic behavior such as constantly touching things or incessantly talking about your past out loud.

Instructions

1. Identify and rate your stressful thoughts.

Use this stressful thoughts inventory to help you assess which recurrent thoughts are the most painful and intrusive.

Stressful Thoughts Inventory

Put a check mark after each item that applies to you. For items which you check, rate them in column **A** from 1 to 5, based on these statements:

1. **Sensible.** This is quite a sensible and reasonable thing for me to think.
2. **Habit.** This is just a habit. I think it automatically, without really worrying about it.
3. **Not Necessary.** I often realize that this thought is not really necessary, but I don't try to stop it.
4. **Try To Stop.** I know this thought is not necessary. It bothers me, and I try to stop it.
5. **Try Very Hard To Stop.** This thought upsets me a great deal, and I try very hard to stop it.

For items which you check, rate them in column B from 1 to 4, based on the following statements:

1. **No Interference.**   This thought does not interfere with other activities.

2. **Interferes A Little.**   This thought interferes a little with other activities, or wastes a little of my time.

3. **Interferes Moderately.**   This thought interferes with other activities, or wastes some of my time.

4. **Interferes A Great Deal.**   This thought stops me from doing a lot of things, and wastes a lot of time every day.

	Check here if your answer is yes	**A** If yes, rate from 1 to 5	**B** rate from 1 to 4
Do you worry about being on time?	☐	___	___
Do you worry about leaving the lights or the gas on, or whether the doors are locked?	☐	___	___
Do you worry about your personal belongings?	☐	___	___
Do you worry about keeping the house always clean and tidy?	☐	___	___
Do you worry about keeping things in their right place?	☐	___	___
Do you worry about your physical health?	☐	___	___
Do you worry about doing things in their right order?	☐	___	___
Do you ever have to count things several times or go through numbers in your mind?	☐	___	___
Are you a person who often has a guilty conscience over quite ordinary things?	☐	___	___
Do unpleasant or frightening thoughts or words ever keep going over and over in your mind?	☐	___	___
Have you ever been troubled by certain thoughts of harming yourself or others—thoughts which come and go without any particular reason?	☐	___	___
Do you worry about household things that might chip or splinter if they were to be knocked over or broken?	☐	___	___
Do you ever have persistent ideas that someone you know might be having an accident or that something might have happened to them?	☐	___	___
Are you preoccupied with the fear of being raped or assaulted?	☐	___	___

	Check here if your answer is yes	A If yes, rate from 1 to 5	B rate from 1 to 4
Do you go back and think about a task you have already completed, wondering how you could have done it better?	☐	———	———
Do you find yourself concerned with germs?	☐	———	———
Do you have to turn things over and over in your mind before being able to decide about what to do?	☐	———	———
Do you ask yourself questions or have doubts about a lot of things that you do?	☐	———	———
Are there any particular things that you try to keep away from or that you avoid doing, because you know that you would be upset by them?	☐	———	———
Do you worry about money a lot?	☐	———	———
Do you frequently think that things will not get better and may, in fact, get worse?	☐	———	———
Do you become preoccupied with angry or irritated thoughts when people don't do things carefully or correctly?	☐	———	———
Do you ruminate about details?	☐	———	———
Do guilt-tinged memories return to you over and over?	☐	———	———
Do you have recurring feelings of jealousy, or fear of being left?	☐	———	———
Do you feel nervous about heights?	☐	———	———
Are you at times preoccupied with desire for things you cannot have?	☐	———	———
Do you worry about auto accidents?	☐	———	———
Do you find yourself returning to thoughts about your faults?	☐	———	———
Do you worry about growing old?	☐	———	———
Do you feel nervous when thinking about being alone?	☐	———	———
Do you worry about dirt and/or dirty things?	☐	———	———
Are you ever worried about knives, hammers, hatchets or other possibly dangerous things?	☐	———	———
Do you tend to worry a bit about personal cleanliness or tidiness?	☐	———	———
Does a negative feature of your appearance or makeup preoccupy you at times?	☐	———	———

	Check here if your answer is yes	A If yes, rate from 1 to 5	B rate from 1 to 4
Do you worry about getting trapped in crowds, on bridges, elevators, etc. ?	☐	_____	_____
Do you think again and again about your failures?	☐	_____	_____
Sometimes do you think about your home burning?	☐	_____	_____
Do you think frequently of certain things of which you are ashamed?	☐	_____	_____
Are you preoccupied with uncomfortable thoughts about sex or sexual adequacy?	☐	_____	_____

(Adapted from the Leyton Scale, devised by J. E. Cooper, University of Nottingham Medical School.)

2. Arrange a timed interruption.

Get an egg timer or alarm clock and have it handy. Close your eyes and focus on the thought that you have chosen. Remember the situation or any associated thoughts that go with it. Try to include normal as well as obsessive or fearful thoughts. In that way you can interrupt the stressful thoughts while allowing a continuing flow of healthy thinking. If you start feeling your usual nervousness or fear, that's fine. It's a good sign, since if you can voluntarily increase your fear, you can voluntarily reduce it too.

When you can easily imagine your thought, open your eyes and set the timer or clock for two minutes. Then close your eyes and continue to mull over your thought. As the bell goes off, shout "Stop!" out loud and either raise your hand, snap your fingers, or stand up. Let your mind empty of every trace of the distressing thought, but allow any neutral or pleasant thoughts to continue.

Try to keep your mind blank or on neutral topics for about 30 seconds. If the upsetting thought recurs within 30 seconds, shout "Stop!" again.

After you have mastered thought interruption with the egg timer or alarm clock you can proceed to using a tape recorder. Record yourself shouting "Stop!" at random intervals of three minutes, one minute, two minutes, and one and a half minutes. If you have had trouble stopping the thought before, you might want to record yourself saying "Stop!" three or four times in a row, instead of just once at each interval.

Proceed with the tape recording in the same way as with the egg timer or clock. The tape recording reinforces your thought control.

3. Practice unaided thought interruption.

While ruminating on your distressing thought, shout "Stop!" without the aid of timer, clock, or recorder. Keep doing this until you have successfully extinguished the thought several times in a row.

When you can completely interrupt the thought by shouting, start saying "Stop" in a normal tone of voice. Practice this until it is just as effective as shouting.

Then teach yourself to fully interrupt the thought with "Stop" said in a faint whisper. Finally, make the "Stop" subvocal—imagine hearing it shouted inside your head while moving your tongue and throat as if you were saying it, but without making a sound. When you master this you can interrupt thoughts covertly, at any place or time without drawing attention to yourself.

4. Prepare your covert assertions.

As you practiced thought interruption, you probably noticed that the mind, like nature, abhors a vacuum. As soon as you inerrupt one train of thought, another seems to step right in to take its place. You can take advantage of this phenomenon by selecting effective covert assertions to substitute for your stressful thoughts.

Covert Assertion and Anxiety

Although anxiety may seem to come on like a single overwhelming wave, it is actually a series of reactions that takes place in four distinct phases. First there is anticipatory anxiety, which you experience when getting ready for or thinking about a stressful situation or event. A good example is preparing for a test or a job interview.

The second phase of anxiety is the initial confrontation when you first see the prospective employer, the test paper, the threatening dog, or whatever it is you fear. It may be the first action in a series of actions that you find unpleasant: picking up the phone, ringing a doorbell, saying hello to someone.

The third phase of anxiety occurs while you are actually trying to cope with the situation or thoughts that make you anxious: talking to your new boyfriend, working on the first question on the test, explaining yourself to your boss, driving the steep, winding road.

The fourth phase of anxiety actually occurs after the situation or event, when you look back and worry about how you did. For example, you may fret for hours after a test or interview, worrying about what you said or didn't say or could have said better or different and what he must have thought of you and why didn't you wear the blue coat instead of the brown, and so on.

To cope with these four phases of anxiety you need to prepare four kinds of covert assertions that you can say to yourself before, at the beginning of, during, and after potentially disturbing situations. The following are examples of assertions that others have used successfully:

Before Event

Worry won't make it any different.
What exactly do you have to do?
Just think rationally. Negative thoughts aren't rational.
You can plan how to deal with it.

Beginning of Event

Just get a grip on yourself. You can handle this.
You only have to take it one step at a time.
Keep your mind on what you have to do, not on the fear.
This anxiety is a signal to relax.

During Event

Take a deep breath, pause, and relax.
What is the next step? Focus on that.
Fear is natural. It arises and subsides, and you can keep it under control.
It will be over soon. Nothing lasts forever.
Worse things could happen.
Do something to take your mind off the fear.

After Event

You did it!
That wasn't so bad.
It's getting easier.
You could do it again with half the trouble.
Your thoughts about it were worse than the thing itself.
Once again you were bigger than your fear.
This really works.

You may want to use some of these statements. However, the best ones will be those you make up yourself. Take a moment now to write down three statements for each of the four phases.

Before Event

Beginning of Event

During Event

After Event

Anger and Depression

The following examples of covert assertions are designed to replace thoughts which generate anger and depression. Use them as models to write ones that apply specifically to you.

> You're strong enough to handle criticism.
> Expect less from her and then you can calm down.
> Take a deep breath—in an hour it won't matter.
> Life isn't fair.
> Go slow and see it from his perspective.
> Memories make you feel worse.
> Decide something, one way or the other.
> Think about what you can do right now.
> Say goodbye to the past. It's OK to forget.
> Look for what you like about you.

Perfecting Your Covert Assertions

Covert Assertion directly attacks the automatic thoughts that invariably precede unpleasant emotions of fear or even depression and anger. Your automatic thoughts determine how you will react to any situation, according to a system that is consistent with its own internal logic. To combat these thoughts, your covert assertions must be worded to correspond to the rules of your personal logic system. Fine-tuning your assertions in this way is a form of "reframing," a powerful technique for accomplishing change and growth.

Your logic is revealed in whatever you are saying to yourself that makes you anxious, depressed, or angry. If you have trouble noticing your automatic thoughts, refer to Chapter Two.

Review the assertions you have composed. Reword any of them that are merely denials or contradictions of your thoughts. Repeating over and over to yourself during a speech, "I am not afraid" will not be very helpful. Instead you should frame an assertion that reinforces your ability to cope with the nervousness, such as "When I talk slowly I feel calm...I have my notes and I'm well prepared... I am entitled to a quota of three bloopers."

Likewise, if you are depressed over the loss of a close relationship, it will not be convincing to assert "She didn't really matter to me." Focus instead on your ability to cope with the feelings of loss and your ability to grow and develop new interests as a single person. Better assertions would be, "It's OK to feel sadness, then let it pass naturally...There are lots of other people to know and things to do...I'm getting good at being with myself."

By editing your assertions to eliminate denials you are doing more than merely introducing a positive tone. You are composing assertions that will remind you that your goal is to cope with unpleasant emotions, not to eliminate them entirely. Effective covert assertions do not deny the existence of anxiety, anger, or depression—they acknowledge the reality of these emotions and redefine them as cues for coping, not collapsing.

Effective assertions also remind you of your power to control your reactions. That is why "you" statements like "You feel calm and in control" are more effective than "I" statements like "I feel calm and in control." Putting your assertions in the second person imposes some distance between you and your reactions and implies a degree of outside control.

Another way covert assertions work is by focusing your attention on facts, directing your mind to the task or situation at hand, instead of allowing it to turn inward and concentrate on automatic thoughts of danger, fear, or loss. That's why many people use assertions such as, "Take one step at a time . . . What's the next thing to do? . . . Describe exactly what's happening."

5. Practice Overt and Covert Assertion.

Close your eyes and imagine a situation that typically triggers fearful or obsessive thoughts. When it is very real for you and you sense the thoughts beginning, say "Stop" out loud. Then say one of your prepared assertions out loud. Repeat this each time the thought comes back. At this point you may want to experiment with different phrasings or different statements to see which ones are most effective.

Repeat the procedure by barely moving your lips and whispering instead of talking out loud. Then repeat covertly, saying the "Stops" and assertions to yourself.

6. Use Covert Assertion in Real Life Situations.

Now that you have developed your skill by practicing in imaginary situations, all that remains is to use it in real life situations. When you know that you will soon be doing something or will be in a situation that is stressful, plan the covert assertions you will use. If the situation is anxiety provoking, run through the four phases of anxiety in your imagination, using appropriate assertions at each step, and see yourself getting through successfully.

Always interrupt stressful thoughts at their inception. Be diligent and don't let them get a foothold. And don't leave a vacuum—the stressful thoughts will come sneaking back if you fail to fill the space with your covert assertions.

Example

Ann was a young woman who felt very nervous around strangers. She could deal with her husband and her two small children, but she often became very anxious and tongue-tied when interacting with anyone outside her family. She thought that they would see that she was too tense to do anything right. She was afraid of confrontations in which she would appear to be stupid or at fault.

Ann needed extra money at Christmas time, and a friend got her a job wrapping gifts at a department store. The first day on the job a customer complained that Ann had given her the wrong color paper and made Ann wrap two packages all over again. While Ann was rewrapping the packages, some of the other customers in line began griping loudly about how slow she was and about how incompetent "these Christmas temporaries" are.

Ann burst into tears and had to take an extra long coffee break to pull herself together. When she went home she felt exhausted and nervous, and never wanted to go back to the store again. However, she had plans for the extra money she would earn, and was mad at herself for letting a few hostile customers get her so upset. She decided to apply Covert Assertion to deal with her problem.

Ann sat at the kitchen table with the egg timer set for three minutes, thinking about how she felt when the woman complained about the packages. When the timer went off, she shouted, "Stop" and stood up. She did this three times before she was able to interrupt the thoughts of failure and embarrassment.

Next she recorded herself shouting "Stop!" at random intervals. She listened to this tape while imagining how nervous she felt going to work on the bus, or as the first customer of the day charged up to the gift wrap counter. Each time the tape said "Stop!" she emptied her mind of the automatic thoughts going through her mind. She continued to think about how pretty the Christmas decorations looked, how she would spend the extra money, and how pleasant it was to be away from the kids for a few hours.

Ann got so that she could blank out her mind of all but the pleasant thoughts just by whispering "Stop" to herself. Finally she could interrupt the thoughts by saying it to herself silently.

While she had been learning to interrupt her thoughts, she had noticed a few things about herself and her fears, and she used this information to write four kinds of assertions that seemed to fit her circumstances and the way her mind worked. Still sitting at the kitchen table, she wrote:

Before Work

You've made it this far in life. This is just the next stage you're going through.
Plan it just like planning a trip.

Beginning Work

They're just like me.
A deep breath, a smile, and you're already started.

During Work, Especially Complaints

One thing at a time. Complete each package before starting the next.
It's only four hours out of your life.
When it's over you'll feel great.
Nothing here is worth taking personally.

After Work

You did it.
You can do it any time you want to.

Ann practiced thought interruption and these assertions out loud and to herself that night while sitting at the kitchen table. The next day she went to work and the assertions worked as long as she remembered them. It was a tough day, but she made it through to the end. The next day was easier because she was gaining in skill and confidence. By the time her three week job was over she was actually enjoying parts of it. When she felt nervous dealing with strangers, she took it as a reminder to use her new skill, instead of as a signal to fall apart.

After Christmas she found herself using the same assertions at a New Year's party and they worked as well as they had at the store.

Special Considerations

1. If you fail at Covert Assertion the first time you try it in a real life situation, you have probably picked one that is too frightening or too disruptive to your life. Covert Assertion is a skill like skiing. Just as you learn to ski on gentle slopes, you should pick an only slightly disturbing situation for your first trial of Covert Assertion.

2. Subvocalizing the word "Stop!" doesn't work for everyone, and most are too embarrassed to shout it out loud. If this is your case, try putting a rubber band unobtrusively around your wrist. When disturbing thoughts intrude, snap the band. You can also pinch yourself. Any sharp, distracting sensation will do.

3. Because it is a learned skill, Covert Assertion takes time to work. if you experience setbacks and reverses, that's normal. Your fears took a long time to learn in the first place, and may take a long time to unlearn.

4. If you forget your prepared assertions or they seem to be meaningless or have little effect, you should reword them until they "feel" right. Your mind has a language all its own and you have to speak its language.

Further Reading

Gambrill, E. D. **Behavior Modification: Handbook of Assessment, Intervention, and Evaluation.** San Francisco: Jossey-Bass, 1978.

Lazarus, A. A. **Behavior Therapy and Beyond.** New York: McGraw Hill, 1971.

Rimm, D. C. and Masters, J. C. **Behavior Therapy: Techniques and Empirical Findings.** New York: Academic Press, 1974.

Wolpe, J. **The Practice of Behavior Therapy.** Oxford: Pergamon Press, 1969.

Chapter 5

Problem Solving

Problems that elude solution result in chronic emotional pain. When your usual coping strategies fail, a growing sense of helplessness makes the search for novel solutions more difficult. The possibility of relief seems to recede, the problem begins to appear insoluble, and anxiety or despair can increase to crippling levels.

In 1971 Thomas D'Zurella and Marvin Goldried devised a five-step problem solving strategy for generating novel solutions to any kind of problem. They defined a problem as *failure to find an effective response.* For example, the fact that you can't find one of your shoes in the morning is not in itself a problem. It becomes a problem only if you neglect to look under the bed where the shoe is most likely to be found. If you look in the sink, the medicine cabinet, and the garbage disposal, you are beginning to create a problem—your response is not effective in finding the missing shoe and therefore the situation becomes "problematic" for you.

Often you may make a situation problematic by employing a response that seems effective at the time, but proves to be disastrous in the end. If you spend hours playing golf every weekend and your mate is irritated about it, you don't necessarily have a problem. You have a problem only if your response is ultimately ineffective. You might develop a strategy of blowing up every time she mentions your golf game, as a way of discouraging further comment. Your solution is a short term success insofar as she gives up mentioning golf, but in the long run she may take a lover and file for divorce. Your response is ineffective in the long run and you have created a big problem. The five-step problem solving process outlined in this chapter will help you assess the consequences of such false short term "solutions" and come up with alternative responses that pay off in the long run.

Applying the five steps taught in this chapter will give you practice in viewing life as an endless series of situations that require some kind of response. Looked at from this point of view, no situation is inherently problematic. It is the inappropriateness of your response that makes it problematic. You will learn to define problems not in terms of impossible situations, but rather in terms of inappropriate solutions. It is helpful to remind yourself that "the *problem* is not the problem—the *solution* is the problem." As this statement begins to make sense to you, you will grasp the essence of problem solving.

A convenient acronym for the five steps of problem solving is "SOLVE," which stands for:

State your problem.
Outline your response.
List your alternatives.
View the consequences.
Evaluate your results.

Symptom Effectiveness

Problem solving is effective for reducing anxiety associated with procrastination and the inability to make decisions. It is useful for relieving the feelings of powerlessness or anger associated with chronic problems for which no alternative solution has been found. Problem solving is not recommended for the treatment of phobias or conditions of global, free-floating anxiety.

Time for Mastery

Problem solving techniques can be put into effect the same day they are learned. After several weeks of practice, applying the steps becomes largely automatic.

Instructions

1. State Your Problem

The first step in problem solving is to identify the problem situations in your life. No situation is inherently problematic, but with endless chances for making ineffective responses to different situations you're bound to *create* some problems. In fact, creating problems is natural and unavoidable. You wouldn't be human if you didn't do it. Also life is basically unfair—you may actually have more problem situations than your friends, relatives, or acquaintances. It's important to realize and accept the fact that problems are normal.

People normally experience problems in areas such as finances, work, social relationships, and family life. The following checklist will help you identify the area in which you operate least effectively and have the most problems. This is the area you will concentrate on as you develop problem solving skills.

Problem Checklist

After each situation listed, check the box that best describes how much of a problem it is for you. If you have trouble determining whether a situation is a significant problem for you, imagine yourself in that situation. Include lots of sights and sounds and actions to make it seem real. In that situation, do you feel angry? depressed? anxious? confused? These are "red flag" emotions. When you experience anger, depression, anxiety, or confusion, you are probably in a situation that is a problem for you—something about the way you are responding to the situation isn't working for you. Mark the appropriate box:

A. **No Interference**—This doesn't apply to me or doesn't bother me.

B. **Interferes a Little**—This mildly affects my life and is a small drain on my energy.

C. **Interferes Moderately**—This has a significant impact on my life.

D. **Interferes a Great Deal**—This greatly disrupts my day-to-day existence and strongly affects my sense of well being.

Health

	A	B	C	D
Difficulty sleeping	☐	☐	☐	☐
Weight problems	☐	☐	☐	☐
Feeling physically tired and run down	☐	☐	☐	☐
Stomach trouble	☐	☐	☐	☐
Chronic physical problems	☐	☐	☐	☐
Difficulty getting up in the morning	☐	☐	☐	☐
Poor diet and nutrition	☐	☐	☐	☐

Finances

	A	B	C	D
Difficulty making ends meet	☐	☐	☐	☐
Insufficient money for basic necessities	☐	☐	☐	☐
Increasing amounts of debt	☐	☐	☐	☐
Unexpected expenses	☐	☐	☐	☐
Too little money for hobbies and recreation	☐	☐	☐	☐
No steady source of income	☐	☐	☐	☐
Too many financial dependents	☐	☐	☐	☐

Work

	A	B	C	D
Work monotonous and boring	☐	☐	☐	☐
Poor relations with boss or supervisor	☐	☐	☐	☐
Rushing and under stress	☐	☐	☐	☐
Wanting a different job or career	☐	☐	☐	☐
Needing more education or experience	☐	☐	☐	☐
Afraid of losing job	☐	☐	☐	☐
Not getting along with co-workers	☐	☐	☐	☐

	A	B	C	D
Unemployed.	☐	☐	☐	☐
Unpleasant working conditions.	☐	☐	☐	☐
Needing more freedom at work.	☐	☐	☐	☐

Living Situation

	A	B	C	D
Bad neighborhood.	☐	☐	☐	☐
Too far from work or school	☐	☐	☐	☐
Too small.	☐	☐	☐	☐
Unpleasant conditions	☐	☐	☐	☐
Things need repair.	☐	☐	☐	☐
Poor relationship with landlord.	☐	☐	☐	☐

Social Relationships

	A	B	C	D
Timid or shy around the opposite sex.	☐	☐	☐	☐
Not having many friends	☐	☐	☐	☐
Too little contact with the opposite sex	☐	☐	☐	☐
Feeling lonely.	☐	☐	☐	☐
Not getting along well with certain people.	☐	☐	☐	☐
A failed or failing love affair.	☐	☐	☐	☐
Feeling left out.	☐	☐	☐	☐
Lack of love and affection	☐	☐	☐	☐
Vulnerable to the criticism of others.	☐	☐	☐	☐
Wanting more closeness to people.	☐	☐	☐	☐
Not understood by others.	☐	☐	☐	☐
Not really knowing how to converse.	☐	☐	☐	☐
Not finding the right mate	☐	☐	☐	☐

Recreation

	A	B	C	D
Not having enough fun.	☐	☐	☐	☐
Not good at sports or games	☐	☐	☐	☐
Too little leisure time	☐	☐	☐	☐
Wanting more chance to enjoy art or self-expression	☐	☐	☐	☐
Little chance to enjoy nature	☐	☐	☐	☐
Wanting to travel.	☐	☐	☐	☐
Needing a vacation	☐	☐	☐	☐
Can't think of anything fun to do	☐	☐	☐	☐

Family

	A	B	C	D
Feeling rejected by family.	☐	☐	☐	☐
Discord at home with mate	☐	☐	☐	☐
Not getting along with one or more of the children.	☐	☐	☐	☐
Feeling trapped in painful family situation.	☐	☐	☐	☐
Insecure—afraid of losing mate.	☐	☐	☐	☐
Unable to be open and honest with family members.	☐	☐	☐	☐
Wanting sexual contact with someone other than mate.	☐	☐	☐	☐
Conflict with parents	☐	☐	☐	☐

	A	B	C	D
Having different interests from mate.	☐	☐	☐	☐
Interference by relatives	☐	☐	☐	☐
Marriage breaking up	☐	☐	☐	☐
Children having problems at school	☐	☐	☐	☐
Sick family member.	☐	☐	☐	☐
Excessive quarreling at home.	☐	☐	☐	☐
Anger, resentment toward mate	☐	☐	☐	☐
Irritated with habits of a family member	☐	☐	☐	☐
Worried about family member.	☐	☐	☐	☐

Psychological

	A	B	C	D
Having a particular bad habit	☐	☐	☐	☐
Religious problems	☐	☐	☐	☐
Problems with authority.	☐	☐	☐	☐
Competing goals or demands.	☐	☐	☐	☐
Obsessed with distant or unobtainable goals	☐	☐	☐	☐
Lacking motivation.	☐	☐	☐	☐
Feeling very depressed at times	☐	☐	☐	☐
Feeling nervous at certain times.	☐	☐	☐	☐
Feeling blocked from attaining goals.	☐	☐	☐	☐
Feeling angry a lot.	☐	☐	☐	☐
Worrying	☐	☐	☐	☐

Other   (If particular situations not listed above significantly interfere in your life, write them here and rate them.)

	A	B	C	D
_____	☐	☐	☐	☐
_____	☐	☐	☐	☐
_____	☐	☐	☐	☐
_____	☐	☐	☐	☐

2. Outline Your Response

The second step in problem solving is to describe the problem and your usual response in great detail. From the problem checklist you have just completed, determine the general area that causes the most interference in your life. From that area, pick one of the situations that you have ranked as interfering moderately or a great deal.

Using the situation you have chosen, fill out the following problem outline. Try to put at least one word in each blank. When a blank isn't large enough for all you have to write, use a separate sheet of paper.

By describing the situation and your response in terms of who, what, where, when, how, and why, you will get your problem clearer in your mind. You'll also uncover many more details than you usually have available for consideration. Take your time. The details of place, mood, feelings, and thoughts are important because they will provide clues for generating alternative solutions later.

Problem Outline

I Situation (from problem checklist or briefly in your own words)

_____

Who is involved—the other people

_____

What happens—what is done or not done that bothers you

_____

Where it happens—location

_____

When it happens—time of day, how often, how long it lasts

_____

How it happens—the rules it seems to follow, the moods involved

_____

Why it happens—the reasons you or others give for the problem at the time

_____

II Response—Summarize what you do or don't do.

_____

Where I do it—location

_____

When I do it—reaction time, duration of response

_____

How I do it—style, mood, degree of force or restraint

_____

How I feel—emotions of anger, depression, confusion, etc.

_____

Why I do it—thoughts about it, theories, explanations, rationalizations

_____

What I want—goals that, if accomplished, would mean that the problem is
  solved

_____

Example

This is the outline completed by Jane, the mother of a rebellious twelve year old son:

I Situation (from problem checklist or briefly in your own words)

Not getting along with child

Who is involved—the other people

12-year-old son Jim

What happens—what is done or not done that bothers you

He won't do chores—take out garbage, water garden, set table.

Where it happens—location

At home, especially in family room in front of TV

When it happens—time of day, how often, how long it lasts

Afternoon & evening, for about two hours, nearly every day

How it happens—the rules it seems to follow, the moods involved

_The more I remind him of chores, the more sullen he gets. Just sits there
while I get madder. Does chores resentfully after I threaten no TV._

Why it happens—the reasons you or others give for the problem at the time

He's going through a stage. I expect too much. He doesn't care how I feel.

II Response—Summarize what you do or don't do

Suffer in silence, then remind, then nag, then yell and threaten.

Where I do it—location

In house

When I do it—reaction time, duration of response

When busy or tired. The more tired I am, the more likely I am to blow up.

How I do it—style, mood, degree of force or restraint

Start quiet then escalate to yelling.

How I feel—emotions of anger, depression, confusion, etc.

*Angry at Jim, feel he doesn't care about me, feel pressured, resentful I have
    to put up with it and husband doesn't.*

Why I do it—thoughts about it, theories, explanations, rationalizations

I'm a failure as a mother. Jim will never learn responsibility and it's my fault.

What I want—goals that, if accomplished, would mean that the problem is solved

I want Jim to obey me.

Using your outline to reclassify your problem

Now that you have outlined your problem in detail you can reclassify it by
trying different ways of thinking about it. You have probably already indulged in
reclassification as you created the outline: you may have gone back to add, delete,

or change information as you went along. Now you will continue this process of reclassification in a more systematic way. Go back over your outline and use the information you have written to complete these statements:

The real problem isn't_____:
Who is involved

    the real problem is_____.
Where you respond

The real problem isn't_____:
What's done that bothers you

    the real problem is_____.
When you respond

The real problem isn't_____:
How it happens

    the real problem is_____.
How you feel

The real problem isn't_____:
Why it happens

    the real problem is_____.
*Why you respond the way you do—
thoughts, theories, rationalizations*

The real problem isn't_____:
The situation

    the real problem is_____.
How you respond

Some of the statements you create in this way won't make sense. Some will have the power of penetrating insights that throw new light on the problem. The real problem is likely to be your response to a situation you want to change. In Jane's case, the problem is not so much that her son doesn't obey as it is that Jane is frequently angry and yelling at him. She has attempted to motivate him with aversive threats which only serve to increase his stubborness. Examine your solutions to determine if they have not actually become the problem.

The purpose of going back over your outline in this way is to generate goals that you can use in the next step of problem solving. As you engage in this process you will see that your goals can change as your way of classifying the problem changes. Examine your responses to the problem—what you do, how you feel, what you want. From these statements you can generate new alternative goals.

For example, Jane found three statements to be particularly enlightening:

"The real problem is the more tired I am, the more likely I am to blow up."

"The real problem is he doesn't care how I feel."

"The real problem is I feel pressured."

From these statements Jane formed three alternative goals:

A. Live with less tiredness

B. Feel cared for by son

C. Feel calm

Using your own reclassifying statements, formulate alternative goals to carry forward to the next step:

Alternative goal A. _____

Alternative goal B. _____

Alternative goal C. _____

If you come up with one goal and have difficulty finding others, ask yourself, "Why do I want this goal?" The answer may be several subgoals that you haven't yet identified.

3. List Your Alternatives

In this phase of problem solving you "brainstorm" strategies to achieve your newly formulated goals. The brainstorming technique set forth by Osborn in 1963 has four basic rules:

Criticism is ruled out. This means that you write down any new idea or possible solution without judging it as good or bad. Evaluation is deferred to a later decision-making phase.

Freewheeling is welcomed. The crazier and wilder your idea is, the better. Following this rule can help lift you out of mental ruts. You may suddenly break free of your old limited view of the problem and see it in an entirely different light.

Quantity is best. The more ideas you generate, the better your chances are of having a few good ones. Just write them down, one after another, without thinking a lot about each idea. Don't stop until you have a good, long list.

Combination and improvement are sought. Go back over your list to see how some ideas might be combined or improved. Sometimes two pretty good ideas can be joined into an even better idea.

Brainstorming during this phase should be limited to *general strategies* for achievement of goals. Leave the nuts and bolts of specific actions for later. You need a good overall strategy first. Particular behavioral steps come in the next phase.

Use this form to list at least ten alternative strategies for accomplishing your goals:

Goal A. _____

1. _____
2. _____
3. _____
4. _____
5. _____
6. _____
7. _____
8. _____
9. _____
10. _____

Goal B. _____

1. _____
2. _____
3. _____
4. _____
5. _____
6. _____
7. _____
8. _____
9. _____
10. _____

Goal C. _____

1. _____
2. _____
3. _____
4. _____
5. _____
6. _____
7. _____
8. _____
9. _____
10. _____

Jane used brainstorming techniques to generate the following strategies for achieving her three goals:

Goal A. Live with less tiredness

Let the chore stay undone if the children don't do it.
Take periodic rest breaks during the day.
Schedule something fun for around 3:00 PM.
Blow up the TV, the noise drives me crazy.
Spend time alone each day.
Hire a maid.
Work out a deal with a highschool girl in the neighborhood to do some of the chores.
Get my husband to barbecue dinner every Saturday.
Stop cleaning the kids' rooms. Let them live like pigs if they want to.
Get support hose.
Unplug the TV during the day.
Have the kids make their own lunches.

Goal B. Feel cared for by son

No matter what he does or doesn't do, stop yelling at him.
Talk to him instead of blasting him.
Let my husband do the disciplining.
"Spontaneously" hug him two or three times a day.
Reward him with a hug when he actually does his chore.
Praise him a lot.

Ask him about school and "check in" with him at least once a day.

If he doesn't obey, take a few minutes with him and find out if anything's wrong.

It's more important to me to have a good feeling with my son than to have him do his chores every day.

Explain my problems to him and ask his help.

Goal C. Feel calm

No matter what, stop yelling.

Rest whenever I start feeling upset or angry.

Blow up the TV.

Husband does disciplining.

Take a week off and go to the mountains.

Get a massage vibrator.

Take a course in relaxation.

Exchange massages with husband after the kids are in bed.

Take Valium.

Start to swim again.

It is important not to give up the search for alternative strategies too quickly. Your tenth idea may be the best one. Jane went over her list and combined some of the ideas. For example, she combined checking in with her son once a day with telling him about her problems and asking his help. She combined spending time alone each day with a scheduled fun activity at 3:00 PM.

4. View the Consequences

By now you should have several alternative goals, each with ten strategies for its accomplishment. The next step is to select the most promising strategies and view the consequences of putting them into action. For some people this process of figuring and weighing consequences happens automatically as soon as they think of a possible strategy for getting what they want. Others are slower and more likely to consciously ponder the consequences. Whichever category best describes you, it will be helpful to do this step thoroughly and conscientiously.

Pick the one alternative goal that is the most attractive to you. Go over its 10 strategies and cross out any obviously bad ideas. Combine several strategies into one whenever possible. You should end up with three promising strategies that are mutually exclusive in some way (can't be combined into fewer strategies).

List these three strategies in the spaces provided on the following Evaluating Consequences form. Under each strategy list any negative and positive consequences you can think of. How would putting that strategy into action affect what you feel, need, or want? How would it affect the people in your life? How would it change their reaction to you? How would it affect your life right now, next month, or next year? Take some time to get *both* positive and negative consequences for each possible strategy.

When you have the major consequences listed, go over each one and ask yourself how likely it is to come about. If the consequence is unlikely, cross it out—you're telling yourself horror stories or being falsely optimistic.

Then score the likely consequences you have left as follows:

If the consequence is predominantly personal in nature, give 2 points.

If the consequence is predominantly social in nature, give 1 point.

If the consequence is predominantly long range in nature, give 2 points.

If the consequence is predominantly short range in nature, give 1 point.

Note that consequences can be both personal and long range at the same time (total score of 4), social and long range (total score of 3), and so on.

Evaluating Consequences

Strategy: _____

Positive Consequences	Score	Negative Consequences	Score
_____	____	_____	____
_____	____	_____	____
_____	____	_____	____
total: ____		total: ____	

Strategy: _____

_____	____	_____	____
_____	____	_____	____
_____	____	_____	____
total: ____		total: ____	

Strategy: _____

_____	____	_____	____
_____	____	_____	____
_____	____	_____	____
total: ____		total: ____	

Example

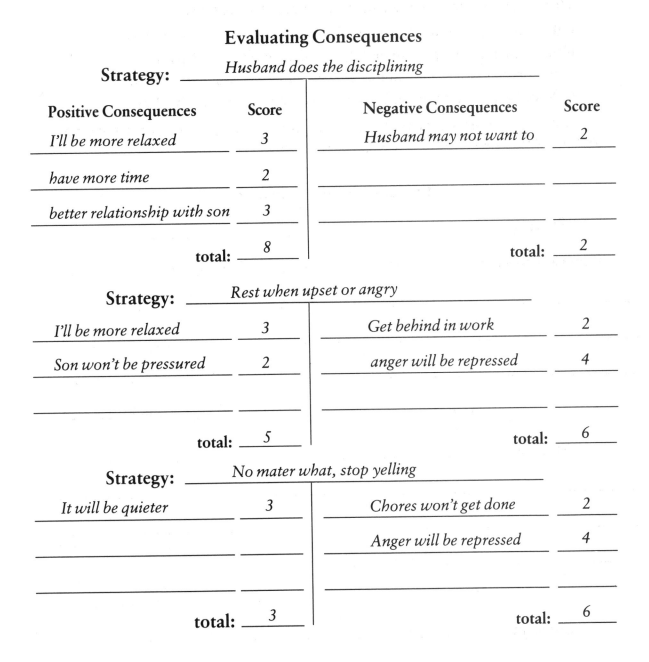

Evaluating Consequences

Strategy: ___Husband does the disciplining___

Positive Consequences	Score	Negative Consequences	Score
I'll be more relaxed	3	Husband may not want to	2
have more time	2		
better relationship with son	3		
total:	8	**total:**	2

Strategy: ___Rest when upset or angry___

I'll be more relaxed	3	Get behind in work	2
Son won't be pressured	2	anger will be repressed	4
total:	5	**total:**	6

Strategy: ___No mater what, stop yelling___

It will be quieter	3	Chores won't get done	2
		Anger will be repressed	4
total:	3	**total:**	6

Add up the scores for each strategy to see whether the positive consequences outweigh the negative. The strategy that has the greatest preponderance of positive consequences is the one you probably should put into action.

Select the strategy whose positive consequences most greatly outweigh the negative consequences. Decide on the steps you will have to take to put your strategy into action. Jane thought of four steps to put "Husband does the disciplining" into action:

Discuss the subject with husband Tuesday after son goes to bed.

Take five minutes each day after work to discuss with husband how well chores are being done.

Have husband spend time with son each evening and focus on how well chores are being done.

Use time I used to spend disciplining to do something nice for husband: bake a special dessert, give a backrub.

You may have trouble thinking of concrete behavioral steps. If so, return to brainstorming to develop a list of alternative steps. Then explore the consequences of the likely steps using the same technique you learned for selecting your overall strategy.

5. Evaluate Your Results

The last step is the hardest, since you now have to act. You've selected some new responses to an old situation. It is time to put your decisions into effect.

Once you have tried the new response, observe the consequences. Are things happening as you predicted? Are you *satisfied* with the outcome? Satisfied means that the new response is helping you reach your goals in a way your old "solution" was not.

If you are still not reaching your goals, if the outcome is not satisfactory, return to your alternative strategies list. You can either generate more ideas at this point or select one or more strategies that you had passed over before. You may repeat steps 3, 4, and 5 of the problem solving procedure.

Example

Al was a travel agent in his late forties. He had become increasingly dissatisfied with his job. He was bored by arranging the same tours and cruises. Six months previously a new computer system had been installed in his office. He was given basic instructions for handling the computer terminals and soon found himself fascinated with computer systems. He hatched the idea of cutting back to half time at work in order to return to school for instruction in computer science.

Al's boss wasn't interested in his plan. They had several confrontations about the issue. Al felt resentful and became inattentive to the detailed travel arrangements that were his responsibility.   This provoked still more confrontations with his boss.

Al applied the **SOLVE** system to his problem like this:

State Your Problem. My job is boring. I want to go to school and switch careers. I have poor relations with my boss.

Outline Response. The situation is that I want time off from a boring job to attend school but my boss won't let me. The response is to ask the boss, get turned down, feel angry, complain, and take it out on customers by being rude and forgetting details.

Al went on to list who, what, where, when, how, and why for both his situation and the response. Then he filled in the blanks of the "real problem" exercise. Some of his results didn't make sense, but two statements shed new light on his problem. They were, "The real problem isn't a mean boss: the real problem is complaining and taking it out on the customers" and "The real problem isn't a boring job: the real problem is *feeling* bored on the job."

From this exercise Al came up with three alternative goals: to achieve better relations with his boss, to give better service to his customers, and to enjoy his current job more.

List Your Alternatives. These are some of the alternatives that Al came up with for his goals:

Better relations with boss
> Get involved creating the new Russia tour package.
> Stop complaining and picking fights.
> Quit, go to school, support myself with some mail order scam.

Better service to customers
> Develop more personal relationships with them.
> Realize I'm providing a real service.

Enjoy job more
> Become very expert with computers.
> Find a way to get just a little time off for one computer class.

View the Consequences. Al crossed off several obviously bad alternatives, such as quitting outright. He considered the consequences in terms of long versus short range benefits, and personal versus social benefits. This showed him that his best options were to get busy on the new tour package, stop complaining, and concentrate on serving his customers. His intention was to improve relations with his boss to the point where he could resume negotiation about getting some time off.

Al did some more brainstorming to develop some concrete steps to follow day-by-day. He put his plans into effect for five weeks.

Evaluate Results. As he expected, Al's relationship with his boss improved. Since he was busy and not fighting with the boss, he enjoyed the job more. He showed his boss how he could take a couple of hours off on Tuesdays and Thursdays and still serve all his customers well. His boss agreed. Al spent those two afternoons a week in a computer science class.

Special Considerations

Some people feel a little overwhelmed by the complex steps involved in problem solving. Their response is, "Do I really have to do all that?" The answer is yes—the first time. You've been stuck for a while in a problematic situation. Your old, habitual solutions haven't worked. You need to follow each step of the technique to identify and then achieve your goals. Later, you can tailor the procedures to fit your particular style and much of it will have become automatic.

Further Reading

D'Zurilla, T. J. and Goldfried, M. R. "Problem Solving and Behavior Modification." **Journal of Abnormal Psychology.** 1971, 78, 107-26.

Karlins, M. and Schroder, H. M. "Discovery Learning, Creativity and the Inductive Teaching Program." **Psychological Reports.** 1967, 20, 867-76.

McGuire, M. T. and Sifneas, P. E. "Problem Solving in Psychotherapy." **Psychiatric Quarterly.** 1970, 44, 667-73.

Osborn, A. F. **Applied Imagination: Principles and Procedures of Creative Problem Solving.** 3rd. ed. New York: Scribner's, 1963.

Perlman, H. H. "In Quest of Coping." **Social Casework.** 1975, 20, 213-25.

Watzlawick, P., Weakland, J. and Fisch, R. **Change.** New York: W. W. Norton, 1974.

Chapter 6

Systematic Desensitization

With Systematic Desensitization, you can train yourself to cope with things and situations that are particularly threatening to you. You learn to relax while imagining scenes that are progressively more anxiety provoking.

Systematic Desensitization was developed by the behavior therapist Joseph Wolpe in 1958. He was influenced by Edmund Jacobson's use of Progressive Relaxation to inhibit high levels of anxiety. Wolpe's early technique was to train people in Progressive Relaxation and then have them seek out real life situations with graduated levels of stress. Later, he found that imaginary scenes were vastly easier to structure, evoked almost identical levels of anxiety, and produced results that were transferable to real life situations.

The two basic principles underlying Systematic Desensitization are simple: One emotion can be used to counteract another, and threatening situations can be "gotten used to." An example Wolpe gives is from everyday experience: A child at the beach for the first time with his father experiences fear of the water, but that emotion is countered by the reassurance engendered by his father's presence. The father "desensitizes" his son to the fear by letting him get used to the water gradually, in easy steps—watching the waves, dipping a toe in the foam while holding hands, getting a foot wet, and so on, until the child is playing happily in the surf.

Symptom Effectiveness

Systematic Desensitization is effective in overcoming classic phobias, chronic fears, and some interpersonal anxiety reactions. It is especially valuable in inhibiting anxieties aroused by stimuli which have no appropriate overt response, such as fear of aloneness, rejection, or being ridiculed.   The first step in Systematic Desensitization is mastering Progressive Relaxation, which is in itself very effective in reducing muscular tension.

Systematic Desensitization is not indicated for multiphobic symptoms, generalized anxiety, or interpersonal situations that require assertive behavior.

Time for Mastery

Learning to relax your four major muscle groups will take four days. Constructing your fear inventory and threatening events hierarchy can go on at the same time. Then the systematic visualization of scenes can be done daily. Results will usually be noticed immediately, with the average fear taking a week to ease and disappear in the imagined scenes. Results in real life situations will lag a little behind those in the visualization sessions.

Instructions

Mastery of Systematic Desensitization is a simple four-step process of learning to relax your muscles at will, listing all of your fears, constructing a hierarchy of threatening scenes, and working your way through the scenes in imagination.

Learning to Relax

It is impossible to be relaxed physically and tense emotionally at the same time. You can learn to take advantage of this direct physiological link between your body and your mind. In four days of doing three practice sessions a day, you can learn to relax your muscles at will. This ability to relax will then be used to desensitize you to your fears later.

Progressive Relaxation can be practiced lying down or sitting in a chair that supports your head. You can read the instructions that follow, then close your eyes and do the exercises. It is a great help to tape record the instructions, repeating them into the machine several times, so that you can play the tape and put all your concentration on relaxing.

Day One. The first day you will learn to tense and relax the muscles of your hands, forearms, and biceps. Do the following brief exercise three times during the day.

Get into a comfortable position. Clench your right fist tighter and tighter, noticing the tension in your fist, your hand, and your forearm. Now relax. Feel the looseness in your hand and notice the contrast with the tension. Do this once more with your right fist. Do the procedure twice with your left fist, then do it twice with both fists at once. Now bend your elbows and tense your biceps, then relax and notice the difference. Repeat twice.

You may notice sensations of heaviness, warmth or tingling in your arms. That is normal. While untensing try saying to yourself, "Let go of tension...I'm feeling calm and rested...relax and smooth out the muscles" over and over. This mental reinforcement will greatly enhance the physical relaxation.

Day Two. Today you will work on your head, neck, and shoulders. Special attention will be given to the head, since from an emotional point of view, the most important muscles in the body are in the head. That's where most people carry their tension. Do the arm exercises from day one, then do the following:

Wrinkle your forehead as tight as you can. Relax and smooth it out. Frown and notice the strain spreading. Let go and allow your brow to become smooth again. Close your eyes and squint them down as tight as you can. Relax your eyes until they are just gently closed and comfortable. Now clench your jaw. Relax your jaw until your lips are just slightly parted. Really notice the difference between tension and relaxation. Press your tongue against the roof of your mouth. Relax. Purse your lips into an "O" and relax. Enjoy your relaxed forehead, scalp, eyes, jaw, tongue, and lips.

Press your head back as far as it can comfortably go and notice the tension in your neck. Roll it to the right slowly, then to the left. Notice the shifting location of tension. Straighten your head and bring it forward, pressing your chin against your chest. Feel the tension in your throat and the strain at the back of your neck. Relax, allowing your head to come back to a comfortable position. Let the relaxation deepen. Shrug your shoulders up hard, hunching your head down between them. Relax your shoulders. Drop them back and feel the relaxation spreading throughout your neck and shoulders. Go through this whole sequence one more time.

Day Three. Now you will shift your attention to your chest, stomach, and lower back, noticing how tension in these areas affects your breathing and how breathing deeply and slowly can relax you. Do the exercises from days one and two, then add the following:

Get into a comfortable position and relax. Breathe in and fill your lungs completely. Hold your breath and notice the tension. Now exhale, letting your chest relax and become loose, and letting the air hiss out. Continue to breathe deeply and slowly several times, feeling the tension flow out of your body with each expelled breath. Then tighten your stomach and hold it. Notice the tension, then relax. Place your hand on your stomach and breathe deeply into your stomach, pushing your hand out. Hold a moment, then exhale, sensing the relaxation as the air hisses out. Now arch your back without straining. Keep the rest of your body as relaxed as possible. Focus on the tension in your lower back. Now relax deeper and deeper. Repeat this whole sequence again.

Day Four. Finally, you will learn to relax your thighs, buttocks, calves, and feet. To the exercises of days one, two, and three, add the following:

Get into a comfortable position. Tighten your buttocks and thighs by pressing down your heels as hard as you can. Relax and feel the difference. Curl your toes downward to make your calves tense. Observe the tension, then relax your calves. Bend your toes back toward your face, putting tension on your shins. Study the tension, then relax. Feel how heavy and relaxed your legs are. Repeat this sequence once more.

Abbreviated Relaxation Sequence

Now that you have done intensive work on these four major muscle groups, you can use an abbreviated form of the exercises to quickly relax your whole body. Tense each muscle group from five to seven seconds, and then relax from 20 to 30 seconds: 1. Tense your fists, forearms, and biceps in a Charles Atlas pose; relax. 2. Wrinkle up all the muscles in your face like a walnut, and roll your head around in a circle to loosen your neck; relax. 3. Take two deep breaths, one into your chest and one into your stomach; hold and relax. 4. Tense legs twice, one with toes pulled back and once with toes curled down; relax.

Breathing deeply is a major key to relaxation. Between each exercise, take deep breaths into your stomach. Repeat to yourself words such as "relax...calm...letting go" while you are breathing. Whenever tension occurs during Systematic Desensitization, take a deep breath and say to yourself, "Relax."

The more you practice Progressive Relaxation the deeper your relaxation will be.

Fear Inventory

While you are learning the relaxation techniques, you can be making a list of the things and experiences that bother you. The following questionnaire will help you remember and rate your fears. After each item, check the one box that best describes how much you are disturbed by it these days.

	Not At All	A Little	A Fair Amount	Much	Very Much
Noise of vacuum cleaners	☐	☐	☐	☐	☐
Open wounds	☐	☐	☐	☐	☐
Being alone	☐	☐	☐	☐	☐
Being in a strange place	☐	☐	☐	☐	☐
Loud voices	☐	☐	☐	☐	☐
Dead people	☐	☐	☐	☐	☐
Speaking in public	☐	☐	☐	☐	☐
Crossing streets	☐	☐	☐	☐	☐
People who seem insane	☐	☐	☐	☐	☐
Falling	☐	☐	☐	☐	☐

	Not At All	A Little	A Fair Amount	Much	Very Much
Automobiles	☐	☐	☐	☐	☐
Being teased	☐	☐	☐	☐	☐
Dentists	☐	☐	☐	☐	☐
Thunder	☐	☐	☐	☐	☐
Sirens	☐	☐	☐	☐	☐
Failure	☐	☐	☐	☐	☐
Entering a room where other people are already seated	☐	☐	☐	☐	☐
High places on land	☐	☐	☐	☐	☐
Looking down from high buildings	☐	☐	☐	☐	☐
Worms	☐	☐	☐	☐	☐
Imaginary creatures	☐	☐	☐	☐	☐
Strangers	☐	☐	☐	☐	☐
Receiving injections	☐	☐	☐	☐	☐
Bats	☐	☐	☐	☐	☐
Journeys by train	☐	☐	☐	☐	☐
Journeys by bus	☐	☐	☐	☐	☐
Journeys by car	☐	☐	☐	☐	☐
Feeling angry	☐	☐	☐	☐	☐
People in authority	☐	☐	☐	☐	☐
Flying insects	☐	☐	☐	☐	☐
Seeing other people injected	☐	☐	☐	☐	☐
Sudden noises	☐	☐	☐	☐	☐
Dull weather	☐	☐	☐	☐	☐
Crowds	☐	☐	☐	☐	☐
Large open spaces	☐	☐	☐	☐	☐
Cats	☐	☐	☐	☐	☐
One person bullying another	☐	☐	☐	☐	☐
Tough looking people	☐	☐	☐	☐	☐
Birds	☐	☐	☐	☐	☐
Sight of deep water	☐	☐	☐	☐	☐
Being watched working	☐	☐	☐	☐	☐
Dead animals	☐	☐	☐	☐	☐
Weapons	☐	☐	☐	☐	☐
Dirt	☐	☐	☐	☐	☐
Crawling insects	☐	☐	☐	☐	☐
Sight of fighting	☐	☐	☐	☐	☐
Ugly people	☐	☐	☐	☐	☐
Fire	☐	☐	☐	☐	☐
Sick people	☐	☐	☐	☐	☐
Dogs	☐	☐	☐	☐	☐
Being criticized	☐	☐	☐	☐	☐
Strange shapes	☐	☐	☐	☐	☐
Being in an elevator	☐	☐	☐	☐	☐

	Not At All	A Little	A Fair Amount	Much	Very Much
Witnessing surgical operations...........	☐	☐	☐	☐	☐
Angry people......................	☐	☐	☐	☐	☐
Mice...........................	☐	☐	☐	☐	☐
Human blood.....................	☐	☐	☐	☐	☐
Animal blood.....................	☐	☐	☐	☐	☐
Parting from friends.................	☐	☐	☐	☐	☐
Enclosed places...................	☐	☐	☐	☐	☐
Prospect of a surgical operation..........	☐	☐	☐	☐	☐
Feeling rejected by others.............	☐	☐	☐	☐	☐
Airplanes........................	☐	☐	☐	☐	☐
Medical odors....................	☐	☐	☐	☐	☐
Feeling disapproved of...............	☐	☐	☐	☐	☐
Harmless snakes...................	☐	☐	☐	☐	☐
Cemeteries......................	☐	☐	☐	☐	☐
Being ignored	☐	☐	☐	☐	☐
Darkness........................	☐	☐	☐	☐	☐
Premature heartbeats (missing a beat)................	☐	☐	☐	☐	☐
Nude men.......................	☐	☐	☐	☐	☐
Nude women.....................	☐	☐	☐	☐	☐
Fighting........................	☐	☐	☐	☐	☐
Doctors.........................	☐	☐	☐	☐	☐
People with deformities..............	☐	☐	☐	☐	☐
Making mistakes....................	☐	☐	☐	☐	☐
Looking foolish....................	☐	☐	☐	☐	☐
Losing control....................	☐	☐	☐	☐	☐
Fainting........................	☐	☐	☐	☐	☐
Becoming nauseous..................	☐	☐	☐	☐	☐
Spiders.........................	☐	☐	☐	☐	☐
Being in charge or responsible for decisions....................	☐	☐	☐	☐	☐
Sight of knives or sharp objects..........	☐	☐	☐	☐	☐
Becoming mentally ill.................	☐	☐	☐	☐	☐
Being with a member of the opposite sex....................	☐	☐	☐	☐	☐
Taking written tests.................	☐	☐	☐	☐	☐
Being touched by others..............	☐	☐	☐	☐	☐
Feeling different from others...........	☐	☐	☐	☐	☐
A lull in conversation................	☐	☐	☐	☐	☐
Other:					
_____	☐	☐	☐	☐	☐
_____	☐	☐	☐	☐	☐
_____	☐	☐	☐	☐	☐
_____	☐	☐	☐	☐	☐

Now add any other things or experiences that bother you and are not on the questionnaire. What embarrasses you? What makes you want to keep quiet or leave? What would you cross the street to avoid? You can list things that are external to yourself, like animals or loud noises. You can also put down internal experiences such as losing control or feeling nauseated. They may be things that you have not even directly experienced but that you would expect to upset you if you encountered them in real life today.

Thematic Grouping. Now group all the items that bother you according to their common themes. Usually there will be three or four themes and the broad outlines will be fairly obvious. For example, here is a list of fears set down in random order by a thirty-year-old woman:

1. mountain roads
2. locked in closet
3. serious car accident
4. dark theaters
5. being alone
6. death
7. elevator rides
8. fire
9. asked to dance
10. people laughing at me
11. steep staircases
12. going crazy
13. roller coasters
14. complications in pregnancy
15. big crowds

After thinking about her list in detail she was able to group her items under these four themes:

Fear of Confined Places
 2. locked in closet
 4. dark theaters
 7. elevator rides
 15. big crowds

Fear of Heights
 1. mountain roads
 11. steep staircases
 13. roller coasters

Fear of Rejection
 5. being alone
 9. asked to dance
 10. people laughing at me

Fears That Are Basically Reasonable
 3. serious car accident
 6. death
 8. fire
 14. complications in pregnancy

You'll note that some fears such as fear of serious injury in a car accident are reasonable and even necessary to survival in some cases. However if such a fear becomes so strong that you can't stand to ride in a car, then it moves out of the reasonable category and becomes a good target for Systematic Desensitization.

Your groupings will be individual to you. While you may place "walking alone at night" under "Fear of the unknown," others might group it with "Fear of the dark" or "Fear of being attacked." Carefully consider what it is about each item that disturbs you and move items around or change the wording of your theme categories until you are satisfied.

Threatening Scene Hierarchy

From your list of themes, pick the one area that disrupts your life the most. From that theme, choose a specific fear or type of situation that causes you a considerable amount of emotional pain. For example, if you are most hampered in your life by worries about illness and the thing that most upsets you about getting sick is having to receive injections, that's the fear to work on.

Next, imagine a very mild instance of the fear you have chosen—one that would bother you almost not at all. In the case of injections, this might be "watching a movie in which a minor character gets a shot." Really set the scene and include specific details about time and place.

Then imagine the worst thing that could happen regarding your fear, and describe the scene vividly in a phrase. For example, "getting a rabies series injection in the stomach."

Give your mildest scene a rating of five, and your worst scene a rating of 100. Wolpe calls these ratings "suds, " which stands for "subjective units of distress." Total relaxation would be zero suds.

The example becomes a complete hierarchy by filling in threatening scenes of varying intensity, in equal increments:

Item	Scene	suds (Subjective units of distress)
1.	watching a movie in which a minor character gets a shot	5
2.	a friend talks about her flu shot	10
3.	prick finger with pin	15
4.	make routine doctors appointment	20
5.	driving to medical center	25

6.	parking car in medical center parking lot	30
7.	thinking about shots in doctor's waiting room	35
8.	woman comes out of treatment room rubbing her arm	40
9.	nurse with tray of syringes walks past	45
10.	entering examination room	50
11.	doctor asks about symptoms	55
12.	doctor says I need an injection	60
13.	nurse enters room with injection materials	65
14.	doctor fills syringe	70
15.	smell of alcohol on cotton ball	75
16.	seeing hypodermic poised in doctor's hand	80
17.	receive penicillin shot in buttocks	85
18.	get flu shot in arm	90
19.	having a large blood sample taken	95
20.	receiving a rabies series shot in the stomach	100

Use the form provided to construct your own threatening scenes hierarchy. Try to get a full 20 items and construct scenes that are separated by even increments of distress. You may have to widen or narrow the range between your top and bottom items. The more specific the scenes and the more even their progression, the greater your success will be.

There are several ways to increase the gradient of distress from scene to scene. It can be a temporal sequence in which a dreaded event gets closer and closer in time. Or it can be a spatial progression in which you approach closer and closer to a feared object. It can be a combination of these two approaches, or just a series of apparently unrelated scenes that are increasingly threatening examples of a particular experience or emotion. Experiment until you find the arrangement that makes sense to you.

Item	Scene	suds (subjective units of distress)
1.	_____	5
2.	_____	10
3.	_____	15
4.	_____	20
5.	_____	25
6.	_____	30
7.	_____	35
8.	_____	40
9.	_____	45
10.	_____	50
11.	_____	55
12.	_____	60
13.	_____	65
14.	_____	70
15.	_____	75
16.	_____	80
17.	_____	85
18.	_____	90
19.	_____	95
20.	_____	100

Systematic Visualization of Threatening Scenes

Now you are ready to begin systematic desensitization sessions. The technique is based on the simple fact that lowering your anxiety reaction to the weakest item on your hierarchy lowers your reaction to all the other items to the same degree. It's a process as natural and simple as easing into a hot tub of bathwater—by the time you get all the way in, you're used to the heat and can take it with no discomfort at all.

Get into a comfortable position where you won't be disturbed for the next 15 minutes. Have your hierarchy handy, and follow these simple steps:

1. Sitting or lying with your eyes closed, use your relaxation skills to progressively relax all the muscles in your body. Use the short form or the long form of the exercises for the main muscle groups and let relaxation flood your body.

2. When you are totally relaxed, allow the first scene on your hierarchy to enter your mind. Visualize the scene for five to ten seconds, making it as real as possible for yourself. Some kinds of scenes will take longer to visualize, such as imagining taking a long trip or cooking a fancy dinner. Use all your senses to create the scene, including awareness of color, sound, touch, and smell.

3. Notice any tension resulting from the scene, and assign it a "suds" value in your mind.

4. Staying in the scene, take a deep breath, hold it for a count of three and release it slowly. Say to yourself, "I am relaxing...tension is draining away...I am now relaxed." Or you can use simpler phrases such as "relax...calm...letting go."

5. Notice how much your level of tension has decreased, then switch off the scene. If you want, you can end the scene by visualizing a specially relaxing place that is associated in your mind with peace and safety.

6. Repeat this series of steps with the same scene, noticing how much your anxiety level decreases in suds each time.

7. When twice in a row you no longer experience any anxiety, then go on to the next scene in your hierarchy.

It generally takes three or four visualizations of a scene to bring your response to it down to zero. Your first session should be about 15 minutes long, and will probably handle the first three or four items on your hierarchy. If you are having trouble visualizing, see the "Special Considerations" at the end of this chapter.

As you gain skill and speed in relaxation and visualization you can lengthen the sessions to thirty minutes. Stop any session if you're getting tired, bored, or overly upset. You can do sessions every other day, daily, or even twice a day—the only limiting factor is fatigue.

As you go through your hierarchy you will notice that your ability to cope with the real life situations in that area improves. When you encounter similar situations in real life, notice any tension and use it as a cue to relax: breathe deeply and repeat your calming statements to yourself.

When you have completed your first hierarchy you may wish to construct another to work on a different area. Most people who experience chronic anxiety reactions can develop hierarchies in two or three areas that can be handled effectively with Systematic Desensitization.

Individuals are different. Don't worry if you seem to be progressing more slowly or quickly than average.

Example

Jennifer was a twenty-year-old student who checked these items on the fear inventory as bothering her "very much":

Speaking in public

Being criticized

Feeling rejected by others

Feeling disapproved of

Looking foolish

She found all of these items seemed to fit under a general theme of "feeling rejected," and resolved to use Systematic Desensitization to overcome these fears.

Jennifer began practicing Progressive Relaxation on a Monday, the same day she did her fear inventory. She learned to tense and relax her arms, and practiced deep breathing. On Tuesday, she continued relaxation exercises, concentrating on her head, neck, and shoulders. Wednesday she focused on her trunk, and Thursday on her legs. She did her relaxation exercises three times a day.

While she was learning progressive relaxation Jennifer also perfected this threatening scene hierarchy:

Item	Scene	suds (subjective units of distress)
1.	Sitting in history class, wondering if I'm going to be invited to Monica's party next month.	5
2.	Seeing Monica outside class. She walks right by.	10
3.	Monica calls and invites me to party. She doesn't seem very sincere. I start worrying about what to wear, what to say.	15

4. Shopping for dress three weeks before party. Everything I try on looks awful. Leave store empty-handed.   20

5. Monica tells me who's coming to party—lots of strangers.   25

6. Looking in mirror and wishing I could lose 10 pounds before the party.   30

7. Two weeks till the party, thinking about whether I should get a permanent.   35

8. Ten days till the party. I make an appointment to get my hair done.   40

9. Finally decide on new pants and a top to wear, but worried I'll be underdressed.   45

10. Monica reminds me about the party. She says there will be several unattached guys there.   50

11. Having hair done a week before the party.   55

12. Hair looks terrible! I'll have to go with a sack over my head.   60

13. Four days before the party and I wake up with a big pimple on my chin. Look like a witch.   65

14. Two days to go. In a class discussion I notice how funny my voice sounds and how I always say obvious, dumb things.   70

15. The day of the party. I'm getting dressed, brushing hair.   75

16. Driving to the party, feeling like no one will talk to me. Wanting to turn around and go home.   80

17. Walking up Monica's front steps, hearing music and laughter inside the apartment.   85

18. Walking into the livingroom. Heads turn in my direction, then turn away.   90

19. Sipping wine alone in the corner, standing around like a complete wallflower.   95

20. A good-looking guy asks me to dance. I'm afraid I'll look foolish and he'll want to get away from me.   100

Jennifer began Systematic Desensitization on Friday morning. She unplugged the phone, put out the cat, and sat in a comfortable armchair. She closed her eyes and relaxed all the major muscle groups in her body using the abbreviated form of Progressive Relaxation.

When she was relaxed, she visualized the first scene on her hierarchy: sitting in class wondering if Monica would invite her to the party. She evoked the sight of the sun slanting through the windows, the empty feeling in her stomach, the sound of the professor droning away, the smell of chalk and paper dust, the feel of the plastic desktop.

After ten seconds of this, she noticed her feeling of tension and assigned it a suds value of four.

Still visualizing the classroom scene, she took a deep breath and slowly released it, saying to herself, "relax . . . calm."

She noticed how her tension decreased, then switched off the scene. To quickly and completely clear her mind, she imagined a relaxing alternate scene of lying on a beach in the sun, hearing the surf.

Jennifer went through these steps four more times. In the last two repetitions, she found that she rated worrying about the invitation at zero suds. She didn't feel at all nervous about being rejected when she imagined the classroom scene.

She went on to the next scene, which took three tries to become undisturbing. She finished her Friday morning session by imagining the third scene: on the phone with Monica, worrying about what to wear to the party. She visualized this scene four times, until it could be rated at zero suds.

By Sunday Jennifer had worked through all 20 items on her hierarchy. During the next week she noticed that she worried less about rejection. She went on to use Systematic Desensitization on two other hierarchies, one dealing with speaking in public, and another dealing with receiving critical comments on term papers.

Special Considerations

If you experience difficulties in practicing Systematic Desensitization, they are likely to be in one of three common problem areas:

1. **Incomplete Relaxation.** If you can't relax at the beginning of a session, try to imagine lying on a soft lawn on a calm summer day, watching clouds slowly floating by. Or imagine watching leaves float by on a broad, slow river. Each cloud or leaf takes some of your muscular tension away with it.

    You may also want to record your relaxation routine on tape and play it at the beginning of each session or scene.

2. **Visualization Difficulty.** If you find that your scenes seem flat, unreal, and unevocative of the distress you would feel in real life scenes, you probably have trouble visualizing things clearly. To strengthen your powers of imagination, ask questions of all your senses to make your scenes real:

Sight: What colors are there in the scene? What color are the walls, the landscape, people's clothes, cars, furnishings? Is the light bright or dim? What details are there—books on the table, pets, chairs, rugs? What pictures are on the walls, what words can you read on signs?

Sound: What are the tones of voices? Are there plane or traffic noises, or dogs barking or music playing in the background? Wind in the trees? Can you hear your own voice speaking?

Touch: Reach out and feel things—are they rough or smooth? Hard or soft? Rounded or flat? What's the weather like? Are you hot or cold? Do you itch, sweat, have to sneeze? What are you wearing? How does it feel against your skin?

Smell: Can you smell dinner cooking? Flowers? Tobacco smoke? Sewage? Perfume or aftershave? Chemicals? Decay? Pine trees?

Taste: Are you eating food or drinking water? Are the tastes sweet? Sour? Salty? Bitter?

It also helps to go to the real setting of one of your scenes—your bedroom for example—and lie down and practice visualization. Close your eyes and try to see the room in all its details, then open your eyes and notice what you missed. Close your eyes and try again. Describe the scene out loud to yourself. Open your eyes and see what you missed this time, and what you changed in your mind. Close your eyes and describe the room again, adding the sounds and textures and smells and temperatures. Keep this up until you have a vivid sense picture of the room.

3. **Misconstructed Hierarchies.** If you find no reduction in anxiety with repetitions of a particular scene, your hierarchy probably needs to be reconstructed with a milder starting point, a more gradual gradient, or both. For example, you might begin with a completely neutral scene.

If you can visualize your scenes clearly and experience little or no anxiety, your hierarchy probably needs to be reconstructed with a steeper gradient between scenes, or with a greater variety of content in the scenes.

If you can visualize your scenes clearly, and experience erratic levels of tension, either the scenes on your hierarchy aren't evenly spaced with regard to intensity, or you have scenes depicting different kinds of items mixed together. In either case, reconstruct the hierarchy and try again.

Further Reading

Bower, S. A. and Bower, G. H. **Asserting Your Self.** Reading, Massachusetts: Addison-Wesley, 1976.

Lazarus, A. A. **Behavior Therapy and Beyond.** New York: McGraw Hill, 1971.

Wolpe, J. **The Practice of Behavior Therapy.** 2nd. ed. New York: Pergamon Press, 1973.

Chapter 7

Stress Inoculation

Stress Inoculation teaches you to cope with and relax away a broad spectrum of stressful experience. You no longer have to avoid or deaden yourself to situations which trigger stress. Rather, you can develop new ways to react, learning to relax in place of your old habitual response of anger or fear.

The basic procedures were formulated as "Coping Skills Training" by Marvin Goldfried in 1973 and by Suin and Richardson in 1971 as an outgrowth of Wolpe's work with deep muscle relaxation and Systematic Desensitization. These techniques were expanded by Meichenbaum and Cameron in 1974 in their Stress Innoculation program.

Donald Meichenbaum argued in his book, *Cognitive Behavior Modification,* that a fear or anger response can be conceived as an interaction of two main elements: 1. heightened physiological arousal (increased heart and respiration rates, sweating, muscle tension, chills, the "lump in the throat") and 2. thoughts which interpret your situation as dangerous, threatening, or unfair, and attribute your physiological arousal to the emotions of fear or anger. The actual stressful situation has very little to do with your emotional response. Your appraisal of the danger, the outcome you expect, the motive you ascribe to others, and how you interpret your own body's response are the real forces that create your emotions.

The sorts of things you tell yourself in stressful situations are habitual. Some people automatically magnify the danger, some habitually see themselves as the victims of malice, and some expect to fall apart or fail. Stress Inoculation helps you to relax away tension and arousal and supplant your old negative interpretations with an arsenal of stress coping thoughts.

Stress Inoculation training involves learning to relax using deep breathing and Progressive Relaxation, so that whenever or wherever you are experiencing stress, you can relax away the tension. The first step is to construct your personal list of stressful situations and arrange the list vertically from the least to the most stressful items. You will learn eventually how to evoke each of these situations in your imagination, and how to relax away your tension while clearly picturing the stressful situation. The second step is the creation of a private arsenal of stress coping thoughts. These will be used to counteract your old habitual automatic thoughts. The third step is to use your relaxation and coping skills "in vivo," to press on through the real life events you find disturbing while breathing deeply, loosening your muscles, and using stress coping thoughts.

Symptom Effectiveness

Stress Inoculation is effective in the reduction of interpersonal and general anxiety, as well as interview, speech, and test anxiety. Studies have shown its usefulness in the treatment of phobias, particularly the fear of heights. Novaco adapted Stress Inoculation to treat chronic anger in 1975.

Time for Mastery

Learning Progressive Relaxation will take four days. The development of a Stress Inoculation hierarchy and a list of effective stress coping thoughts will take approximately one week. Once you are able to relax away tension in situations conjured up in your imagination, you need to put the skill to work during actual stressful events. The time it takes to replace your old habitual responses with this new habit will depend on the amount of practice and commitment.

Instructions

Learning to Relax

How well you succeed in a Stress Inoculation program depends on how well you have learned to relax. First, you need to master Progressive Relaxation, as outlined in the previous chapter on Systematic Desensitization. You should be able to achieve deep muscle relaxation in one to two minutes. Progressive Relaxation should be "over-learned" so that it can be done automatically, without having to think about each step. The same unconscious coordination with which you walk or drive a car can be applied so that the sequence of tensing and relaxing muscles is achieved with smooth precision.

The second component of relaxation is deep breathing. Deep breathing isn't just filling your lungs up with air. It means pushing the air downward into your abdomen, relaxing those tight diaphragm and stomach muscles at the same time. To achieve deep breathing, place both hands on your belly, just above the pubic area. Breathe in so that the air expands your belly and pushes your hands. Push your hands as much as feels comfortable, at a rhythm that feels right to you. Exhale with a sigh, and imagine the tension is flowing out of your body as you release each breath. While you are deep breathing, think to yourself: "relax...calm...letting go." Use these words when you feel the slightest bit of tension, as cues to relax your muscles and breathe deeply. These words may elicit images or memories of pleasant scenes. Use the words and images together to deepen your relaxation.

Making a Stressful Events Hierarchy

Having learned how to relax, you are now ready to make a list of current situations in your life which you find stressful. Include on the list stressful events which are likely to occur in the near future. Think of the major areas of your life—work, family, sexual relationships, friends, daily responsibilities, health—and think of the specific settings and persons involved in situations that you typically associate with painful emotions. Try to get twenty items on your list, running the full gamut from very mild discomfort to your most dreaded experiences.

You can turn the list into a hierarchy by ranking the stressful experiences in order, from the least to the most disturbing. Each item on the list should be slightly more stressful than the item which preceded it, and the increases should be in approximately equal increments.

Wolpe devised a system for the ranking of stressful events based on a measurement called "subjective units of distress" (suds). Complete relaxation is rated as zero suds, and the most stressful event in your hierarchy is assigned a value of 100 suds. All of the other items are ranged somewhere in between, and are assigned suds scores depending on your subjective impression of where each situation falls relative to your least and most stressful items. If the most stressful item on your hierarchy is "ex-husband depressed and wants to move back home" and is ranked at 100 suds, then "facing enormous mastercharge bill" might be rated 60 suds, and "rushing to pick up kids from babysitter" might fall around 25 suds. Since you are an expert on yourself and know how you react to things, you can decide where each stressful event fits relative to the others. It is advisable, on a list of 20 items, to separate each item with increments of five suds. In that way the items will progress in relatively equal steps.

The following sample hierarchy was constructed by a nurse who was also a single parent:

Rank	Item	suds (subjective units of distress)
1.	Children slightly rude to boyfriend.	5
2.	Night of weekly encounter group, worried about what to say.	10
3.	Something breaks and needs repair in house.	15
4.	Cooking dinner for guests.	20

5. Kids have poor report cards. Letter comes from teacher requesting a special conference.   25

6. Assigned too many patients who need a lot of attention and care.   30

7. Car doesn't work.   35

8. Leaving kids at home alone at night.   40

9. Having to say "no," particularly to boyfriend or family.   45

10. Kids leave house a mess on Sunday after long hard weekend of work.   50

11. Bleeding gums, chronic dental problem.   55

12. Overslept, late for work.   60

13. Can't find kids, they're long overdue and I've called everyone.   65

14. A much-liked patient is dying.   70

15. Doctor extremely angry, criticized quality of work.   75

16. Assigned role of being charge nurse for the day, responsible for operations of entire ward.   80

17. Kids sick at home and I have to go to work.   85

18. Patient given wrong medication at work, have to report error.   90

19. Boyfriend withdrawn and very rejecting.   95

20. Huge fight with boyfriend and he drives away angry.   100

You may notice that this hierarchy is a mixture of many different cconcerns. The stressors include work, family, health, friends, mechanical breakdowns, and range from anxiety about possible calamities to irritation with a messy livingroom. A good hierarchy doesn't focus on just one kind of problem, but gives you the opportunity to practice relaxation and coping skills with a variety of stressful situations.

With your hierarchy complete, it can now be used for learning how to relax while experiencing stress. Start with your first scene (lowest suds) and construct it in your imagination. Include a clear picture of where you are, who is with you, sounds, smells, whatever is important to really get into the scene. Hold onto the stressful image for 30 to 40 seconds. Notice how your body reacts: changes in heart rate and respiration, particularly the beginning of any muscle tension. Use these sensations as signals for deep muscle relaxation and deep breathing.

Tightening in your body is like an early warning system of what later will be real emotional discomfort. If you interpret the feelings of arousal in your body as anxiety or anger, you will experience these emotions. But if you label the same arousal as a signal to relax, you can stop being nervous or angry and start coping. It is possible to relax away the tension even as you imagine a particularly stressful situation. Keep the scene clearly in mind while you relax. Use the words "relax. . .calm. . .letting go" as verbal cues to release tension.

When you have twice imagined a particular scene without tension or anxiety, holding the clear image 30 seconds each time, go on to the next item in your hierarchy. Over a three or four day period, move slowly up your entire hierarchy of stressful situations. Using this same procedure of relaxing away stress, progress from the least to the most difficult items. At the end you will have gained important knowledge of where and how tension builds in your body. You will welcome early signs of tension as your signal to relax. As you achieve relaxation on your items with the highest suds, you will be building confidence that stress reduction is possible, even in the most threatening situations.

For your hierarchy to work best, each scene must be vivid and real to you. Use all your senses to build the image: sound, smell, color, familiar shapes, temperature, and texture. Initially it may be hard to feel "in it" at all. However, as you practice you will be able to use a variety of sense impressions to put yourself in the picture. If you have trouble evoking a scene, describe it vividly and completely into a tape recorder. Play it back with your eyes closed, letting the words call up particulars of the problem situation. Include on the tape both sides of dialogues you have with others that you find distressing. As you are listening and visualizing the scene, notice the beginnings of any physical tension and start the relaxation response. Rather than a signal for anxiety or anger, physical tension is now your signal to relax.

On the first day that you initiate work with your hierarchy, don't go beyond three or four scenes. Stop before getting tired or bored. Going a little bit at a time, you should make it through your hierarchy in four days. When you have relaxed your way through the list two or three times, you can expect a feeling of greater confidence when confronting the same situations in real life.

Stress Coping Thoughts

You have learned how to relax with imagined stressors. Before dealing with real life situations, you need to master one more skill. The greatest source of emotional pain is the negative things you say to yourself: "Something awful is going to happen. . .I can't take this. . .they're setting me up. . .I'm going to do a bad job. . .he's too selfish to give a damn."

While you are trying to deal with a situation, fighting to make the best choices and somehow get through, you are also blasting yourself with a steady stream of negative automatic thoughts. Meichenbaum has called this the "internal dialog of conflict." A dentist who became very distressed when his wife got angry used to think, "Oh no, this will level me. . .I ought to stand up to her. . .maybe she really wants to leave me. . .this is going to be an awful evening. . .I'll reason with her . . . what an ugly, ugly mood." On the one hand, he was trying to coach himself to stand his ground, on the other he was convincing himself that things were horrible and he would shortly be abandoned.

To overcome these automatic thoughts you will need to create a personal list of stress coping thoughts. Stress coping thoughts act as a circuit breaker for painful emotions. To understand how they work, examine the components of an emotional response:

The stimulus situation: The dentist's wife has just complained about his late arrival from the office.

Physical reactions: His autonomic nervous system produces symptoms such as hand tremor, tightness in stomach, sweating, palpitations. He begins taking short, quick breaths.

Thoughts: He interprets his wife's emotions and intentions, he predicts the outcome of the situation, he evaluates her actions and his own as good or bad, and finally he labels the sensations inside his own body: "I'm scared, angry." While he is interpreting her remarks and his physical reactions, he begins to feel an emotion. That emotion in turn may increase the hand tremor, stomach tightness, etc. When he notices the symptoms of tension increasing, he may think, "Now I'm getting really frightened" or "Now I'm really angry." A feedback loop is thereby created in which negative thoughts increase physical tension and tension intensifies negative thoughts.

The feedback loop can work for you as well as against you. Your thoughts don't have to intensify fear or anger. Instead they can calm you, push away painful emotions, and act as a tranquilizer for a tense stomach. Stress coping thoughts tell your body there is no need for arousal—it can relax.

In Meichenbaum and Cameron's Stress Inoculation program, they suggest four steps for coping with any stressful situation: preparing, actually confronting the situation, coping with emotional arousal during the situation, and reinforcing success. Below you will find suggested stress coping statements for each of these steps. Some of them may work for you, but the best ones will probably be those you write yourself.

1. Preparing

There's nothing to worry about.
I'm going to be all right.
I've succeeded with this before.
What exactly do I have to do?
I know I can do each one of these tasks.
It's easier once you get started.
I'll jump in and be all right.
Tomorrow I'll be through it.
Don't let negative thoughts creep in.

2. Confronting the stressful situation

Stay organized.
Take it step by step, don't rush.
I can do this, I'm doing it now.
I can only do my best.
Any tension I feel is a signal to use my coping exercises.
I can get help if I need it.
If I don't think about fear I won't be afraid.
If I get tense, I'll take a breather and relax.
It's OK to make mistakes.

3. Coping with emotional arousal

Relax now!
Just breathe deeply.
There's an end to it.
Keep my mind on right now, on the task at hand.
I can keep this within limits I can handle.
I can always call_____.
I am only afraid because I decided to be. I can decide not to be.
I've survived this and worse before.
Being active will lessen the fear.

4. Reinforcing success

I did it!
I did all right. I did well.
Next time I won't have to worry as much.
I am able to relax away anxiety.
I've got to tell_____ about this.
It's possible not to be scared. All I have to do is stop thinking I'm scared.

Adapted from "The Clinical Potential of Modifying What Clients Say to Themselves" by D. Meichenbaum and R. Cameron. In M. J. Mahoney and C. E. Thorensen, *Self-Control: Power to the Person.* Copyright © 1974 by Wadsworth, Inc. Reprinted by permission of the publisher, Brooks/Cole Publishing Co., Monterey, California.

At this point you should create you own list of stress coping thoughts. Memorize a number of them for each of the four coping stages. Make the coping statements relevant and meaningful to you. Change them if they begin to lose effectiveness. Keep your list handy at all times: tape the most powerful stress coping thoughts to your nightstand, on the front door, on the inside flap of a purse or briefcase. Attach a list to the sun visor of your car. Read them again and again until they become second nature.

Of all the coping steps, the most easily forgotten is reinforcing your own success. Taking credit for coping forces you to acknowledge your ability to change old habits and patterns. Reinforcing success also helps you remember to use your coping skills next time you encounter a stress syndrome.

Coping in Real Life

The final step in Stress Inoculation is applying your skills in real life situations. Select an item on your hierarchy that is low in suds and that you can easily arrange to encounter "in vivo." When you feel prepared, actually place yourself in that situation. As you begin to cope, your body tension will be used as a cue to relax away tightness. Simultaneously, stress coping thoughts will flow in a continual stream of reassurance.

Arrange in advance so that you can leave the stressful situation when you need to. Stay long enought to relax away some of your tension and use your repertoire of coping thoughts, but don't get overwhelmed.

It is expected that coping "in vivo" will be more difficult than relaxing away tension in imagined scenes. Some setbacks are inevitable. But practice will make relaxation and stress coping thoughts so natural that they will quietly begin at the first sign of tension.

Example

A ranger employed in a large regional park created the following hierarchy:

Rank	Item	suds
1.	Assigned to patrol isolated trails.	5
2.	Chain saw breaks, must return to toolshed to install new chain.	10
3.	Forced to punish son for eating wild and possibly poisonous plants.	15
4.	Four-year-old son growling and crawling all over me in chair, pulling, punching.	
5.	Driving huge dump or water truck over narrow mountain roads.	25
6.	Nightly problem with son refusing to go to bed. Crying and screaming when put down for the night.	30
7.	Seeing people litter, having to insist on compliance with litter law.	35
8.	Attend grievance session as shop steward for union.	40
9.	Confronting campers who violate fire or noise regulations.	45
10.	Electrical storm. Fear that lightning will hit trees near house.	50

11. Cutting back undergrowth in a poison oak area.   55

12. Dealing with an auto accident in the park.   60

13. Car breaks down, major repair necessary. Worry about money.   65

14. Wife complains about loneliness. Is irritable and withdrawn.   70

15. Helping a snakebite victim.   75

16. Fighting a brush fire, digging trenches in intense smoke and heat.   80

17. Stomach begins to act up. Continual heartburn for several days.   85

18. Seeing a snake. Hearing the rattle.   90

19. Boss ill, temporary supervisor officious and authoritarian.   95

20. Wife unhappy with isolation, leaves to spend week with parents.
     Feeling very alone and worried about marriage.   100

When the ranger had mastered relaxation procedures, he began to apply them to his hierarchy. He attempted to imagine the first stressful situation (five suds) by visualizing lonely trails at dusk. He had difficulty, however, so he wrote down all the things he usually noticed in a dark forest: smell of pines, coolness of the air, bird sounds, tall trees keeping the trail in shadow, dead stumps the red bark of manzanita, the forest floor full of pinecones and needles, the trail climbing steeply around the curve of a hill. The elements of the scene were then tape recorded and played back. He repeated the tape until he could construct a vivid image of the setting in imagination. The efforts invested in sharpening his imagination in the first scene paid off as he progressed through the hierarchy. Other scenes were easier and he knew he could tape record a vivid picture if there was any difficulty.

Throughout the hierarchy, he gained increasing skill in spotting the first signs of tension. Muscle tightness usually occured first in his diaphram and upper abdomen. This became the signal to relax away stress. Holding the image of a scene for 30 to 40 seconds, he monitored the changes in his body while focusing on deep breathing and Progressive Relaxation. After visualizing a scene twice for at least 30 seconds without tension or emotional arousal, he went on to the next item in the hierarchy. Sometimes he would have to visualize a situation six or more times before the image was stress-free.

Practice was scheduled mornings and evenings for 20 minutes. He was able to successfully relax away tension in about five scenes per day, and within four days completed the hierarchy. The hierarchy was then repeated two more times.

Learning to relax was only half the battle. The ranger had also been working on his list of stress coping thoughts, writing at least five for each of the stages of a stressful situation:

1. Preparing

I can handle this, I've done it before.
I can relax rather than get tight.
I'll take one thing at a time.
I'll make a plan for coping.
Turn off the worry and *do* something.

2. Confronting the stressful situation

It will be over soon enough.
No scary thoughts.
I'll follow each step of my plan.
If I take care of myself, I'll be all right.
I won't worry about what others think.

3. Coping with emotional arousal

Where is my body tight? I can relax it.
Concentrate on breathing.
I'll tighten, then relax my stomach.
Breathe deeply and think only of coping.
Negative thoughts are the enemy. Stop them now.

4. Reinforcing success

I can turn off my worry now.
I relaxed and made it through.
I'm getting good at coping under stress.
I'm not so afraid of things.
I did a good job just then.

He typed a file card with the phrase, "I can relax rather than get tight," and taped it to his truck dashboard. He made additional signs for the shaving mirror, his key case, his locker.

When the ranger began using his skills in real life, he started with item number five, "Driving huge dump or water truck over narrow mountain roads." He took the water truck to a remote campsite, breathing deeply and relaxing while he drove. He told himself, "No scary thoughts. . .just concentrate on breathing. . .where is my body tight? I can relax it." When he got back he noted that he'd done a good job. Over the next few days he followed the same procedure while confronting campers who had violated fire regulations and while he was working near poison oak.

During normally occuring real life stresses, he began to apply the relaxation skills and to select appropriate stress coping thoughts. He refined and added coping thoughts as he went along. For the first few weeks he kept forgetting his training. In time he developed the ability to spot stress coming and begin coping thoughts immediately. He noticed the first clutch of physical tension. The process of "checking in" with his body and starting coping skills was becoming automatic.

Stress Inoculation in the Control of Anger

Anger is one of the most devastating and physically harmful emotions. Stress Inoculation training was extended to the treatment of anger by Novaco in 1975. In his book, *Anger Control: the Development and Evaluation of an Experimental Treatment,* Novaco argued that anger could be redefined as a problem that calls for a solution rather than as a threat that calls for an attack. Attention should be focused. on coping mechanisms rather than on anger-escalating automatic thoughts such as, "He's doing that deliberately . . . who the hell does she think she is . . . he doesn't give a damn about me."

There are five steps in Novaco's Stress Inoculation treatment for anger: Redefining anger, conducting a situational analysis of trigger mechanisms, learning relaxation skills and a sequence of stress coping thoughts, applying coping skills to a hierarchy of anger-provoking situations, and applying coping skills to real life provocations.

Redefining Anger

Whether you get angry in response to some provocation depends on what you think, what happens inside your body, and what behavioral choices you make. Cognitively, your anger is determined by attributions (motives you ascribe to others), appraisals (what you think is being done to you), and expectations. If you decide that people are deliberately harming or attacking you, that they are bad or that you are a victim of injustice, then your self statements will provoke anger. You can prime the anger pump even more by imagining scenes of retribution in which you blow up or hit someone, and by saying things to yourself like, "I'll show him."

Anger is also influenced by what occurs inside your body. Tension and agitation increase the likelihood of an anger response. Your interpersonal behavior also serves to escalate anger. Small acts of antagonism trigger retaliatory behavior in others and the vicious circle begins.

Rigid belief structures are a fertile field in which to grow chronic anger. An intolerance for mistakes, a belief in the value of retaliation, strict expectations about how people should act, a feeling that all criticism is true and therefore must be defended against, or unreasonable demands for success are setups for an angry life. Anger acts as a barricade against threats to these beliefs.

The underlying source of all anger is what you think. Novaco says that "anger is fomented, maintained, and influenced by the self-statements that are made in provocative situations." (p. 33). Changing an angry response therefore requires changing the structure of your thoughts.

Conducting a Situational Analysis

You need specific information on how you trigger anger. Relive a recent anger experience by closing your eyes and "running a movie" of all the things you thought, the things you felt inside your body, and how you actually behaved. Pay particular attention to your attributions, appraisals, and how you think things *ought* to have been. What motives did you ascribe to others? How did you label what they were doing? Did you entertain automatic thoughts such as, "I should have let him have it . . . I'm not going to take that . . . she has no right, I won't let her get away with it"? Did you rehearse in your mind exploding or getting revenge?

While still running the movie, notice how your body felt and where the tension was. Notice if there were any signals in your body which you interpreted as growing anger.

Finally, recall what you actually did. What was your first response and what effect did it have? Did your responses tend to escalate the situation or cool it down?

Conduct a situational analysis on at least five recent anger-provoking situations. Run the movie in slow motion until you have detailed information about your thoughts, feelings, and actions.

Relaxation Skills and Stress Coping Thoughts

Read and follow the earlier instructions for learning Progressive Relaxation and deep breathing. They are the basic skills you will need to counteract the physiological tension that can lower your anger threshold. When you can relax at will within one or two minutes, you will be able to encounter provocative situations without tightening up.

Once you have mastered relaxation skills, you must work on your thoughts. Anger reactions can be divided into the same four coping stages discussed earlier in this chapter. Novaco recommends the following stress coping thoughts for the four stages:

1. Preparing for provocation

This is going to upset me, but I know how to deal with it.
What is it that I have to do?
I can work out a plan to handle this.
I can manage the situation, I know how to regulate my anger.
If I find myself getting upset, I'll know what to do.
There won't be any need for an argument.
Try not to take this too seriously.
This could be a testy situation, but I believe in myself.

Time for a few deep breaths of relaxation. Feel comfortable, relaxed, and
   at ease.
Easy does it, remember to keep your sense of humor.

2. Impact and confrontation

Stay calm. Just continue to relax.
Just as long as I keep my cool, I'm in control.
Just roll with the punches. Don't get bent out of shape.
Think of what you want to get out of this.
You don't need to prove yourself.
There is no point in getting mad.
Don't make more out of this than you have to.
I'm not going to let him get to me.
Look for positives. Don't assume the worst or jump to conclusions.
It's really a shame that he has to act like this.
For someone to be that irritable, he must be awfully unhappy.
If I start to get mad, I'll just be banging my head against the wall. So I
   might as well just relax.
There is no need to doubt myself. What he says doesn't matter.
I can't change him with anger, I'll just upset myself.
I'm on top of this situation, and it's under control.

3. Coping with arousal

My muscles are starting to feel tight. Time to relax and slow things down.
Getting upset won't help.
It's just not worth it to get so angry.
I'll let him make a fool of himself.
I have a right to be annoyed, but let's keep the lid on.
Time to take a deep breath.
Let's take the issue point by point.
I'll stay rational, anger won't solve anything.
My anger is a signal of what I need to do. Time to cope.
I'm not going to get pushed around, but I'm not going haywire either.
Try to reason it out. Treat each other with respect.
Let's try a cooperative approach. Maybe we are both right.
Negatives lead to more negatives. Work constructively.
He'd probably like me to get really angry. Well, I'm going to disappoint
   him.
I can't expect people to act the way I want them to.
Take it easy, don't get pushy.

4. Reflecting on the provocation

a) when the problem is unresolved

Forget about the aggravation. Thinking about it only makes you upset.
These are difficult situations, and they take time to straighten out.
Try to shake it off. Don't let it interfere.
I'll get better at this as I get more practice.
Remember relaxation. It's a lot better than anger.
Can you laugh about it? It's probably not so serious.
Don't take it personally.
Take a deep breath.

b) when the conflict is resolved or coping is successful

I handled that one pretty well. It worked!
That wasn't as hard as I thought.
It could have been a lot worse.
I could have gotten more upset than it was worth.
I actually got through that without getting angry.
My pride can sure get me into trouble, but when I don't take things too
    seriously I'm better off.
I guess I've been getting upset for too long when it wasn't even necessary.
I'm doing better at this all the time.
(from Novaco, 1975)

Select from this list the stress coping thoughts that seem to relate to you. Add your own, since the ones you compose yourself will probably be the most effective for you. Memorize at least five stress coping thoughts for each of the coping stages. In the future, as you confront provoking situations, your thoughts will consist of coping statements rather than your old, anger-instigating automatic thoughts.

Coping With Your Anger Hierarchy

As with the hierarchies used earlier in this chapter, rank anger-provoking scenes from the least to the most upsetting. Rate the disturbing scenes from zero suds (no anger) to 100 suds (the angriest you get). Create a hierarchy of 20 items, ranking them at five sud increments. It is important that the items progress in equal steps.

Use your anger hierarchy in a similar way to the stress hierarchies described earlier in this chapter. Move from the lowest to the highest suds scene. Get a clear picture of each item in your imagination, including sight, smell, sound, and feel. Hold on to the image and notice how your body reacts. Use stress coping thoughts and relaxation procedures to control your anger. Occasionally imagine yourself losing control and starting to respond angrily. You can use the loss of control as a cue to increase coping procedures. Continually instruct yourself with the new stress coping thoughts rather than your old angry automatic thoughts. Imagine having the impulse to really blow up, then inhibiting the impulse and deciding not to attack.

Any tightening in your body or symptoms such as racing heart or perspiration should be your early warning system that anger is imminent. Use these physiological cues to increase relaxation and breathe deeply. When you have twice imagined a particular scene without tension or anger, go on to the next item in the hierarchy. Over a period of several days, you can slowly move through your entire list of anger-provoking situations.

The following anger hierarchy was constructed by a retired legal secretary:

Rank	Item	suds
1.	Cleaning lady bangs into hardwood baseboards with vacuum.	5
2.	Reading about the trillion dollar national debt.	10
3.	A friend is very bossy and demanding, hurries me while eating just because she is through with her meal.	15
4.	Watching people speed in their automobiles. Angry and worried about being hit.	20
5.	Telephoning city offices and being shifted from person to person and finally being cut off.	25
6.	Husband stores old car in garage, blocking cabinets I want to use. The car collect dust and gets piled with junk.	30
7.	A friend gets angry when anyone is late. She withdraws and pouts.	35
8.	Husband makes me repeat questions many times before answering. Seems to deliberately tune me out.	40
9.	Sister prods to know too much about personal affairs and then blabs to others.	45
10.	Read article in paper about government giving away money to other countries and spending on porkbarrel legislation while taxes keep going up.	50
11.	Husband goes to a party in an old sports shirt when I have gone to the trouble to get really nicely dressed for the occasion.	55
12.	In-laws demand help with elderly relative while I'm rushed and in the middle of planning a dinner party.	60
13.	Husband leaves things lying around livingroom every day and I have to clean them up.	65

14. Elderly sister eats continually and keeps gaining weight against doctor's orders. Get worried and angry when watching her gluttony.   70

15. Husband spends money to buy steak for "the boys" but won't take me out to a nice restaurant.   75

16. A part-time employer is cool and gives no commitment about the availability of future work.   80

17. Husband fails to provide sufficient money from paycheck for household expenses, but splurges on an expensive car, fine liquors, and personal pleasures.   85

18. Husband staying up late with TV and then not wanting to do anything the next day.   90

19. Expected to cook an elaborate meal at the end of the day when I feel tired. Treated coolly if I refuse.   95

20. Husband spends his day off until 3 AM each week at in-law's house, then sleeps all day the next day. Spend no time together during his days off. No rides or trips because he's always at in-laws's.   100

It was a formidable list. In some situations she let the anger out and in others she seethed quietly. She went back to her situational analysis, and realized that she typically said to herself, "It's not fair . . . he doesn't care an iota . . . no one who really loves someone would act like this . . . I can't stand this . . . it's disgusting."

She noted that she frequently assumed that things were done deliberately to annoy her, or at least done in total disregard for her needs and feelings. This assumption seemed to increase her anger. Going back and "running a movie" of her anger experiences, she remembered that her stomach would start to tighten, her heart start to pound, and a hot flush would extend up her shoulders and neck. She usually interpreted this as a signal that she was "really steamed." When she expressed anger, she usually started with a question such as, "Why don't you cut out the bullshit?"

Learning to cope with the anger scenes meant doing three things. First, she had to replace her negative, anger-instigating thoughts with coping thoughts. Second, she needed to relax away tension in her body to prevent symptoms of physiological arousal. Third, she had to instruct herself to inhibit her usual sarcastic remarks so that she wouldn't escalate the situation with her comments.

In addition to making her hierarchy, she wrote several stress coping thoughts for each of the four stages of coping. These were tailored to her personality and were effective antidotes to her usual automatic thoughts:

1. **Preparing for provocation**

   I won't let this get to me.
   My health comes first, whatever I do I won't get upset.

2. **Impact and confrontation**

   It's a lot of fuss about nothing.
   That's the way it is, you can't change people.
   Let it go, let it go.

3. **Coping with arousal**

   Calm, calm, calm. I'll sit down and relax.
   At the first sign of getting tight, relax.

4. **Reflecting on provocation**
   a) **unresolved**

   OK, to hell with it, forget it and relax.
   Stop dwelling on it, read your Agatha Christie and relax.

   b) **resolved and successful**

   I'm getting the hang of this, wait till I tell _____.

She added her own stress coping thoughts to several that seemed right to her from Novaco's list. She memorized the coping thoughts and used them as she moved from scene to scene in her anger hierarchy.

Coping With Anger in Real Life

Start with a low suds situation. The retired legal secretary started with item one: "Cleaning lady bangs into hardwood baseboards with vacuum." When the cleaning lady next visited, she paid particular attention to the battering of the baseboards. She noticed that when her stomach started to tighten she was thinking, "Is she just trying to annoy me? She doesn't give a rap about my house." She used these thoughts as cues to relax away tension and to begin her stress coping thoughts. As she felt herself getting aroused, she thought, "Calm, calm, calm, I'll sit down and relax...time to take a deep breath...I can't expect people to always act the way I want."

After exposing herself to the anger-provoking situation for a few moments, she went upstairs to get away from it. She knew that she had stayed long enough to get some practice with her stress coping thoughts, but not so long that she became upset. After successfully coping, she thought to herself, "I'm getting the hang of this . . . I actually got through that without getting angry."

After making it through the baseboard scene, she selected an item somewhat higher on the suds scale. She arranged to be a little late for luncheon with her friend and the usual problem of withdrawal and pouting ensued. She had prepared for the situation by thinking, "I won't let this get to me . . . this could upset me, but I know how to deal with it." As her friend started to pout, she thought, "There is no point in getting mad . . . let it go, let it go." She took several deep breaths. At one point she almost lost control, and she reminded herself, "At the first sign of getting tight, relax."

She repeated the procedure with additional items on her hierarchy, until relaxation and coping thoughts were almost automatic. She made a firm commitment to herself to use coping skills whenever she felt the first tickle of anger, long before she began to lose control.

Further Reading

Goldfried, M. R. "Reduction of Generalized Anxiety Through a Variant of Systematic Desensitization." In **Behavior Change Through Self-Control** by Goldfried, M. R. and Merbaum, M., eds. New York: Holt, Rinehart and Winston, 1973.

Meichenbaum, D. **Cognitive Behavior Modification.** New York: Plenum Press, 1977.

Meichenbaum, D. "Self Instructional Methods." In **Helping People Change** by Kanfur, F. K. and Goldstein, A. P., eds. New York: Pergamon Press, 1974.

Mahoney, M. J. and Thorensen, C. E. **Self-Control: Power to the Person.** Monterey, California: Brooks/Cole, 1974.

Novaco, R. **Anger Control: The Development and Evaluation of an Experimental Treatment.** Lexington, Massachusetts: D. C. Heath, 1975.

Suinn, R. M. and Richardson, F. "Anxiety Mangement Training: A Non-Specific Behavior Therapy Program for Anxiety Control." **Behavior Therapy.** 1971, 2, 498-510.

Chapter 8

Covert Sensitization

Among the greatest sources of painful emotions are destructive habits. These are the vices, the things you have learned to do that feel good for the moment and for which you later pay dearly. There is pleasure, for example, in a three-hour martini lunch. It's a nice way to blot out tension, unwind, and socialize. Unfortunately, a habit of martini lunches wastes time and may leave you quite disfunctional for the rest of the afternoon. As a consequence you suffer *more* stress trying to catch up on missed work while wrestling with alcohol-induced weariness.

The hallmark of destructive habits is short-term gain coupled with long-term loss. You nightly gorge yourself right up to and including the chocolate mousse, and over the months you are sad to observe your slow evolution into a blimp. After each paycheck you spend a fourth of your income at several favorite department stores. It's always fun, but you have those ever-mounting bills and finance charges.

Covert Sensitization was developed and popularized by Joseph Cautela as a treatment for destructive habits. It is called "covert" because the basic treatment takes place inside your mind. The theory behind Covert Sensitization is that behaviors that become strong habits are learned because they are consistently reinforced by a great deal of pleasure. One way to eliminate the habit is to begin associating your habitual behavior with some very unpleasant, imagined stimulus. As a result, your old habit no longer evokes images of enjoyment, but becomes associated with something noxious and repulsive. This association is formed by pairing the pleasurable images of your habit with painful images of nausea, physical injury, social ostracism, or some other unpleasant experience. Covert Sensitization can help the old habit lose most, if not all, of its appeal.

Symptom Effectiveness

Covert Sensitization has had consistent success in the treatment of sexual deviations such as sadistic fantasies, pedophilia, transvestism, and exhibitionism. It has also been used to reduce stealing, fingernail biting, compulsive gambling, compulsive lying, and compulsive shopping. It has been helpful in curtailing use of non-addictive drugs such as marijuana. Although there is no published research, Covert Sensitization may be useful in reducing compulsive recreations such as television watching and pinball.

Covert Sensitization has been used with mixed results on alcohol, obesity, and smoking problems. The weight of research evidence indicates that it is not particularly effective with smoking. If is not effective in treating alcoholism *per se,* but has been used to treat a habit of alcohol indulgence on particular occasions and in particular environments. The previously discussed martini lunch at a favorite watering hole can lose its appeal with Covert Sensitization. Although it is not the final answer to obesity, Covert Sensitization can be used to treat a weight problem that is exacerbated by a few particular foods or by a certain eating environment.

In short, Covert Sensitization is effective when the habit is confined to a particular substance, setting, or situation. It is not very effective with generalized habits such as smoking and compulsive eating or drinking. The reason appears to lie in the word *sensitization.* You become sensitized to something unpleasant, which you associate with your habit in particular settings and situations. A sensitization to one particular food, drink, or setting does not seem to generalize. It is nearly impossible to become sensitized to all food, all drink, or all situations associated with compulsive eating, drinking, and smoking. And thus the technique has diminished effectiveness with such pervasive habits.

Time for Mastery

It will take four days to master Progressive Relaxation and an additional two weeks to begin getting results from the Covert Sensitization procedure.

Instructions

1. Learn Progressive Relaxation.

The first step in Covert Sensitization is to become relaxed. Jacobson's Progressive Relaxation, outlined in the chapter on Systematic Desensitization, is the quickest and most effective way to let go of your muscular tension. Practice Jacobson's procedure in two 15 minute sessions daily. Once you have mastered the four-step shorthand procedure you will be capable of deep muscle relaxation throughout your entire body in less than two minutes.

2. Analyse your destructive habit.

What environment are you typically in? Who is with you? How did you set the situation up? What's the first thing you do as you prepare to launch into your old habit?

A housepainter who was becoming too stout to climb scaffolding analyzed the conditions under which he tended to gorge himself. He shopped once a week, and usually spent that evening watching television and making endless raids on the icebox. He continued eating until he had polished off the cinnamon bread, ice cream, and fruit pies—his favorite snacks. He also gorged himself at an Italian restaurant a block from his house, and at a McDonald's that was on the way home. He noticed that he was always alone on these occasions because he was embarrassed about friends observing his gluttony. He usually had skipped lunch and felt terribly hungry. The first thing he did before gorging himself was to think of all the wonderful foods he had in the icebox, or to peruse the menu with a sense of excitement as he searched for the most filling meal.

3. Create a pleasure hierarchy.

Make a short list of five to ten scenes in which you enjoy your destructive habit. Rank them from the least to the most pleasurable, and assign pleasure ratings from one to ten. You could make a hierarchy out of a few of your favorite foods, always being certain to include the settings in which they are consumed. The stout house-painter listed these items on his pleasure hierarchy:

Item	Pleasure rating
Leaving work and thinking about a big dinner.	1
Shopping for favorite snacks.	3
Snacking on fruit pies while at home watching TV.	5
Snacking on ice cream while at home watching TV.	6
Snacking on cinnamon bread while at home watching TV	7
Huge, spicy meal at favorite Italian restaurant. Feeling very hungry.	10

Other hierarchies are more complex and contain items revolving around anticipation or preparation for the destructive habit. A compulsive shopper created the following hierarchy:

Item	Pleasure rating
Depositing paycheck and thinking about a favorite department store. Imagining the clothes racks and display cases.	1
Looking through catalogs for "ideas."	2
Fantasizing about some new clothes while making dinner.	5

Walking around Macy's.	5
Selecting clothes to try on.	6
Impulsively splurging on a gift.	7
Getting something "really exciting" like a new stereo or TV.	9
Getting it home to be tried out or tried on.	10

Still other hierarchies focus on various elements of a particular pleasurable situation. A teacher found himself smoking prodigious amounts of marijuana in the hour after he got home from his last class. His hierarchy consisted of the routine steps he took in preparing a joint:

Item	Pleasure rating
Get stashbox, papers, and matches out of bookcase.	1
Sit in reclining chair and spread out newspaper to catch excess.	3
Put on earphones and roll joint.	5
Light up and take first hit.	7
Put last of joint in roach clip, feeling stoned.	9
Smoking, spacing out, forgetting about everything.	10

Use the following form to create your own pleasure hierarchy.

Item	Pleasure rating (1 to 10)
_____	_____
_____	_____
_____	_____
_____	_____
_____	_____
_____	_____
_____	_____
_____	_____
_____	_____

When developing your pleasure hierarchy, write it out completely. The items in the examples are abbreviated, but yours should be much more detailed. You might include where you are, who is with you, what you are doing, what you are thinking, and what is going on inside your body. A typical item in your hierarchy might read like this:

> "The cards are dealt and I pick each one up. I am excited and nervous. Green felt over the kitchen table at Jack's house. A few strangers but mostly the same crowd. The fifth card goes around and they're ready for the first bets. I'm to the left of dealer, I bet a buck."

The more detail you have, the easier it will be to imagine the scene. If you have difficulty getting a mental image of an item in your hierarchy, spice it up with a variety of sense impressions. In addition to what you see, notice how it smells, what you hear, whether you feel warm or cold, etc.

While creating the hierarchy, make sure your first item is no more than a one or two on the ten-point pleasure scale. In other words, select something barely pleasurable to start off with, and then work your way up to the intensely delightful aspects of your habit. Try not to let more than two points separate consecutive items.

4. Create an Aversion Scene.

Find something the *thought* of which deeply repulses or frightens you. Rate the following for degree of repulsion or fear experienced when *imagining* the item:

Open wounds	Crawling insects
Dead people	Raging fire
Getting teeth drilled	Becoming nauseated, throwing up
Thunder	Snakes
Looking down from high places	Heart attack
Falling	Physical injury
Injection, having blood drawn	Fainting
Huge, open places	Looking foolish
Closed spaces	Throwing up in public
Dead animals	Spiders
Rejected, ostracized by friends	Blood
Rejected, ostracized by strangers	Being severely criticized

Select the two or three items which distress you most when you think about them. Nausea is the most commonly used aversive item for Covert Sensitization. Social ostracism and rejection have also been used extensively. The aversive item should be sufficiently repulsive so that when you think about it you can generate a very explicit body sensation. Your ability to really *feel* the repulsion or fear bodily will be very important to the success of this procedure. For example, the thought of nausea should be accompanied by a very specific memory of something that really nauseated you—until you begin to feel a little of the old nausea returning.

5. Combine pleasurable and aversive scenes.

Once you are able to clearly imagine and experience the aversive scene, you are ready to begin pairing it with items on your pleasure hierarchy. The following example shows how it is done. A young man who privately enjoyed certain rituals of transvestism was concerned that it was sapping his motivation to meet women and have a sexual relationship with another person. Here is one of the items from his hierarchy combined with the aversive feeling of nausea:

> "Slowly pulling up the green panties, watching everything in the full-length mirror. Feeling very turned on. The room is warm, the panties cool and smooth. Then suddenly that sick feeling starts and a bad smell. I get really turned off as my stomach turns over and over, and pieces of lunch catch in my throat. I try to gag it back but I can't. I start to vomit all over myself. I quickly pull off the panties and begin feeling better. I run into the bathroom for a cool shower, and begin to feel much more comfortable and relaxed."

Pair each item of your pleasure hierarchy with the aversive scene in just this manner:

a) Start with a detailed description of that particular item on the hierarchy.

b) Introduce the aversive scene so that you feel turned off to whatever you were just enjoying.

c) Imagine yourself feeling better as soon as you stop whatever you were doing.

Write out this three-step scenario for each item on your hierarchy. The aversive scene should be as disgusting as possible, full of detail, and completely eradicate any experience of pleasure. Be sure to turn off the aversive scene *as soon as* you cease the destructive habitual behavior. Let yourself have immediate feelings of relief, comfort, and relaxation.

When you have rewritten your hierarchies to include the aversive scene, you can begin practicing Covert Sensitization. Read over the first item of your hierarchy until you have it clearly in mind. Close your eyes and get relaxed using Progressive Relaxation. Relaxation helps you form clearer images. When the tension is out of your body, imagine the first item. Notice what you see, smell, and hear. Notice everything you are doing. Then move right into the aversive scene until you feel uncomfortable and repulsed.

The stout housepainter sat in his favorite chair and used the shorthand procedure to progressively relax all his muscles. When he felt relaxed he began relishing the thought of cinnamon bread, the fifth item of his hierarchy:

> "The TV is on. There's a blue glow. I'm slumped in my chair and I think of getting a little something to eat. I go into the kitchen and butter five pieces of cinnamon bread. It looks delicious. As I bring it to my mouth I start to feel queasy. It's like that time I ate the bad crab. Just like that and I

feel sick to my stomach. I start to take a bite but everything comes up—all over me and everything. I throw the bread in the garbage and open a window. Immediately I feel relief. While I'm breathing the fresh air the nausea goes away."

Using this procedure, go through each item in your hierarchy three to five times. Limit yourself to one or two items a day, so that over a period of approximately one week you can complete the entire hierarchy.

6. Alter the aversive scene.

Change your hierarchy so that you avoid vomiting, being ostracized, or whatever you have chosen for an aversion. Avoid the aversion by avoiding your destructive habit. At the first sign of feeling queasy you put the food down, get up and leave the bar, quit the card game, etc. and start to feel better. For example, the stout housepainter rewrote the fifth item of his hierarchy to reflect this change:

"I'm relaxed. The TV is on. There's a blue glow. I'm slumped in the chair and I think of getting a little something to eat. I go into the kitchen and butter five pieces of cinnamon bread. I start to bring a piece to my mouth, but I have that queasy feeling and put it down right away. I immediately feel relieved and relaxed again."

Go through your hierarchy again, avoiding rather than experiencing the aversive scene. As you did initially, limit yourself to one or two items a day, practicing each item three to five times before going on to the next one.

7. Practice Covert Sensitization in real life.

Once you have mastered Covert Sensitization with imagined scenes, practice the procedure in the presence of tempting objects or situations when your desire for them is low. As you become more confident about controlling a destructive habit you can begin using Covert Sensitization when the temptation is stronger. For example, if you have been working on controlling pastry cravings, you might pass by a bakery window when you weren't very hungry and practice Covert Sensitization while you look in. Later when you are more sure of yourself you can go down to the bakery just before breakfast and repeat the procedure.

Coverent Control

After going through your hierarchy experiencing the aversive scene in the first week and avoiding it in the next week, you should be significantly less interested in your old destructive habit. Nevertheless you may still have occasional impulses to backslide. These can be combated with a procedure called *Coverent Control*.

Practice Covert Sensitization in real life when you are tempted: Imagine your aversive scene, avoid the habit, and feel better. The perform one or both of these Coverent Control exercises:

1. Reward yourself with a "high probability behavior" to replace doing the old habit. A high probability behavior is something that, if you were left alone, you would do frequently. It feels good and is easy to do. Daydreaming is a high probability behavior for a lot of people. They do it frequently because it is a pleasant, easy way to relax for a moment. A cup of coffee, a brief chat, a stretch and a walk around the office may all be high probability behaviors. Reward yourself with one when you successfully resist the impulse to start up the old habit.

2. Make a list of three to five statements about the positive outcomes of avoiding your old habit. For example, "I'll be able to play tennis again... I'll be so much more attractive...I'll have some money in the bank...I'm feeling a lot better about myself." Read or recall one of these positive outcomes each time you successfully resist temptation.

Special Considerations

1. If you have difficulty remembering or clearly visualizing items in your hierarchy, tape record the entire hierarchy. Speak slowly, leaving pauses for your imagination to fill in additional details.

2. Problems in really experiencing the aversive symptom of nausea may be overcome with the help of an easy-to-obtain chemical. A small vial of valeric acid can be very useful in developing that queasy feeling. It's harmless but has a nasty, nauseating odor.

3. The instructions suggest that you go through your hierarchy twice, once experiencing and once avoiding the aversive scene. You may instead wish to alternate experiencing and avoiding the aversive scene on each trial of a particular item.

4. Always time the nausea or other aversive stimulus to coincide exactly with the moment you begin to engage in the destructive habit. Cut off the aversion as soon as you abandon the destructive habit.

5. The effects of Covert Sensitization can be strengthened with booster sessions. When you feel stronger or more frequent impulses to engage in your destructive habit, go through your hierarchy again and resensitize yourself to the aversive scenes.

Further Reading

Cautela, J. R. "Covert Sensitization." **Psychological Reports.** 1967, 20, 459-68.

Homme, L. E. "Perspectives in Psychology XXIV.   Control of Coverants, the Operants of the Mind." **Psychological Record.** 1965, 15, 501-11.

Horan, J. J. and Johnson, R. G. "Coverant Conditioning Through a Self-Management Application of the Premack Principle: Its Effect on Weight Reduction." **Journal of Behavior Therapy and Experimental Psychiatry.** 1971, 2, 243-9.

Maletzky, B. "Assisted Covert Sensitization." **Behavior Therapy.** 1973, 4, 117-9.

Maletzky, B. "Assisted Covert Sensitization in the Treatment of Exhibitionism." **Journal of Consulting and Clinical Psychology.** 1974, 42, 34-40.

Chapter 9

Visualization

Visualization is a powerful tool you can use to gain control of your mind, emotions, and body and to bring about desired changes in your behavior.

For example, a woman in her seventh month of pregnancy who is experiencing excruciating pain is given a sonargram indicating she has a benign tumor blocking her birth canal. Surgery or medication is out of the question. She uses visual imagery to relax and reduce pain. A month later her pain is gone and she is relaxed. She returns to her doctor for another sonargram. Much to the surprise of her physician, her tumor has disappeared.

A woman has been drinking coffee, often excessively, for 15 years. The coffee contributes to insomnia, nervousness, and stomach problems. Prior attempts to quit have resulted in headaches, depression, and craving. Visualizing herself coffee-free now and in the future enables her to stop drinking coffee abruptly with no withdrawal symptoms. Months later she is able to have an occasional cup of coffee without returning to her old excessive habit. She has lost her craving for coffee.

A young man is tense, nonassertive, and prone to headaches and insomnia. He is in a freak auto accident with his wife driving which adds lower back pain and flashbacks of the accident to his symptoms. Practicing visualization exercises, he learns to relax, control his headaches and back pain, and substitute pleasant images for his frightening flashbacks. He sees himself being assertive in his mind's eye, and eventually is able to confront his wife and stand up to his boss. His insomnia, which he does not specifically work on, improves spontaneously.

The people in these three examples have found that visual imagery can be used as a blueprint to positively modify their lives. The mere suggestion of an alternative way of being or behaving can put into motion subtle changes that soon become manifest in dramatic improvements.

Emil Coué, a French pharmacist, pioneered a movement in the early 1900's to make use of this human suggestibility to overcome the stress syndrome, enhance recovery from illness, and facilitate the accomplishment of positive goals. He believed that you can persuade yourself through your imagination to do anything that is physically possible to do. On the other hand, if you think you will fail you are very likely to do so. Fear of failure becomes the cause of failure. Belief in success inspires success. Coué argued that your thoughts, good or bad, become concrete reality. He was convinced that physical diseases are generally far more easily cured than mental ones.

While Coué stressed positive mental programming in the form of autosuggestions such as, "Every day in every way I am getting better and better," contemporary practitioners have expanded positive thinking to include positive visualization. By forming an image, you can make a clear mental statement of what you want to accomplish. By repeating this image again and again, you come to expect that what you want will occur. Because of this positive expectation, you start behaving in ways that are consistent with achieving your desired goal, and actually help bring it about. For example, a basketball foul-line shooter visualizes shooting perfect baskets. A student envisions getting an A on an exam. An expectant mother imagines a painless delivery. An obese man sees himself in his mind's eye as slender and good-looking.

In addition to consciously programming change through positive images, you can use visualization to gain access to your unconscious mind. You can find out why you persist in certain self-destructive patterns or learn alternative ways of looking at and dealing with problem situations.

Symptom Effectiveness

Positive visualization techniques can be used to relieve muscular tension, reduce or eliminate pain, and facilitate recovery from illness and injury. The ability to visualize vividly is also important to the success of many other Cognitive Stress Intervention techniques.

Time for Mastery

For maximum effectiveness, practice visualization exercises two or three times a day for ten to twenty minutes at a time. How quickly you will see results will depend largely on the goal you set for yourself, your powers of imagination, and your willingness to take the time to practice. The relaxation and pain relief exercises will have some immediate results. Recovery from illness or injury and achieving goals will take longer.

Instructions

Relaxation and Inner Guide Exercise

Whenever you practice visualization it is best to begin by relaxing. You are more receptive to positive suggestions when you are deeply relaxed. The following exercise combines imagery with Progressive Relaxation. Initially it will be worthwhile to tape record the directions or have someone read them to you. Soon you will learn to do the exercise without needing to hear the directions. The more you practice, the more quickly and profoundly you will relax. Do the exercise twice a day, at about the same times each day and in the same place if possible. Feel free to change any part of the instructions you find uncomfortable or disturbing. For example, some people do not like escalators, so for that part of the scene they imagine stepping onto a conveyor belt or walking down a path or hallway.

Arrange some quiet, uninterrupted time in a peaceful room with soft lighting and comfortable temperature. This may require the cooperation of the people with whom you live or work. Wear comfortable clothing. Do not do this exercise within a couple of hours after eating a heavy meal. Sit in a comfortable chair and follow the directions:

Place your feet flat on the floor, close your eyes, and relax your limbs. Move around until every part of your body is supported and tension is minimized. Good posture, including a straight spine, is best.

Begin by focusing on your face and feeling any tension in the muscles of your head...your scalp...across your forehead...around your eyes...your nose...your cheeks...your mouth...your tongue...your jaw. (pause) Make a mental picture of this tension. It may be a metal band around your head, a burning piece of coal behind your eyes, or a tight clamp on your jaw. (pause) Now mentally picture your symbol of tension relaxing. The metal band becomes a crown of soft feathers, the burning coal becomes beautifully cool, or the tight clamp loosens. (pause) Experience the muscles of your head becoming relaxed. (pause) As they relax, feel a wave of warm relaxation spreading throughout your body. (pause) Contract the muscles of your head...wrinkle your forehead, scalp, nose, and cheeks...squeeze your eyelids together...open your mouth wide and stick out your tongue. Maintain this state of tension for about seven seconds, and then relax. (pause) Feel the relaxation deepening in your body. (pause)

Now let yourself concentrate on your neck and shoulders and feel any tension in these muscles. (pause) Make a mental picture of this tension. (pause) Now mentally picture the symbol of tension relaxing. (pause) Experience the muscles of your neck and shoulders becoming relaxed, warm, and heavy. (pause) As they relax, feel your body becoming more relaxed, warm, and heavy. (pause) Tense the muscles of your neck and shoulders by drawing your shoulders upward toward your neck, squeezing tightly for about seven seconds. Then relax, feeling the relaxation moving through your body. (pause)

Now bring your attention to your arms and hands and notice any tension in these muscles. (pause) Make a mental picture of this tension. (pause) Now picture the symbol of tension relaxing. (pause) Experience the muscles of your arms and hands becoming relaxed, warm, and heavy. (pause) As they relax, let your body slip deeper into peaceful relaxation. (pause) Now tense the muscles of your hands and arms by making fists and flexing your biceps. Hold this pose for about seven seconds and then relax, letting your arms flop down, pulled by the force of gravity, very heavy and very relaxed. Study the feeling of relaxation, heaviness, and warmth in your arms and hands and notice that the rest of your body is becoming more and more relaxed. (pause)

Now concentrate on your back and feel any tension in the muscles of your back. (pause) Make a mental picture of this tension. (pause) Mentally picture the symbol of tension relaxing and becoming comfortable. (pause) Experience the muscles of your back becoming relaxed as the rest of your body enters into an even deeper state of relaxation. (pause) Tense the muscles of your back, pulling your shoulders and head backward and arching your back. Be careful not to aggravate any injuries or chronic back trouble you may have. Hold this pose for seven seconds and then relax completely. (pause)

Next focus on your breathing. (pause) Note any tension in the front of your torso...your chest...your lungs...your stomach...your intestines. (pause) Make a mental picture of this tension. (pause) Mentally imagine the symbol of tension relaxing. (pause) As the muscles of your torso become even more relaxed, feel a wave of warm relaxation spreading out through your entire body. (pause) Take a deep, slow breath, filling first the bottom of your lungs, then the middle, then the top...and slowly exhale. Inhale slowly again...this time hold your breath until it just begins to feel uncomfortable and then exhale forcefully through your mouth. Experience a wave of warm relaxation through your body as you continue to breathe slowly and deeply.

Now notice your buttocks, thighs, calves, and feet, and feel any tension in these muscles. (pause) Make a mental picture of this tension. (pause) Now mentally picture the symbol of tension relaxing and becoming comfortable. (pause) Experience the muscles of your buttocks, thighs, calves, and feet becoming heavy, warm, and relaxed, along with the rest of your body. (pause) Now contract the muscles of your buttocks, thighs, calves, and feet by raising your legs straight out in front of you and pointing your toes toward you and squeezing your muscles tightly for seven seconds. Then relax, letting your feet fall slowly to the floor. (pause) Study the sensations of warm relaxation and heaviness. (pause) Now raise your legs straight out in front of you again, this time curling your toes under and tightening the muscles of your buttocks, thighs, and calves for seven seconds. Then let your legs fall to the floor again. Notice how relaxed, heavy, and warm these are. (pause)

Now quickly scan your body for any remaining tension. If you encounter any, mentally picture the tension as a symbol. Picture the symbol of tension relaxing away, and then tighten and relax the muscle.

Now you will use visualization to directly relax your mind. Imagine an escalator that leads down to a wonderfully pleasant place. In your mind's eye, reach out and grasp the railing and step on. As you slowly descend, count backward from ten to one: ten...nine...eight...seven...six...five... four...three...two...one. Step off the escalator and notice the path in front of you. Follow it to a pleasant place of your own choosing that is totally comfortable for you. It may be by some water, in the mountains, in your home, in a museum, or even in the clouds. It may be a place you have been, or would like to go, or would like to create beyond the boundaries of reality. (pause) Mentally fill in the details of shape, color, lighting, temperature, sound, texture, taste, and smell.. Explore your special place. (pause) In your mind's eye look at your hands and feet and notice what you are wearing. Note how you are feeling in this special place, and relax even more. (pause) Continue to imagine yourself relaxed in this very comfortable place for a little while. (pause)

When you are ready to return from your special place, imagine returning to the escalator. (pause) Reach out and grasp the railing and step on. As you ascend, count to ten slowly: one...two...three...four...five...six...seven ...eight...nine...ten. When you reach ten and arrive back at the here-and-now, open your eyes.

In the relaxed state attained by the previous exercise, you can choose to suspend your conscious, rational mind and tune into thoughts and images that normally remain out of consciousness. Your unconscious mind is a rich storehouse of knowledge that can provide you with alternative ways of looking at and coping with everyday life. Although you may already have some awareness of your unconscious processes from dreams, intuitions, and feelings, you probably do not make use of this inner resource on a regular basis to assist you in getting more out of life. Visualization in a relaxed state can help you access unconscious information that will expand your conscious alternatives.

For example, Alice was an attractive, successful hair stylist who entered psychotherapy to find out why she could not allow herself to experience pleasure for more than brief moments before getting depressed and withdrawing from any enjoyable activity. Her therapist directed her to relax and assume an attitude of curiosity in which she would be open to any thoughts or images that might come to mind. She was to ask herself, "I wonder why I don't let myself enjoy myself for more than brief moments? I just wonder..." She then let her mind drift, without forcing any answers. When she did this she saw an image of herself as a child having a wonderful time and suddenly being interrupted by her mother, who glowered at her and said, "Who the hell do you think you are, having a good time when I'm sick and suffering?" Alice realized that, as an adult, she repeated this mental image each time she had a good time, thereby dampening her enjoyment. This memory, long buried in her unconscious, gave Alice important insight into her problem as well as direction for positive change.

Communicating With Your Inner Guide. A more structured way of consulting with your unconscious mind when you are in a state of deep relaxation is to imagine an inner guide. Your inner guide is a wise and helpful messenger who has access to the rich storehouse of knowledge in your unconscious mind. Your inner guide may take many forms: It may be a person, an animal, a plant, a place, or an event. The inner guide may speak, demonstrate, point out, or simply allude to the answer you are looking for.

To consult your inner guide, go through the previous relaxation exercise and enter your special place. Tape record or have someone read you the following instructions:

When you are deeply relaxed in your special place, look off in the distance. Notice that a small, radiant, blue-white light is slowly moving toward you. (pause) As the light comes closer, you discover that it is alive...perhaps a friendly stranger or an animal. (pause) As the person or animal approaches you, notice the details of its appearance: its shape, color, face, posture, sex, and mannerisms. (pause) If you feel relaxed, warm, comfortable, and safe in this being's presence, you know that it can serve as an inner guide. (pause) Ask it what its name is and wait for an answer. If you are not feeling comfortable in its presence, ask it some questions to find out why you are afraid. Wait for the answers. (pause) Once you feel confident that it can serve as your inner guide, ask for assistance with your problem. Discuss your problem as you would with a close friend. Pay close attention to what your guide tells you or to any gesture it might make. Its advice may come in words, something it shows you, an imagined event, or feelings. (pause) When you are finished, agree with your guide to meet at a future time for more discussions. (pause)

Leave your inner guide and special place behind and return to the escalator. Reach out and grasp the railing and step on. As you gradually ascend, count slowly to ten: one...two...three...four...five...six... seven...eight...nine...ten. When you reach the top and return to the here-and-now, open your eyes. Stretch as you become fully awake. Take a moment to notice how you are feeling. (pause) Review the experience, perhaps taking some notes about what you learned. Consider how this experience relates to your life and what action, if any, you will take as a result of the communication with your inner guide.

It may require several attempts to get in touch with your inner guide. Do not be discouraged. After all, you have probably been ignoring it for years.

Example

Ann had been experiencing chest and stomach pain off and on for six months. She felt tired, overworked, and depressed. Her symptoms had become more intense in the last week. She decided to get in touch with her inner guide and ask for some help. She did the relaxation exercise and went to her special place, which was darker than usual.

In the distance she saw a blue-white light that shone like a firefly in the night. As it came closer, it looked like a little fairy. Her first thought was, "Oh no . . . not Tinkerbell!" As the glowing figure approached, it grew into a full-sized woman who became old and turned into a wrinkled old man right before Ann's eyes. Ann felt completely at ease with this old man and she knew she could confide in him.

She began by telling him how she had been feeling and how her life was going. He listened with an ancient, bemused smile. She felt desperate when she asked, "Will I ever get over this?"

He replied, "When the rain stops, a bird will sing."

"That's very Zen of you," Ann said, "but I need something more concrete."

The man remained silent and stared at her. Ann thought about his comment.

"Well," she reflected, "rain doesn't go on forever, and beyond the rain there is something different . . . singing . . . That sounds pretty optimistic. So maybe he thinks there is hope for change. But why do I persist in these painful feelings? Why do I ache so?"

The old man motioned to her to look around her. She saw that her usually green, lush special place had turned into a barren wasteland of beiges and browns. Her next words were said through tears.

"Yes, it's true: I've let my life become a desert by cutting myself off from my friends and working too hard. Ever since I broke up with Steve and my best friend Janis moved away, I haven't really felt very sociable. It's so painful when people leave. It feels safest just to work hard. What can I do about this?"

The old man smiled and said, "Create some free time for yourself and see what happens."

Ann and her guide agreed to meet again in three days to continue their conversation.

Pain Control

The Nature of Pain

Pain is an important survival mechanism. Acute pain is a signal of danger notifying you that something is wrong and you should do something about it. But chronic pain such as the aching of arthritis or a broken arm in a cast is pointless in terms of survival after you have initiated the appropriate treatment. Chronic pain nags, saps your energy, and interferes with your ability to work, think, sleep, and enjoy life. Fortunately, this kind of pain is susceptible to control with Cognitive Stress Intervention techniques.

If pain were merely a mechanism for physical survival it would be a purely physical phenomenon, experienced in exactly the same way by everyone. Actually, different people experience the same kind of pain in many different ways. This is because pain is experienced not only physically, but emotionally and cognitively as well. In their 1965 gate control theory of pain, Melzak and Wall called these three aspects of pain the sensory/discriminatory aspect (physical sensations), the motivational/affective aspect (emotional feelings), and the cognitive/evaluative aspect (thoughts). The exercises in this section are designed to deal with pain in all three of these aspects.

Childbirth is a good example of how thoughts and feelings can affect the experience of pain. In *The Original Approach to Natural Childbirth,* Dr. Dick-Read states that thoughts, especially in the form of visual images, can surround a natural physical function with an aura of pain *or* pleasure so vivid that normal reflexes are altered. Fear of childbirth is learned from the stories of friends and traditional associations of pain with labor. This fear leads to muscular tension, which is interpreted by the brain as pain. A stress syndrome is set up. The fear/tension/pain cycle actually produces true pain through the mechanism of pathological tension. Dr. Dick-Read recommends that pregnant women practice visualizing positive images of childbirth. This replaces fear with pleasurable images, short-circuiting the stress syndrome and replacing it with a positive cycle of pleasurable images leading to muscular relaxation and a relatively painless labor.

You may have noticed that you occasionally feel the first twinges of headache, backache, or stomachache and tense up, recalling previous episodes of pain and anticipating another round of agony. Your fear increases your muscular tension and your tension contributes to your pain, in the same sort of stress syndrome as that described for childbirth.

Relaxation for Pain Control

Progressive Relaxation, presented in the first part of this chapter, helps control pain in two ways. First, it reduces muscular tension, short-circuiting the fear/tension/pain syndrome that so often exacerbates your experience of pain. Second, it shifts your attention away from pain. According to Melzak and Wall's gate control theory of pain, shifting the focus of your attention is a major tactic in pain management.

Refocusing your attention works because you literally cannot feel pain when your attention is elsewhere. You probably recall times when you cut yourself without realizing it and didn't feel anything until you noticed the cut. Elmer Green discusses this in his book *Beyond Biofeedback*. He performed experiments in which subjects were given painful electric shocks while lights flashed, sounds blared, and vibrations shook around them. When the subjects tuned into the lights, sounds, or vibrations, they couldn't feel the electric shocks. They were able to push the discomfort out of conscious awareness by redirecting their attention.

Use your favorite relaxation exercise, or the relaxation exercise presented in the first section of this chapter. Relieve your muscular tension and shift your attention away from your pain using the fantasy of a real or imaginary scene that is incompatible with the experience of pain. For instance, imagine yourself sunbathing on a pleasant, warm beach; fishing in your favorite spot; walking through the woods with a friend; resting on a hill overlooking the city; visiting a museum; sitting in your favorite chair; or looking at your garden.

Visualization for Pain Control

Visualization takes relaxation one step further in the control of pain. Besides reducing muscular tension and redirecting attention away from pain, visualization exercises can actually reduce pain by manipulating images of pain.

Visualization exercises act directly on the emotional and cognitive aspects of how you experience pain, taking advantage of your ability to understand and interpret reality symbolically. You can use the following exercises to transform your pain into visual images which you can then manipulate in your imagination.

Memorize, tape record, or have a friend read to you each of these four exercises. Go through each one slowly, trying it a few times. Continue with the ones you find most helpful:

Size and Shape

1. Note any pain in your body.

2. Give your pain a shape and a size.

3. Make the shape gradually larger and larger until it is as big as you can imagine.

4. Slowly make it smaller and smaller until it returns to its original size.

5. Slowly make it enormous one more time.

6. This time as you make it gradually smaller, let it return to its original size and then continue to shrink until it finally disappears.

7. Note any change in the intensity of your pain.

> Example: Judy imagined her headache as a jagged line about six inches long. She visualized it becoming so big that it filled her entire field of vision. When she diminished it the second time, she spent about three minutes shrinking it to a tiny dot that finally disappeared.

Colored Lights

1. Note any pain in your body.

2. Imagine the painful area filled with red light.

3. Imagine the rest of your body filled with soothing, relaxing, cool blue-white light.

4. Change the red light to blue-white light and let a soothing, cool wave of relaxation flow into the painful area.

5. Change all the blue-white light to red light and feel a wave of warm relaxation flow through your body.

6. Change the red light to blue-white light and let your body enjoy the cool, soothing state of relaxation.

7. Note any change in the intensity of your pain.

> Example: Leroy imagined his broken leg lit up with bright red light, and

the rest of his body radiating cool blue light. The red slowly faded to blue, and he felt a cool relaxation flood his body. As he changed the blue to red, he imagined his body becoming warmer and more relaxed. Finally he let the light change to blue-white again, and again felt the cool type of relaxation.

Color, Shape, and Distance

1. Note any pain in your body.

2. Give this pain a shape and a color.

3. Change the shape and color of your pain.

4. Push this new colored shape away from you in your mind's eye until it is out of your awareness.

5. Notice any change in the intensity of your pain.

    Example: Sam saw his stomach pain as a dark red, heavy-looking ball. He changed the color to green and the shape to a frisby. Then he pushed it away and it gathered momentum and sped off into the universe, beyond his sight.

Pain versus Relaxation Symbols

1. Become aware of any pain in your body.

2. Give this pain a symbol.

3. Give the concept of relaxation a symbol.

4. Let these symbols interact in such a way as to cancel or remove the pain symbol.

5. Notice any change in the intensity of your pain.

    Example: Lynn imagined her headache as a tightly fitting steel band around her head. Her relaxation symbol was a magician's wand that flipped the band off into the sky. As the band flew into the air, it turned into a delicate necklace of gold.

Glove Anesthesia

1. If you are right-handed, imagine your left hand is becoming more and more relaxed. As it relaxes it becomes heavier and heavier.

2. Imagine your hand being slowly immersed in cool water: the fingertips, all of the fingers, the palm, finally the whole hand. Feel the hand becoming more and more heavy and relaxed.

3. As the water is getting colder, notice the hand beginning to tingle and feel numb. Focus on the sensations of cold, tingling, and numbness as you repeat to yourself, "cold, tingly, numb" slowly over and over.

4. Pinch your numb hand with your other hand. You should feel pressure, but no pain. If there is pain, repeat the above procedure.

5. Once the hand is numb, move the feeling of anesthesia to other parts of your body by placing your anesthetized hand on the area and allowing the feeling of anesthesia to flow from your hand to that area. Feel the sensation of cool, tingling numbness flowing into the new area, making it heavy and relaxed and numb.

> Example: Jackie, who had not been able to get relief from a toothache with codeine, used this technique successfully to rid herself of the pain and get a good night's sleep. After she had numbed her hand, she placed it on her jaw and felt the cold numbness dull the ache in her tooth.

Recontextualizing Your Pain

Another way to control pain with visualization is to imagine a different cause for your pain. This transforms the context in which your pain occurs and makes it more tolerable. For example, when you feel the piercing throb of a toothache, imagine eating your favorite ice cream as a child. The cold hurts your teeth, but it tastes delicious.

General aches and pains might be transformed into warm sand hitting your skin during a windstorm on an exciting desert caravan trip. Pain in your shoulder could be imagined as an injury sustained when you made a last-minute touchdown and won the football game. A chronic sore throat can be the result of non-stop speechmaking during the last week of your successful presidential campaign. The more pleasing the fantasy, the more tolerable the recontextualized pain will be.

Why It's Hard to Let Go of Pain: Uncovering Pain's Positive Functions

Pain is adaptive. Starting very early in infancy, you learn to associate painful sensations with increasingly complex meanings. You develop your own idiosyncratic way of perceiving and dealing with pain as you constantly adapt to your environment. If you grew up geared toward a rugged sports career, for example, you would probably develop a stoic, accepting attitude toward the pain of injuries sustained on the football field. On the other hand, if you set your sights on becoming an opera singer, you might view your body as a delicate musical instrument and be extremely sensitive to any pain or potential injury.

Pain can be so adaptive that it sometimes seems worth holding on to. If you're like most people, you have sometimes used pain to avoid a difficult situation, get taken care of, or get extra love, attention, or special consideration. These are some of the positive functions that pain can have in your life.

For example, you can use pain as a way to get help from others by saying, "not for me, but because of my pain. . ." The problem with this tactic is that you have to hold onto your pain in order to get your needs met. The solution is to learn assertiveness so that you can ask directly for love and attention for your own sake, not for your pain's sake. Then you will be free to let your pain go or diminish.

Another example of the adaptive misuses of pain is using it to avoid thinking about unpleasant emotional conflicts that you feel unequipped to resolve. The physical pain may seem more bearable than confronting the emotional pain. For example, a man who was repeatedly taunted by his fellow warehouse workers for not talking and fighting "like a man" developed chest pains that made it impossible to continue working in the warehouse. He dwelt on his pain, rather than dealing with his doubts about his masculinity.

If you are having trouble letting go of persistent, chronic pain, you need to uncover the positive function being served by your pain. To do this, find out what your pain has to say by following these directions:

Get into a comfortable position and close your eyes. Scan your body for muscular tension, relaxing it as you take several deep, slow breaths. When you are relaxed, adopt a curious, accepting attitude.

Address the part of your body that is in pain as if it were a person, perhaps a close friend. Ask it what positive function your pain is serving, and wait patiently for whatever answer comes.

If you do not understand the answer at first, don't worry. Remaining in your relaxed state, recall a time in your past when you did not understand something and yet it came out all right. Dwell on that past experience and its positive outcome for a while. Perhaps the answers to your question about the purpose of your pain will become clear on a conscious level, or perhaps the answer will remain on the unconscious level.

For example, Jerry was a quality control inspector in the production department of a computer company. He was known for his rigid adherence to high standards and for his temper when he discovered a product that fell short of his criteria of excellence. He was also a nice guy who hated to hurt others' feelings. He had had stomach cramping and gas almost daily for years. Elaborate medical tests revealed no organic basis for his discomfort.

Jerry decided to consult with his stomach to find out what positive function his pain might be serving. He first relaxed and assumed a curious yet accepting attitude, and asked his stomach what purpose it had when it became so painful. At first his only response was to feel a little dizzy and nauseated. He recalled a time in his life when he had experienced something he didn't understand that worked out well: falling in love with the woman he eventually married.

After a few sessions of questioning the purpose of his pain, Jerry saw an image of himself as a villain in a melodrama in which the protagonists hated his guts. He realized that in his eagerness to do a good job, he ignored the feelings of the people whose work he inspected. His stomach registered the conflict between his desire to do a perfect job and his need to be liked. While he consciously ignored this conflict, his stomach pain provided a frequent reminder of its existence. As an alternative way of handling the conflict, Jerry learned to express himself in an assertive rather than aggressive way. He also lowered his unreasonable expectations regarding the quality of the finished product.

Overcoming Illness and Injury

The relationship between mind and physical illness cannot be underestimated. Consider a healthy African tribesman who learns that the tribe's witch doctor has put a death curse on him. He will die within a few days unless he is told that the spell has been broken. Also consider the power of the placebo in contemporary western medicine. A patient is told that the pills he is to take will produce specific beneficial results. Although the medication is actually neutral in effect, the patient gets better in a few days.

Western studies of Indian yogis indicate that the mind can exert tremendous influence over the body. For instance, a yogi can jab a large needle into his body and not bleed or feel pain. He can walk on burning coals without experiencing blisters or pain. He can survive in a closed container for many hours after another person would have died from lack of oxygen.

Biofeedback researchers have found that average Americans, not just yogis, can learn to voluntarily control many physical processes normally thought to be under the involuntary control of the autonomic nervous system. Among these processes are heart rate, muscle tension, skin temperature, and sweat gland activity. As Barbara Brown points out in her book *New Mind, New Body*, Biofeedback research has provided the first scientific proof that the mind can relieve illnesses as well as create them.

The following exercise is borrowed from Carl Simonton's book *Getting Well Again:*

1. Relax in a comfortable chair with your feet on the floor and your extremities supported so that they are not strained. Insure quiet, a comfortable temperature, and soft lighting.

2. Use the relaxation exercise described in the first part of this chapter.

3. Relax in your special place for a few minutes.

4. Create a mental picture of your illness or injury. Imagine it in a form that makes sense to you. If you have a broken arm, you could imagine the jagged ends of the bone roughly meeting but not attached. If you have a stomach ulcer, you might see an inflamed, raw sore on the stomach wall.

5. Picture a treatment—magical or scientific—that will eliminate the injury or illness, or strengthen your body's ability to heal itself. If you are under treatment you can visualize it working effectively. Imagine seeing your broken bone resting peacefully, enclosed in a protective case. Imagine milk or antacids coating the ulcer with soothing, healing white liquid that neutralizes the acid and reduces the inflamation.

6. Picture your natural physical defenses and physical processes eliminating the illness or injury. See new, red blood flowing in, multiplying and forming a thick, gluey substance that binds the pieces of bone together. See healthy cells multiplying and covering the ulcer, and white blood cells removing the debris and cleansing the area.

7. See yourself as healthy and free from illness, injury, and pain. See your bone completely healed, stronger than ever. See yourself participating in your favorite activities, feeling happy, healthy, and pain-free. See your stomach lining pink and healthy. See yourself feeling calm and vital, enjoying yourself.

8. See yourself successfully proceeding toward achieving the goals in your life. See yourself participating in your career, in sports, in your community. See yourself raising a healthy, happy family. See yourself taking a trip you have long wanted to take.

9. Congratulate yourself for participating in your own recovery. See yourself doing this exercise three times a day in a relaxed and alert state.

In Elmer Green's *Beyond Biofeedback* Jack Schartz describes a very creative healing visualization in which you can distract your attention away from your pain and focus on healing the injured part of your body. He uses a cut hand as an example:

In a quiet room, sit down in a comfortable chair. Relax, using your favorite relaxation exercise to quiet your body and emotions. In your mind's eye, see yourself sitting in a chair. Allow your body feeling to merge with the visualized figure so that you feel you are the figure sitting in the chair in your mind. Think of your body and your visualization as if they are identical twins, fitted perfectly together.

Look at your hand in your mind's eye. See it slip like a glove from the body. As it moves away from you, it grows larger, until it is as big as a house standing ten yards away from you, sitting on its base at the wrist.

Now rise to your feet in your mind-body and walk toward the hand. When you are halfway there, turn around and see your other body, sitting in the chair. Say to it, "Cross your legs," and it complies. If it doesn't, return to the chair and try again. When you see it cross its legs, psychological conditions are right, and you can walk on to the hand.

When you reach the hand, you notice a door which you open and walk inside. The hand if hollow, and a ladder is leaning against the wall of the hand on the palm side, right alongside of the gash. On the floor are patching materials, some tape and glue. You put these things in a bucket and carry the bucket up the ladder to the cut to begin your repair job.

You repair it in whatever way seems best to you in your visualization. You may want to put glue on the edges of the cut and then put strips of sticky tape over it with glue to hold it firm. After you have patched it up, quietly watch it for a while to be sure it is firm. If you are sure, climb back down the ladder. However, if the patch starts coming off, remove it and start over. Continue in this manner until you have a patch that you know will hold.

When you have the results you want, come down the ladder, put the materials on the floor, go out the door, close it, and walk back to your body, where you turn around and sit down.

You look at your huge mind-hand and notice that there is no wound. The hand gradually shrinks as it slowly moves toward you. Finally, when it is the right size, it slips back into place like a glove.

Thank your body for doing such a good job. See yourself as one whole being, body and mind filled with joy and energy. Open your eyes, feeling good. Ignore your hand initially, allowing the body to integrate the visualization without interference. Later you can let yourself look at it, but do not pick at it emotionally or mentally. Remember, a farmer does not dig up his seeds to see if they are sprouting.

Practice this visualization a couple of times a day as long as it is needed. Practice makes perfect. Take the usual traditional medical precautions along with doing this and any other exercises presented in this chapter. This is a nice exercise to use when you are having dental work done.

Achieving Goals

Setting and achieving goals that fulfill your needs is essential to health and happiness. Striving toward your goals is a statement that you are taking charge of your life, rather than letting life take charge of you.

Visualizing a goal is more important than knowing every detail of how you will reach it. When you set out to climb a hill, you don't need to know every twist the trail will take or the function of your every nerve and muscle. Most of all you need a clear image of the top of the hill.

Seeking visualized goals is a powerful, natural tendency that you follow even if you don't consciously set any goals. It's a tropism like the tendency of plants to seek light—a slight but constant, unreasoning but insistent drive that can eventually crack the hardest granite. If you don't have a clear vision of where you want to go, this urge will be frustrated and you may experience your life as meaningless or directionless. Or you may actually visualize negative goals for yourself. You may see yourself as unhappy, uncreative, sick, in pain, and a failure. Your natural tendency to seek visualized goals will work toward making these negative images a reality. Given this innate power, visualizing positive goals is as important to your happiness as good nutrition is to your physical health.

The first step in goal setting is to get in touch with what you want out of life. Answering the following questions can help you if you don't currently have any specific goals. If answering these questions makes you feel a little trapped or limited in your options, remember that goals change as you change. The important thing is to have some positive goals, not to have the same goals forever.

What specific habit would you like to develop or break?
What personality trait would you like to develop?
What kind of home would you like to own?
What would you like to do on your next vacation?
How can you better communicate with your family members?
What new position or honor would you like to attain?
What person would you like to have as a closer friend?

What professional or occupational skill would you like to strengthen?
What new hobby or activity would you like to begin?
What would solve a problem you now have?
What study habits would you like to acquire?
How much money would you like to earn?
How would you like to improve your physical condition?
What specific financial habit would you like to acquire?
What additional education would you like to have?
What civic interest or public service would you like to begin?
What other things would you like to have happen to you?

When you have answers to some of these questions, use them to fill in the goal planner that follows. Break them down into lifetime goals, one year goals, and one month goals. Then rate them as top, middle, or bottom drawer items. Top drawer items are your most important goals, the ones that are essential to your health, happiness, and sense of self worth. Middle drawer items are moderately important to your enjoyment of life. Bottom drawer items are goals that would be nice to achieve after you have all the rest, but you could live without them.

Visualizing Your Goal

Choose a one month goal that is a top or middle drawer item for you, and is relatively easy to achieve. This is the goal that you will visualize first.

Write the goal out on a separate sheet of paper. Express it as a statement of fact in the present tense. Include any crucial details of time, place, facts, figures, persons, and your feelings about it. Here are some examples of well expressed goals: "I am going on singles club outings once a week and meeting interesting new people." "I am swimming a mile three times a week. I feel stronger and more alive." "I am living comfortably within my budget for food, clothing, and entertainment. I feel financially secure and in control of my spending." "Bob and I are understanding each other and really trusting and loving each other."

Don't use negatives such as, "I am not overeating." Your unconscious tends to drop out negatives, so that this sentence would be reduced to "I am overeating."

When you have your goal clearly expressed to your satisfaction, follow these instructions:

1. Do the relaxation exercise presented earlier in this chapter as a way of quieting your body and mind and making yourself receptive to positive images.

2. Repeat your goal to yourself very slowly, several times.. See the words written on the page. Let the words really sink in.

3. See yourself with the goal already accomplished. How are you feeling now that you have reached your goal? What are you doing? What do you look like? What are your surroundings? What are people saying to you? How are the people who are most important to you responding to your achievement?

Goal Planner

Rank as T, M, or B
(Top, Middle or Bottom drawer items)

Lifetime goals

_____

_____

_____

_____

_____

_____

One year goals

_____

_____

_____

_____

_____

_____

One month goals

_____

_____

_____

_____

_____

_____

4. Look back over the steps you took to reach your goal. What was the first one? Decide to take some action on this first step. Be in touch with a sense of accomplishment for taking the first step. Then add in the details of the other steps.

5. Be happy and thankful that you have reached your goal.

6. Slowly return to the present time, feeling alert and relaxed. Open your eyes and take the first step toward your goal.

To get the best results from this exercise, practice it three times a day. Work on one goal at a time, and when you have reached a goal, be sure to acknowledge your success. If you find your needs changing, change your goals accordingly. As you continue this process, you will find yourself acting in ways compatible with achieving your goals.

As you practice visualizing your goals, you may learn some important things about yourself. You may discover that you want something very different from what you set out to get. You might learn that you are afraid of how others will respond if you achieve your goal. You might find that you are unwilling or unable at this time to perform the necessary steps to reach your goal.

If you are unable to see yourself actually reaching your goal, you may still be questioning your ability to reach the goal. Do not deny your doubts—in fact, explore them freely. Continue your visualization exercises as a way to strengthen your belief that you will meet your goal. Acknowledge the possibility that you may attain your goal or that something even better will occur.

Making Mental Movies

This is a good technique to use when you find that you can visualize yourself having achieved a goal, but you can't imagine the concrete steps to take to reach it. To make mental movies, write out a clear statement of your goal, then:

1. Get into a comfortable position and perform your favorite relaxation exercise to calm your body and mind.

2. Close your eyes and adopt a passive, receptive attitude.

3. Imagine a movie screen. Picture yourself on the screen in a movie, having successfully achieved your goal. Watch and listen to yourself enjoying your success.

4. Run the movie backwards for about ten seconds. See and hear what you did that led up to accomplishing your goal. If you go over ten seconds without getting any clear images, take a deep breath, stretch, and go back to the end of your movie. Roll it backwards again for ten seconds. Keep doing this until you see and hear vivid scenes of the steps you took.

5. Ask yourself, "Is it *possible* for me to do these things to accomplish my goal?" *Don't* ask "Do I *want* to do these things?" Remember that so far merely doing what you want has not netted you success. If you really want

to achieve your goal, you may have to try something new, something out of the ordinary for you. If you can take the necessary steps, go on. If you can't, return to the blank movie screen and run another movie.

6. Now step into the movie. Live through the scenes leading up to your success. Imagine yourself doing, saying, and experiencing all the steps that you will take.

7. Come back gradually to the present time, feeling refreshed, confident, and resolved to take the first step. Open your eyes.

Some people have trouble imagining moving pictures. If that's true for you, visualize a slide show. See your success scene and the scenes that lead up to it as detailed color slides. Run the slide projector backward and forward.

You may get a clear movie of your goal and the scenes that lead up to it, but have mixed feelings about the goal itself. You can also make mental movies to explore this kind of ambivalence. Follow the mental movie procedure up to the point of seeing yourself with your goal accomplished. Then run the projector *forward* into the future. Watch yourself experiencing the long-term consequences of your goal. For example, you may have a goal of achieving an intimate relationship with a particular woman. Running the movie forward from the scene of initial success might reveal an unfolding nightmare of feeling trapped in marriage, disagreements over having or rearing children, financial disasters, and so on. This further information about your unconscious predictions for the future may lead you to rewrite or recast your entire movie.

Example

Rosa felt that she had no influence over her husband's behavior. Often he would do things that bothered her, but she said nothing for fear of making him angry. She seldom suggested any activities because she didn't want to cause friction. She decided to use mental movies to improve her ability to influence her husband's behavior.

She defined her first goal as, "I ask Joe to go to the beach with me instead of watching the game on TV next Saturday. He cheerfully agrees."

1. Rosa relaxed on her bed, using Progressive Relaxation.

2. She closed her eyes and achieved a calm, receptive state of mind.

3. Imagining a wide movie screen, she pictured herself sitting at the dinner table with her husband, who had just agreed to go to the beach with her.

4. She then ran her movie backwards, observing herself carefully. She saw that in the movie her voice was soft when talking to Joe. She noticed that when she leaned forward, so did he. And when she touched him, his face softened and he smiled. She also observed that as she described how much she wanted to go to the beach and why, he became as enthusiastic about going as she was.

5. She asked herself, "Is it *possible* for me to do these things?" Her answer was, "This seems manipulative and I hate being manipulative...but yes, it is possible for me to do it."

6. Rosa turned the projector to forward and stepped into the picture. She experienced what she would see, hear, say, do, and feel in real life.

7. She opened her eyes, resolved to talk to her husband that night after dinner, using the script from her movie.

Rosa went on to make mental movies of other, related goals, such as getting her husband to help with the dishes and take dancing lessons with her. After successfully accomplishing them with her husband, she began to routinely make mental movies of all her goals as a way of loosening up her creative imagination to help her with all sorts of problem solving.

Special Considerations

If you have difficulty visualizing, try the following simple exercise: Close your eyes and recall your bedroom, a pleasant recent or childhood experience, or what you had for breakfast, in as much detail as possible. Pay attention to shapes, colors, and lighting as well as smells, tastes, textures, temperature, sounds, physical sensations, and feelings. Someone who is not a strong visualizer usually has a well-developed memory which favors another sense, such as the sense of smell, physical sensation, or hearing. If this is true for you, recall an experience by tuning into whatever sense is easiest for you, and then imagine associated visual images. You may decide to concentrate on whatever sensory images you can most easily attain, or to expand gradually into images involving two or more senses.

Unrecognized negative visualizations counteract the effects of the positive visualizations you consciously hold in your mind. It is therefore important to deal with any negative visualizations that occur to you in addition to your positive ones. The negative visualizations underlie areas of dissatisfaction in your life. For example, a woman who was 30 pounds overweight had the following negative visualizations:

1. She saw herself as fat in the future as well as now.

2. When she visualized herself as slender, she saw men sexually harrassing her— a very frightening image.

3. When she visualized herself as slender, she also saw people rejecting her for reasons other than her weight.

4. When she visualized herself as fat, she saw her husband loving her "for herself."

Looking at her negative visualizations gave her considerable insight into why it was so difficult for her to lose weight. She programmed visualizations that took her fears into account:

1. She pictured herself as slender and assertive so that she could easily deal with sexually aggressive men.

2. She pictured herself as slender and able to handle criticism and rejection. She saw herself as feeling OK about herself.

3. She pictured her husband loving her "for herself" when she was slender.

Further reading

Brown, B. **New Mind, New Body.** New York: Harper and Row, 1974.

Coué, E. **Self-Mastery Through Conscious Auto-Suggestion.** London: Allen and Unwin, 1922.

Dick-Read, G. **Childbirth Without Fear.** New York: Harper and Row, 1953.

Gawain, S. **Creative Visualization.** Berkeley, California: Whatever Publishing, 1978.

Green, E. and Green, A. **Beyond Biofeedback.** New York: Dell, 1977.

Horowitz, M. **Image Formation and Cognition.** New York: Appleton-Century-Crofts, 1970.

Jung, C. G., ed. **Man and His Symbols.** Garden City, New York: Doubleday, 1968.

Le Shan, L. **You Can Fight For Your Life.** New York: Evans, 1977.

Maltz, M. **Psycho-Cybernetics.** New York: Pocket Books, 1966.

Melzack, R. and Wall, P. "Pain Mechanisms: A New Theory." **Science.** 1965, 150, 971-5.

Samuels, M. and Bennett, H. **Be Well.** New York: Random House, 1974.

Samuels, M. and Samuels, N. **Seeing With the Mind's Eye.** New York: Random House, 1975.

Satir, V. **People Making.** Palo Alto, California: Science and Behavior Books, 1975.

Simonton, O. C., Matthews-Simonton, S. and Creighton, J. L. **Getting Well Again.** New York: Bantam Books, 1980.

Smith, M. J. **When I Say No, I Feel Guilty.** New York: Bantam Books, 1975.

Chapter 10

Covert Reinforcement

Covert Reinforcement is a means of learning to approach situations which you previously avoided out of fear. It involves pairing your desired approach behavior with positive reinforcers. This procedure is first practiced in your imagination. Later you can apply the same procedure in real life.

For example, imagine that you are afraid of heights and you want to work in a highrise office building In your imagination you pair the desired approach behavior (going up in the elevator to the top floor and looking out the window without anxiety) with a positive reinforcer (sitting at home by a cozy fireplace with your spouse). When you are comfortable with imagining this previously anxiety-provoking scenario, you begin to practice it in real life, still visualizing the reinforcer. As you practice this technique you will find that your anxiety level is greatly reduced because your avoidance response to the situation is not being reinforced and the feared danger does not occur.

Symptom Effectiveness

Covert reinforcement is used in the treatment of various types of avoidance behaviors such as test anxiety, phobias, and procrastination. It has also been used to improve self-esteem and promote a positive attitude toward specific groups of people.

Time for Mastery

Two weeks to a month are required to accrue maximum benefits from Covert Reinforcement.

Instructions

1. Describe your avoidance behavior.

Your avoidance behavior is what you do that is a problem for you. You must describe it in specific terms. Here are some examples of well-defined problems suited for this technique:

> "I am a fifth-year collge undergraduate who panics on objective tests (multiple choice, true-false, and fill-in). I know the material, but when I see the questions, my mind goes blank, my heart starts racing, my hands get cold and sweaty, and I leave the room. I want to be able to relax, concentrate, and do sufficiently well on the test to pass it."

> "I am extremely anxious when I have to speak to groups larger than six people. I get tongue-tied and say what I have to say in as few words as possible. As part of my job as an engineer, I must present project proposals in a persuasive manner to the board of directors of my company. My inability to articulate my ideas in a coherent and impactful way often results in worthwhile projects getting shelved. I would like to present proposals in a persuasive enough manner that they are accepted."

> "I feel too ugly and inadequate to ask out any of the women I find attractive. When I go up to a woman to ask her out, I back off, thinking that she will say "no." I want to improve my self concept and overcome my fear of rejection sufficiently to ask attractive women out."

> "My father was an alcoholic and made life miserable for everyone in the family. I grew up detesting alcohol and people who drink it. As an adult, I socialize with people who drink, and I feel tense and withdrawn when I observe others loosening up and having a good time after one or two drinks. I would like to relax and enjoy talking with individuals who happen to be social drinkers."

2. Describe your approach behavior.

Your approach behavior is what you want to happen. Think it through very carefully or, better yet, write it out step by step. Ask yourself what leads up to the approach behavior. What is the actual approach behavior—what you want to happen? What is the logical successful conclusion of the approach behavior? What are the surroundings? How do you look? How do you feel? Who else is involved? What is their response to you and your approach behavior?

For example, imagine again that you have a fear of heights. Your approach behavior is being able to work comfortably in a highrise office building. The logical sequence of events would begin with you walking into the building lobby. You go directly to the elevator. You watch the light flicker from fifty down to one. The door opens and people pour out. You get on with some others. The elevator starts upward. You feel slightly anxious, but remember to relax and take a deep breath. You study the people around you. The elevator stops at various floors and people get off and on. You continue to observe, being aware of clothes, facial expressions, hair styles, and conversations. You feel the elevator moving. At the fiftieth floor you get off and walk casually over to the window. You look out over the city. You feel queasy for a moment and then remember to relax and breathe deeply. You enjoy the view without further uneasiness. Your boss comes over and says hello. You chat pleasantly while you both admire the view.

3. List your positive reinforcers.

Positive reinforcers are pleasant situations or experiences that have the following four qualities: You can enjoy them thoroughly, you can easily imagine them, imagining them creates a feeling very similar to the feeling created in real life, and you can easily erase the imagined scene from your mind at will.

From the following list, select three or four items that give you the most pleasure:

Eating certain foods or drinking certain beverages
Watching or participating in a specific sport
Listening to or making music
Observing or being with members of the opposite sex
Engaging in your favorite hobby
Doing something you enjoy with friends or family
Reading, watching TV, listening to the radio, or going to the movies
Solving problems
Being right
Being praised for something you are or do
Winning
Peace and quiet
Taking a bath or shower
Sleeping
Shopping
Being in nature

Note: If you are unable to think of any enjoyable activities or situations, go directly to the second technique presented in this chapter, Covert Negative Reinforcement.

4. Practice relaxation.

Find a quiet place where you will not be interrupted. Sit in a comfortable position with your body fully supported and relaxed. Close your eyes, take a few slow, deep breaths and let the tension drain out of your body. Scan your body for tension. If you find any, let it dissolve away. The more relaxed you are, the more easily you will be able to imagine your scenes.

5. Practice imagining reinforcers.

For example, imagine sitting at home in the Jacuzzi, peacefully chatting with a friend. Fill in the details of the five senses as much as possible. Notice the feeling of the warm jets of water on your body, the contrast of warm water and cool air, the floating feeling in your arms, the sounds of bubbling water and your friend's voice, the smell of pine trees surrounding you, the sight of your friend sitting in the steaming, churning water, and so forth.

You may find that you are better at imagining in one sensory modality than another—perhaps the sense of hearing or touch instead of vision brings the scene more alive for you. That's fine. With practice you can gradually increase the number of sensory modes through which you imagine the scene. If you find that you absolutely cannot imagine any enjoyable situations, go directly to the second technique presented in this chapter, Covert Negative Reinforcement.

After successfully imagining the first scene, go on to the other enjoyable scenes you have selected. See how quickly and vividly you can bring these scenes to mind. When you have one clearly in mind, hold it for about 20 seconds and then let it go. Relax for 20 seconds.

The time intervals suggested are arbitrary. Some people can form a clear image of a scene in seven seconds, instantaneously erase it, and rest for just five seconds before calling up the next scene. Others take 30 seconds or more to get a scene clearly in mind, and require a correspondingly longer time to rest between scenes. Find the intervals that work best for you.

6. Record your approach behavior scene.

Tape record the scene describing your approach behavior. At each point where you would normally become anxious, insert the word "Reinforce" and pause for about 20 seconds before resuming your description of the scene. The following is an approach behavior scene recorded by a student who experienced acute test anxiety:

"Ten minutes before the final exam, I walk into the lecture hall. (Reinforce) I notice hundreds of other students milling around looking for seats, and two proctors standing at the front of the room with a stack of exams. (Reinforce) I find a seat just as one of the proctors begins to explain the instructions for taking the exam, the policy regarding cheating, needing to leave the room, and so forth. (Reinforce) The other proctor hands out the exam. I get mine and wait for the signal to open to the first page and start. (Reinforce) We are told to begin and I open to the first page and see the multiple choice questions. (Reinforce) I read the first question and answer it correctly. (Reinforce) I go on and finish the first page. I am not sure of three of my answers and I mark the questions so that I can come back to them later. (Reinforce) On the fourth page is a series of questions covering a lecture I missed. I start to get anxious and lose my ability to concentrate. I remember to take a deep breath and relax. (Reinforce) I finish the exam with fifteen minutes to spare and return to look at the questions I was not sure of. (Reinforce) I change one of my answers. When

I am finished I give my exam to the proctor and leave, feeling worried that I didn't know quite a few of the answers. (Reinforce) A week later the test results are posted and I learn that I passed the exam. I feel ecstatic! (Reinforce)"

An alternative to tape recording your scene is to have a friend read it to you while you relax with your eyes closed. That way, you can raise your finger to indicate that you have a clear image of the part of the scene being described, at which the reader *immediately* says, "Reinforce." After you have clearly imagined the reinforcer scene, erased it, and relaxed, you can raise your finger again as a signal to the reader to immediately resume. Covert Reinforcement is one technique for which using a reader can be superior to using a tape recorder.

7. Listen to your approach behavior scene.

You are now ready to put the preceding steps together. Select for your reinforcer an enjoyable scene that is very easy to visualize. Relax as described in step four. Listen to your approach behavior scene, putting yourself fully into the situation being described. When you hear the word "Reinforce," clearly imagine your enjoyable scene for about 20 seconds, then erase it and relax as the description of the approach behavior resumes.

Do this at least twice a day, going through the entire approach behavior scene twice each time. Practice every day until you can listen to the entire scene without feeling anxious.

When you feel at ease with the imagined scene, rewrite and retape it, dropping out every other "Reinforce." Listen to this revised scene for a few more days, until you feel at ease with only half the original "Reinforcers."

Return to the original script of your approach behavior scene and retape it leaving in every third "Reinforce." Practice for a couple of days with this version. Then tape a version with only one-fifth the number of "Reinforcers," and use that for another two days.

As the days go on, the enjoyable scene you are using as a reinforcer may lose its effectiveness. If that happens, switch to one of the other enjoyable scenes you have practiced imagining.

8. Use Covert Reinforcement in real life.

When you feel comfortable practicing your approach behavior scene with one-fifth the reinforcer scenes you started with, you are ready to practice in real life. As you move through the actual events, make use of the imagined reinforcer scenes whenever you start feeling anxious.

If you don't feel quite ready to face the actual experience, you might want to *simulate* it first. For example, you could go to the lecture hall and take an old exam, using your reinforcer scene whenever you felt a wave of anxiety beginning to rise. From there it's a short step to successfully applying Covert Reinforcement to real life scenes.

Special Considerations

If a reinforcer scene seems to be losing its strength with frequent use, try changing the time of day when you practice, and practice for relatively shorter periods of time. When a reinforcer scene finally does lose its power, shift to a new reinforcer scene.

If your reinforcer scene involves drive-related activities like eating, you can increase the power of the reinforcer scene by practicing Covert Reinforcement when you are hungry.

Your ability to listen to your approach behavior scene without anxiety should be "overlearned" to make sure that your avoidance behavior doesn't recur. A good maxim to remember is "what becomes boring will never again be frightening." Therefore, continue practice sessions for at least a week after you have successfully used Covert Reinforcement in real life.

Covert Negative Reinforcement

This procedure is used when you cannot think of any positive reinforcers in your life. It involves imagining some feared stimulus, then shifting to your desired approach behavior. You eventually come to prefer the approach behavior because it is paired with escape from the feared stimulus. For example, if your approach behavior is driving across bridges without anxiety, you might begin by imagining a feared stimulus such as receiving a painful injection. After you have a clear image of the injection and the accompanying unpleasant feelings, you erase the image of the injection and shift to a scene in which you are fearlessly crossing a bridge.

Instructions

1. **Describe your avoidance behavior**—what you want to change (same as Covert Reinforcement).

2. **Describe your approach behavior**—what you want to happen (same as Covert Reinforcement).

3. **List your negative reinforcers.**

Negative reinforcers are things, people, situations, and events that elicit fear in you. To act as an effective negative reinforcer, a feared item should have the following three qualities: you can clearly imagine it, imagining it produces a response in you similar to your response in real life, and you can erase the image quickly, with little or no residual discomfort. With this in mind, select from the following list three items you fear. You will use these items as your negative reinforcers.

Failure	Being in a crowd	Open space
Thunder	Certain animals	Closed space
Some aspect of death	Certain noises	Deformities
Fighting	A lull in conversation	Certain places
Accidents	Some aspect of sex	Loss of control
Dentists or doctors	Traveling	Being wrong or imperfect
Ridicule	Fires	Nausea
Being alone	Illness	Knives or other sharp objects
Falling	Strangers or novelty	Guns
Insanity	Rejection	Tests
Wounds or blood	Injections	Speaking in groups

4. Practice relaxation (same as Covert Reinforcement)

5. Practice imagining negative reinforcers.

Focus on as many senses as possible. For each feared item, bring it into focus and hold it in focus for about 20 seconds. Then erase the scene and rest for 20 seconds. Note which negative reinforcer scene is easiest to visualize.

6. Record your approach behavior.

Tape record a script to assist you in practice. Start with the words "Negative reinforcer." Pause 20 seconds, then state the words "Approach behavior" and describe the first segment of your approach behavior scene. Pause another 20 seconds, and then say the words "Erase and rest." Pause another 20 seconds. Repeat this sequence until you have recorded all the segments of your approach behavior scene.

As with Covert Reinforcement, having a friend read your script to you works very well. With a reader you can arrange finger signals to control the length of the pauses.

7. Listen to your approach behavior.

The format for practicing Negative Covert Reinforcement is as follows:

The words "Negative reinforcer" signal you to imagine your chosen feared item for 20 seconds. If you are having the script read to you, you can adjust the length of time you spend imagining the item by signaling the reader with your index finger when you are ready to go on.

The words "Approach behavior" and the description of the appropriate segment of your approach behavior scene signal you to shift from imagining the unpleasant item to imagining your desired approach behavior. Clearly imagine the segment for 20 seconds.

The words "erase and rest" signal you to stop imagining your approach behavior and rest for 20 seconds.

Listen to your script at least twice a day, going all the way through it two times. When you feel comfortable with imagining your approach behavior, make a new recording with fewer negative reinforcers, just as described for positive reinforcers in step seven of Covert Reinforcement. If your negative reinforcer scene begins to lose its power, choose another from your list of three.

8. Practice Covert Negative Reinforcement in real life.

When you feel comfortable imagining your approach behavior with one-fifth the original negative reinforcers, you are ready to perform the approach behavior in real life.

Example

Nancy, a young divorcée, reported that she was fearful of driving on freeways and drove only on familiar, though inconvenient surface roads. This severely limited her ability to take long trips and her efficiency in getting around town. Since she was unable to think of any positive reinforcements, she was unable to use Covert Reinforcement and decided to use Covert Negative Reinforcement instead.

She began by identifying three things that she was afraid of: Saying "no" to a nice guy, failing, and being in a crowded room.

Nancy practiced imagining each of these negative reinforcers until she was able to get a clear image with all of her senses. She decided to use failure as the negative reinforcer in her first practice sessions.

She wrote out and tape recorded this approach behavior scene in the Covert Negative Reinforcement format:

"Negative reinforcer" (Imagine 20 seconds.) "Approach behavior: I am getting out my keys, unlocking the car door, getting in and sitting down in my car. I put the keys in the ignition." (Imagine 20 seconds.) "Erase and rest." (Rest 20 seconds.)

"Negative reinforcer" (Imagine 20 seconds.) "Approach behavior: I start the car and look in the rear view mirror to see if it's safe to pull out." (Imagine 20 seconds.) "Erase and rest." (Rest 20 seconds.)

"Negative reinforcer" (Imagine 20 seconds.) "Approach behavior: The car is warmed up and I pull out slowly into traffic, looking back to be sure it's safe. I drive the car down old, familiar, uncrowded streets." (Imagine 20 seconds.) "Erase and rest." (Rest 20 seconds.)

"Negative reinforcer" (Imagine 20 seconds.) "Approach behavior: I see a sign indicating the freeway entrance. I move over into the right lane to prepare to go on the freeway." (Imagine 20 seconds.) "Erase and rest." (Rest 20 seconds.)

"Negative reinforcer" (Imagine 20 seconds.) "Approach behavior: I drive onto the freeway. I'm going 55 m.p.h. The traffic is very light." (Imagine 20 seconds.) "Erase and rest." (Rest 20 seconds.)

"Negative reinforcer" (Imagine 20 seconds.) "Approach behavior: I know that I am a good driver and that I have an excellent, safe car. The traffic becomes moderately heavy." (Imagine 20 seconds.) "Erase and rest." (Rest 20 seconds.)

"Negative reinforcer" (Imagine 20 seconds.) "Approach behavior: I know that I can get off the freeway, but that it's much faster and convenient to take the freeway. I continue as the traffic gets heavier and I get a little more nervous." (Imagine 20 seconds.) "Erase and rest." (Rest 20 seconds.)

"Negative reinforcer" (Imagine 20 seconds.) "Approach behavior: I turn on my favorite radio station and listen to music as the traffic crawls along, bumper to bumper." (Imagine 20 seconds.) "Erase and rest." (Rest 20 seconds.)

"Negative reinforcer" (Imagine 20 seconds.) "Approach behavior: The traffic picks up and then suddenly slows down. I have to slam on my brakes. I feel shaken, but in control." (Imagine 20 seconds.) "Erase and rest." (Rest 20 seconds.)

"Negative reinforcer" (Imagine 20 seconds.) "Approach behavior: My exit comes up and I get off the freeway, drive a few blocks, and park in front of my office." (Imagine 20 seconds.) "Erase and rest." (Rest 20 seconds.)

Nancy listened to her tape recording twice a day, twice through at each sitting. As often happens, her first negative reinforcer scene of failure gradually lost its power to make her afraid. She switched to her second negative reinforcer scene, and then to her third by the end of one week of daily practice.

When she felt at ease with the imagined approach behavior scene, she retaped the scene, dropping out every other "Negative reinforcer." She continued to practice the approach behavior scene for several more days, then retaped it with one-third the original "Negative reinforcer" statements. After two more days she made a final tape with only one-fifth of the original "Negative reinforcer" statements. When she felt comfortable with that tape, she got in her car and went for a short, fearless drive on the freeway. To "overlearn" her approach behavior, she listened to her tape for a week after she began to drive the freeways regularly.

Further Reading

Cautela, J. R. "Covert Negative Reinforcement." **Journal of Behavior Therapy and Experimental Psychiatry.** 1970, 1, 273-8.

Cautela, J. R. "Covert Reinforcement." **Behavior Therapy.** 1970, 1, 33-50.

Marshall, W. L., Boutilier, J. and Minnes, P. "The Modification of Phobic Behavior by Covert Reinforcement." **Behavior Therapy.** 1974, 5, 469-80.

Wisocki, P. "An Application of Covert Reinforcement for the Treatment of Test Anxiety." Unpublished Doctoral Dissertation. Boston College, 1971.

Chapter 11

Covert Modeling

Covert Modeling is an effective way of altering an existing negative sequence of behavior, or of learning a new behavior pattern. You can probably think of a number of behavior patterns that you find unsatisfactory and want to change. You may want to improve your performance at work, in a personal relationship, or in a sport. You might have fallen into some routine that you don't like, such as sitting in front of the TV with a can of beer instead of playing with your kids. Or you may find yourself repeatedly coming home tired at the end of a long work day and getting into an argument with your spouse. You might feel bored and uncommunicative every time you go to visit your in-laws. Some situation may be so anxiety-provoking for you that you avoid them entirely: high places, enclosed or crowded rooms, being alone, novelty, panoramic vistas, or the presence of certain animals such as snakes, dogs, or spiders.

Likewise, there are probably some new patterns of behavior that you would like to add to your repertoire that might not require any change in your existing behavior. You may want to learn assertive skills to aid you in looking for a new job, asking for a raise, or returning to the dating scene after a divorce. Covert Modeling can be useful in learning such new behavior patterns.

One of the most important ways that you learn to perform a new behavior is to observe and imitate someone else doing it successfully. A young musician may learn to perform on stage by watching his favorite artists on television or at concerts, and then modeling his behavior after theirs. In assertiveness training, shy individuals often watch videotapes of people who initiate and maintain conversations, and then imitate these videotaped models.

However, good models are not always readily available when you need them. In 1971 Joseph Cautela found that you can learn new behavior sequences by *imagining* people performing the desired behavior successfully. He called his technique "Covert Modeling." Covert Modeling enables you to identify, refine, and practice in your mind the necessary steps for completing a desired behavior. Once you feel confident imagining yourself doing a particular activity, you can more effectively perform it in real life.

Covert Modeling is most effective when you imagine a variety of models, including yourself, performing your desired behavior. Also, it is most successful when you imagine these models struggling with and eventually overcoming difficulties, rather than when you imagine them succeeding effortlessly.

Symptom Effectiveness

Covert Modeling can be used to improve any already existing behavior sequence, or to learn a new behavior sequence that is a major departure from the usual way you act. It is helpful in reducing avoidance behavior such as phobias and test anxiety, and in increasing assertive behavior. Covert Modeling can be used to reduce depression, resentment, and procrastination associated with the failure to perform desired behavior or solve problems adequately.

If you are unable to attain clear and detailed images, Covert Modeling will probably be of little help to you. However, vivid *visual* images are not absolutely necessary. You may be able to get strong physical or auditory impressions that will allow you to use this technique with success.

Psychologists Thase and Moss found in 1976 that Guided Behavior Rehearsal was more effective than Covert Modeling in reducing avoidance behavior. Unfortunately, avoidance behavior does not always lend itself to rehearsing in real life, making Covert Modeling a useful alternative.

Time for Mastery

You should get results after four 15 minute sessions. Personal preference will determine how quickly you change over from Covert Modeling to practice in real life.

Instructions

Practice Imagining

Sit down in a comfortable, quiet place where you can be uninterrupted for about 15 minutes. Close your eyes and scan your body for tension, using your favorite relaxation exercise. After you have let go of the tension in your body, take a few deep breaths, focusing on your breathing and allowing yourself to become more and more relaxed.

With your eyes closed, practice recalling what the room you are sitting in looks like. What are the various objects in the room? How are they positioned? What are their colors, textures, shapes? What are the walls, ceiling, and floor like? After imagining the room, open your eyes and see how much of the detail you captured. Repeat this exercise until you are satisfied with your imagery of the room. You may also want to try this exercise in a variety of settings to develop your ability further.

Next, imagine a nature spot in your mind's eye. Notice the green trees rustling in the gentle warm breeze. Notice the rough mottled bark of the trees, and their shining leaves. Feel the earth beneath you, paying attention to its color and texture. Listen to the water flowing nearby and to the birds as they flit from branch to branch. Smell the various scents that fill this natural place. Feel the pleasantly warm sun through the trees. Allow yourself to fantasize what your eyes, ears, nose, and skin would tell you about this spot in as much detail as possible. Then imagine that an old friend walks up to you through the trees and greets you. What does he or she look like? What does he or she have to say? What does the voice sound like? What do you have to say?

Once you have developed some facility in imagining scenes using sight, sound, smell, and feeling, you are ready to begin Covert Modeling proper. It is not necessary for your images to be as clear as a motion picture or a record, but they should be as vivid as practice can make them.

Covert Modeling

1. Write out your problem behavior as a sequence of separate steps. (If you are learning an entirely new behavior, start with number two below.)

> Example: My poor form when serving in tennis:
> a) When going to serve in tennis, I face the net,
> b) look down to be sure that I do not step over the service line,
> c) look at the point where I intend to hit the ball.
> d) I throw the ball into the air as I pull my racket back right behind my head.
> e) I glance at the ball as it goes into the air, and then focus again on the place I am trying to hit.
> f) I know as soon as I have hit the ball whether it will be good, depending on the angle of my racket arm at the moment I hit the ball.
> g) I move to position to return my opponent's shot.

2. Write out your desired behavior. You do this by analyzing your problem behavior and making whatever changes, additions, or deletions you want. You may decide to combine steps or break one step down into several.

> Example: In reviewing the steps to my lousy serve, I realize that I need to make changes at a, d, e, f, and g. The rewritten steps are:
> a) When going to serve in tennis, I turn *sideways* to the net,
> b) look down to be sure that I don't step over the service line,
> c) look at the point where I intend to hit the ball.
> d) I throw the ball into the air as I pull my racket back *as far as it will go, arching my back and bending my knees slightly.*

e & f) I *keep my eye on the ball* as it goes into the air and my racket comes forward to hit it. I evaluate *visually* whether I have made a good toss, and *do not hit the ball if the toss looks bad*. I *keep my eye on the ball* until I have hit it.

g) I allow my racket arm to *follow through before moving* to position to return my opponent's ball.

3. Practice imagining the context in which the problem behavior occurs. Hold this clear image twice, for 15 seconds each time.

> Example: I imagine the view of our neighborhood tennis court from the vantage point of the service line. I hear the sounds of tennis shoes on concrete, people yelling, and the "thunk" of rackets hitting balls. The sun is shining and there's a light breeze.

4. Imagine someone very different from you in age, sex, and attire. Visualize this dissimilar model in the context in which your problem behavior occurs. See this different person performing your desired behavior. Imagine the model struggling to do the behavior correctly, encountering all the problems that you would be likely to face in the real situation. Imagine the person finally doing the desired behavior perfectly. See the person doing it correctly twice, holding the scene in your mind for 15 seconds each time.

> Example: I imagine my old tennis instructor standing at the service line in his moth-eaten blue sweat suit, racket in hand. He's pretending to be a beginning tennis player learning to serve. Gradually, after many trials, he achieves the serving form I described. I imagine the perfect serve twice, holding it in my mind for 15 seconds each time.

5. Imagine someone similar to you performing the desired sequence of behavior with difficulty at first, then successfully. Visualize the successful sequence twice.

> Example: I imagine my tennis partner at the service line in her tennis whites. She's the same age and sex as I, but a better tennis player. I imagine her serving rather badly at first. Gradually she improves until she serves perfectly. I imagine her serving perfectly twice, holding the scene in my mind for 15 seconds each time.

6. Imagine yourself performing the desired behavior and gradually mastering it. See yourself performing perfectly twice.

> Example: I imagine myself at the service line, dressed in my cut-off jeans and striped teeshirt. I serve, making all my usual mistakes at first, then gradually improving. Finally I deliver two perfect serves.

7. Role play your desired behavior. This is an optional step. If you are ready to try the desired behavior in real life, go on to number nine.

There are several ways of role playing your desired behavior. You can rehearse it in front of a mirror. Or you can take both parts of a dialogue by sitting in a chair and saying what you would say, shifting to another chair and saying what the other person would say, shifting back to your chair to respond, and so on. Another method is to rehearse the desired behavior with friends acting out the parts of significant characters in a scene while you play yourself. Make the scene as realistic as possible. Finally, you can tape record yourself and practice what you want to say, playing it back to get used to hearing yourself say assertive things.

Example: I practice throwing an imaginary ball in the air and hitting it with an imaginary racket, focusing on good form.

8. Prepare some coping statements. This is also an optional step. If you feel confident, go on to number nine.

Even after all this practice, you may still have some pessimistic thoughts that inhibit you from applying what you have learned to real life situations. If so, make a list of coping statements. These are short, positive statements that you can memorize or write down on a card to have handy. Compose four kinds of statements: preparing for a situation, confronting the situation, coping with stress, and reinforcing success. For a more detailed explanation of coping statements, see the chapter on Stress Inoculation.

Example: To counter my pessimistic thoughts about my serving ability, I wrote out and repeated to myself the following coping statements:

Preparation:
What exactly do I have to do to serve well?
I know I will get this right eventually.
Let all the parts flow smoothly together.

Confronting the situation:
One step at a time.
Practice makes perfect.
Go slowly.

Coping with stress:
Concentrate.
Remember to breathe.
Let it flow.

Reinforce success:
I've improved a lot.
My serving feels much better to me now.
Many of my serves were great!

9. Perform the desired behavior in real life.

Example: On Saturday I played tennis with my partner. When serving, I slowly went through the behavior sequence I outlined as the perfect serve. My serves weren't perfect, but they were a lot better than usual.

Examples

Frank and Sharon

Frank and his twelve-year-old daughter Sharon had had a good relationship until recently when they began to quarrel over her math homework. Frank resolved to use Covert Modeling to change this problem behavior.

Step 1. Frank described their problem behavior in sequential order:
   a) I'm watching television while Sharon is playing in her room.
   b) At 9:30 she asks for help with a math problem.
   c) I say "sure" and we sit down at her desk together.
   d) I have to read the whole chapter in order to understand the problem.
   e) It's after ten (her bedtime) before we figure out the first problem, and there are four equally hard problems to go.
   f) I start to feel testy and ask her why she didn't start earlier, and she says I don't want to help her anyway.
   g) I feel incredibly irritated that she has been so irresponsible and is dumping it all on me. I start to get loud. She starts to cry.
   h) Her crying gets worse, and I tell her I'm going to figure out the other four problems by myself.
   i) She stays up for half an hour while I am trying to do the problems, and I finally insist that she go to bed.

Step 2. Frank rewrote the behavior for a, b, e, f, g, and h:
   a) I will check in with her at intervals during the evening to see how she is doing on her homework.
   b) I will set up a rule that she cannot ask for help with her homework after 9:00.
   e) I will make up another rule that she cannot count on help after 10:00 and if the homework is not finished by 10:00, she goes to school with it incomplete.
   f) When I feel testy, I will tell her I feel pressured and am willing to do only one more problem. Also, I will joke with her about not wanting to burn the midnight oil with her again.
   g) I will take a deep breath when I notice that I'm starting to get loud and quiet my voice down. I will get some punch and cool off in the kitchen.
   h, i) I will give her a hug when she cries, tuck her into bed, and remind her that we do not do homework after her bedtime.

Step 3. Frank imagined the context as being his daughter's desk in her room. He clearly visualized this twice for 15 seconds each time.

Steps 4, 5, and 6. Frank chose to practice Covert Modeling on the sofa in the living room after Sharon went to bed. He made a point of relaxing before he started imagining. He would take three slow breaths, telling himself to relax and noticing the tension drain out of his body. He ran through the desired behavioral sequence in his mind, using his ex-wife as his dissimilar model. She had to face many of the same problems that he did with Sharon in real life. He imagined her able to deal with them effectively and getting the desired results.

Next he pictured his older brother (a similar model) performing the desired behavioral sequence. Finally, he imagined himself performing the desired behavioral sequence, succeeding only after struggling through the usual problems.

Step 7. After practicing steps four through six for about 15 minutes a day for four days, he decided to role play the desired behavior. He practiced in front of a mirror out loud, speaking his own and his daughter's roles.

Step 8. Frank made up the following list of coping statements to be used when he talked to his daughter:

Preparation:
    It will be easier once I get started.
    Sharon and I are both going to
        profit from this.

Confrontation:
    Keep it simple and sensible.
    Use a gentle voice.

Coping with stress:
    Focus on the new plan.
    Breathe and relax.
    Time out if I start to get angry.

Reinforce success:
    She understands and
        agrees—success!
    I did it!
    Let's celebrate.

Step 9. Satisfied with his role playing and coping statements, Frank proceeded to carry out the desired behavior sequence in real life.

Sandra and her boss

It had never occurred to Sandra to ask for a raise until her friend Jan who held the same level clerical position in another department asked for and got a substantial salary increase. Since this was an entirely new behavior for Sandra, she started with step two, writing out her desired behavior. It was a long list of steps because there were at least two confrontations involved and several different ways her boss might react. After several revisions, this is what she wrote:

    a) I approach my boss in the staff lounge during the coffee break.
    b) I have difficulty getting his attention, but finally do.
    c) I ask for 15 minutes of his time in the next couple of days to discuss a raise.
    d) He tries to put me off on his secretary, and I have to repeatedly ask for and finally get his cooperation.
    e) At the appointed time I walk into his office and greet him.
    f) I sit in the blue chair he reserves for guests.
    g) We make some small talk about the weather and how busy the office has been.
    h) I explain that I'm here to request a ten percent raise.
    i) I mention my good performance record and how long I've been working at the same salary level.

j) He looks displeased and replies that in these days the department is not doing well and we all have to learn to live with less.

k) I point out that it would be more cost effective to give me a raise than to train a new employee to take over my responsibilities.

l) He continues to be negative.

m) I say that if I can't get the raise I deserve, I'll have to start looking for a new job.

n) He offers a five percent raise.

o) I stick to my demand.

p) He eventually agrees, after seeing that I won't be budged.

q) I thank him, make sure to ask when the raise goes into effect, and walk out of his office feeling elated.

Sandra practiced visualizing the staff lounge and her boss's office until she could clearly imagine the sights and sounds.

She visualized her uncle George as a dissimilar model going through all the steps of successfully asking for a raise. Then she imagined her friend Jan, someone very much like herself, performing the same steps. Finally she imagined herself asking for and getting a ten percent raise.

Sandra role played the desired behavioral sequence with her husband playing the role of her boss. Her husband made a point of being a particularly tough boss to talk to.

Because she was still very nervous about asking for the raise, Sandra made up some coping statements. She wrote them on a card and kept it in the middle drawer of her desk at the office, referring to it frequently to counteract negative thoughts about asking for a raise.

Armed with her coping statements, Sandra went ahead and made her appointment, presented her case, and got her ten percent raise.

Further Reading

Cautela, J. "Covert Modeling." Paper presented at the fifth annual meeting of the Association for the Advancement of Behavior Therapy, Washington, D.C., Sept. 1971.

Kazdin, A. "Comparative Effects of Some Variations of Covert Modeling." **Journal of Behavior Therapy and Experimental Psychiatry.** 1974, 5, 225-31.

Kazdin, A. "Covert Modeling and the Reduction of Avoidance Behavior." **Journal of Abnormal Psychology.** 1973, 11, 87-95.

Kazdin, A. "Covert Modeling, Imagery Assessment and Assertive Behavior." **Journal of Consulting and Clinical Psychology.** 1975, 43(5), 716-24.

Kazdin, A. "Covert Modeling, Model Similarity, and Reduction of Avoidance Behavior." **Behavior Therapy.** 1974, 5, 325-40.

Kazdin, A. "Effects of Covert Modeling and Reinforcement on Assertive Behavior." **Journal of Abnormal Psychology.** 1974, 83, 240-52.

Kazdin, A. "The Effect of Model Identity and Fear-Relevant Similarity on Covert Modeling." **Behavior Therapy.** 1974, 5, 624-35.

Thase, M. E. and Moss, M. K. "The Relative Efficacy of Covert Modeling Procedures and Guided Participant Modeling on the Reduction of Avoidance Behavior." **Journal of Behavior Therapy and Experimental Psychiatry.** 1976, 7(1), 7-12.

Chapter 12

Values Clarification

Life is a series of tiny and large decisions. All are based, consciously or unconsciously, on your values. Values are the rules you live by. They run the gamut from purely arbitrary preferences like "Add the salt before the pepper" to life and death moral commandments like "Thou shalt not kill."

In this chapter you will learn:

- how values are formed,
- how to distinguish different kinds of values,
- how conflicting or unrealistic values create emotional pain,
- how to examine and clarify your personal values in order to make genuine, positive decisions.

Values influence you more than most of the real or imagined consequences of your actions. You tend to do what you think you should or ought to do. You want to be right, to look good to yourself. Here is a list of typical values which have enormous influence on how people behave:

Looking in style
Always being consistent, trustworthy, and keeping commitments.
Standing your ground, not getting pushed around
Being "up-front," saying exactly what's on your mind
Preferring things that are old, from another era
Preferring natural rather than synthetic
Preferring individual rather than cooperative effort, or vice-versa.
Being "cool," being one of the gang, conforming
Never being influenced by fear

Having prestige, recognition of success
Preferring rest, idleness, not having anything to do
Preferring the artistic and intuitive, as opposed to the rational and scientific
Being safe
Being skilled at doing things, competent
Acting according to the needs of others, altruism
Avoiding pain at all costs
Particular pleasures—good food, drink, sex, etc.
Being in love
Social interaction as opposed to being alone
Avoiding criticism, being approved of
Staying close to your family
Being fiercely independent
Being weird, eccentric, an oddball
Making money, accumulating wealth

There are hundreds, perhaps thousands of similar value statements that dominate people's lives. They are the silent forces behind much decision making. The goal of Values Clarification is for their influence to become conscious, for you to know which values you want to keep and which values are most important.

The formal principles of Values Clarification were set forth by Louis Raths, who built upon the educational theories of John Dewey. In *Values and Teaching*, Raths explained how children learn values from adults. Some adults practice a permissive, "hands off" approach, saying nothing at all about what to do in matters of sexual behavior, aggression, manners, religion, etc. This approach can create more problems than it solves, because children learn reluctance to express their feelings and suffer from a simple lack of information.

Other adults are moralizers. They try to "save" children from the agonizing process of developing values by simply telling them outright what they ought to do, think, and feel. Today's world is too complex and changing a place for this to work very well. Even if a particular adult's off-the-rack value system works well for him, that is no guarantee that it will serve equally well without alteration for the next generation.

One of the most effective ways adults teach values to children is by example. They consciously provide role models for children to emulate. This approach is often fairly successful if an adult is consistent and has a child's respect. However, there are many possible role models these days competing for a young person's attention: parents, teachers, peers, TV characters, religious leaders, political figures, entertainers, etc.

Raths avoids the problem of dictating too much or too little about which values are proper. His techniques of Values Clarification encourage the *process* of valuing without dictating the *content* of values. Instead of saying, "You should not sleep around" or "You should practice birth control," a teacher or group leader using Values Clarification techniques presents hypothetical situations concerning sexual behavior, and invites the group to discuss them from all angles. He or she might say, "What would you do if you had to choose from these options:

1. being a virgin
2. having had one satisfying sexual relationship in the past, but none right now
3. having an ongoing series of not very satisfying sexual relationships
4. being married for life to someone who occasionally turns you on
5. swearing off sex forever?"

The discussion and internal monologues that result will uncover what the participants believe is right or wrong, desirable or undesirable for them in the area of sexuality. There are no right or wrong answers, and no value judgments are made. The teacher or group leader might act as something of a role model by participating in the exercise and revealing, but not espousing, his or her own values.

Different Values Clarification exercises focus on different stages of the valuing process. The process of valuing can be broken down into four steps, although the steps are constantly combining and interacting in your life:

Discovering, clarifying, elaborating, and changing your beliefs

Affirming your beliefs when appropriate

Choosing your actions based on your beliefs—choosing freely, from alternatives, and after consideration of the consequences

Acting on your beliefs consistently

Symptom Effectiveness

You will probably benefit from Values Clarification if you are having trouble deciding about an important change in your life such as enrolling in school, marriage, divorce, buying a house, changing carreers, or retirement. Values Clarification is effective in reducing the situation-specific anxiety that can arise at such times, when you don't know what to do or wonder if you have made the right choice.

Values Clarification is also used to reduce anxiety secondary to ambivalence, which can arise when you want two mutually exclusive things at once. For example, you might want to vote for a friend in a club or union election, but also want to vote for someone else who is not a friend but who you know is better qualified and would do a better job.

With young people, Values Clarification is helpful in overcoming apathy and low self esteem, reducing flighty behavior, moderating over-dissenting, hostile attitudes, combating indecisiveness and procrastination, liberalizing tendencies to over-conform, and improving academic performance.

Time for Mastery

You should experience results immediately upon starting Values Clarification exercises. The exercises themselves can be taken at your own pace and in any order. At first, spend about half an hour on each exercise, and try at least one exercise a day. After a week, you should know which ones you may want to repeat or expand upon.

Mastery of Values Clarification does not mean arriving at the right opinion or doing the right thing. Rather, you will notice an increase in self-awareness, greater clarity about what you value in life, and reduced anxiety and doubt about expressing your values to others and about putting your beliefs into action.

Instructions

A Three Penny History

When you set out to examine your personal values, it's helpful to realize that the same questions of right and wrong that plague you have plagued humanity for centuries. In the fourth century B.C. Socrates and Plato were engaging in Values Clarification with the Greeks of that day. In Plato's *Republic* and Socrates' *Apology* and *Crito*, we find such questions as: When if ever is it right to tell a lie? Under what circumstances should one break a promise? Is law, convention, personal morality, religion, or self preservation the final arbiter of right action?

If Socrates were around today, he would define Values Clarification with the same words he used to define moral philosophy: Hard thought about right action. Early moral philosophers argued that right action is motivated by cardinal virtues. Cardinal virtues were like primary colors—they were the essential traits of good moral character from which all other moral virtues could be derived. Plato held that the cardinal virtues were Wisdom, Courage, Temperance, and Justice.

Modern moralists have abandoned the word "virtue." They tend to speak of ethical principles. A common first principle that is mentioned or implied by most ethicians is Benevolence. The principle of Benevolence is that we should do good and avoid or prevent evil. To this is usually added the principle of Beneficence or Utility: that we should seek the greatest balance of good over evil in the universe. Derived from (or at least closely related to) Beneficence is the principle of Justice: that we should distribute good equally. From these basic principles are derived all sorts of more specific principles such as not injuring anyone, telling the truth, keeping agreements, not interfering with another's liberty, and so on.

As soon as you start thinking about basic ethical principles, this question comes up: What is the "good?" Hedonists would say that the good is pleasure, perhaps going on to define pleasure as including intellectual and spiritual as well as physical pleasure. Others would say that pleasure is just a side effect of achieving or experiencing other desired goods such as wisdom, intimacy, beauty, etc. The following is a list of "goods" compiled from the history of moral philosophy. The items are ranked roughly in order by how much importance they have been given by philosophers and other thinkers. The "goods" that have been traditionally regarded as most important are near the top, and those traditionally accorded less importance are near the bottom. Go ahead and rerank them yourself from 1 to 18, according to what "goods" you hold most important:

_____ Life, consciousness, activity
_____ Health, strength
_____ Pleasures and satisfactions of all or certain kinds

_____ Happiness, beatitude, contentment
_____ Truth
_____ Knowledge and true opinion of various kinds, understanding, wisdom
_____ Beauty, harmony, proportion in objects contemplated
_____ Aesthetic experience
_____ Morally good dispositions or virtues
_____ Mutual affection, love, friendship, cooperation
_____ Just distribution of goods and evils
_____ Harmony and proportion in your own life
_____ Power and experiences of achievement
_____ Self expression
_____ Freedom
_____ Peace, security
_____ Adventure, novelty
_____ Good reputation, honor, esteem

Your Personal Value System

As an infant your only "value" is self preservation. As you grow up you become more socialized and take on a more complex system of values. You draw first from the conventions of your family and peers, and later from law: "Nice girls don't scratch in public...don't steal cars or you will go to jail." As you mature, you choose some of these received rules to make your own, developing a personal morality or value system.

At any point in your development you may have all of the following reasons for acting in a certain way: because it's essential to survival, because it's the law, because it's the conventional thing to do, and because it's the moral thing for you to do. In the final analysis, however, the best guide to right action is your personal value system.

Mere self preservation won't get you very far. Most crises of judgment are social in nature. They have to do with your relationships to others, not your physical survival.

Merely adopting the prevailing rules of law or convention won't serve you very well either. The prevailing rules are usually imprecise, always subject to exception, and sometimes in conflict with each other. The prevailing rules are often too literal, negative, and conservative. For example, the rules about not parking on the north side of the street on Wednesday mornings will tell you nothing about what beliefs you should have about urban sanitation, crowding, or appropriate kinds of public services. Also, the prevailing rules of a society may be morally irrelevant or wrong. It was once considered lewd for a woman to show her ankle in public, while at the same time it was considered perfectly legal and moral to own slaves. Finally, changing circumstances, styles, and legislation can change the prevailing rules. Only you can change your personal value system. And only your value system can provide the positive, creative kinds of rules you need as a healthy individual.

Kinds of Values

All values fall into one of two broad categories: moral values and non-moral values. In this chapter, the terms "moral" and "non-moral" are used without any religious connotations.

Moral values have to do with right and wrong, good and evil. They guide your behavior with the force of obligation. They form the basis for judgments of moral responsibility and guide such ethical behavior as telling the truth, keeping agreements, and not injuring others. Associated with moral values are such character traits as honesty, loyalty, and fairness. Moral statements often contain words such as "must...ought...should...never...always."

Non-moral values have to do with tastes, preferences, and styles. They relate to what is desirable and undesirable, as opposed to what is right and wrong or good and evil. Non-moral values carry no sense of obligation. There is no moral responsibility connected with accepting or rejecting a non-moral value. The traits associated with non-moral values tend to be personality traits like charm, shyness, or cheerfulness, as opposed to character traits like honesty or fairness. The activities that come out of non-moral values are merely preferred, not dictated: going to the ballgame instead of to a movie, reading a book instead of watching television. Non-moral values are a lot more plentiful than moral values, since they are expressions of your attitudes toward all sorts of objects, concepts, and experiences: cars, paintings, art, knowledge, pleasure, democracy, history, sports, hobbies, etc. Statements of non-moral value often contain the same words as statements of moral value, but examination shows that the words are not meant in an absolute, normative sense.

Values and Emotional Pain

There are several ways that you may be creating pain in your life by clinging to inappropriate, conflicting, unrealistic, or confused values:

Arrested Development. This occurs when you are stuck between the two stages of moral development. When you're young you decide what to do by an unthinking adherence to the customs of your family, your social class, and your peer group. As you grow older, there should be a natural shift toward basing your behavior on thought-out, personal, internalized values. If you are trying to make adult decisions with an adolescent value system, you are in for some trouble. For example, a young man grew up in a devout Jewish family that judged the value of his male cousins' and brothers' marriages by whether they married nice Jewish girls. He himself fell in love with a nice Irish girl, who loved him and obviously wanted to get married. Every time he thought of asking her to marry him, he experienced acute anxiety about what his family would think. In order to reduce this anxiety and proceed into married life, he had to work out a more mature value system. He gave up the externally imposed notion that a particular heritage is the most important consideration in choosing a wife. He replaced it with an internalized, personal value that more important considerations are love and compatibility.

Conflicting Non-moral Values.   Conflicting non-moral values are major contributors to stress syndromes. For example, a policeman who placed a very high value on leisure time also held the belief that a man must provide a certain high standard of living for his family. This second value led him to take a moonlighting job as a bartender to earn extra money, which virtually eliminated his leisure time. He was chronically tired, irritable, and unable to function well at either job or at home. Using Values Clarification exercises, he revealed this conflict to himself. He was able to explain his values to his family and to take action to eliminate the conflict. In this case, the policeman chose to give up bartending and accept a lower standard of living with less income, but more leisure time. Another individual practicing Values Clarification might have chosen to pursue a better second job and an even higher standard of living.

As a second example, consider the case of the reluctant cello student. Her parents wanted to pay her tuition to a distant but famous music school. She examined the values involved in a decision to go away to school or stay at home. Going meant:

> Pleasing her parents
> Furthering her music career
> Adventure and new experience

> Staying meant:
> Remaining secure and safe
> Preserving a satisfying relationship with her boyfriend

When she ranked the values in their order of importance, she determined that a satisfying relationship was by far her highest priority. It was difficult to disappoint her parents and to pass up a rare opportunity. Clarifying her values, however, made the decision easier.

As both these examples illustrate, the point of Values Clarification is not to arrive at the "best" or "only" decision. The point is to arrive at a clear understanding of which values you are going to use as a basis for decision in your life, and then to act on them.

Moral Dilemmas.   Most of the time, you are only aware of your non-moral values, since there are so many of them and since they guide so many of your daily decisions. However, when there is a decision to be made and both kinds of values are in direct conflict, you can become painfully aware of your moral values.

For example, a woman with a high school education who wanted to live in a warm climate was going to apply for a transfer from Buffalo to Los Angeles. She learned that the only opening available in Los Angeles required someone with a college degree. She knew that she could do the job without the degree, and that if she simply claimed to have a degree, her company would give her the job in Los Angeles and never catch her in the lie. However, she was an honest person who believed in telling the truth. Her non-moral value of wanting to move to a warmer climate was in direct conflict with the moral value of telling the truth. She agonized over the transfer application for some time.

Finally she came up with the rationalization that the lie wasn't so bad because it wouldn't really hurt anybody, and the benefit of living in a warmer climate justified a little lie. She sent in the fraudulent application, got the job, moved west, and almost immediately began sabotaging her own chances of success at the new job by coming in late and making stupid mistakes. She was nervous and apprehensive all the time, even though she knew that no one would check up on her imaginary college degree.

Eventually Values Clarification exercises showed her that she was punishing herself for having broken her own moral code. Once she faced the fact that she had transgressed, she was able to live with the occasional twinge of guilt, and began to do better at her new job.

The point of this example is not whether the woman was morally right, morally wrong, over-scrupulous, or just plain silly. The point is that if you hold a value to be morally binding on yourself and you run counter to it in pursuit of one of your non-moral values, you will experience conflict. And you will often find some way to blame or punish yourself.

The Whim of Iron. If you apply non-moral values like "people should dress nicely" with the same strictness as truly moral values like "people should not murder each other," your unreasonable expectations will make life miserable for you. You will see every sloppy person as the moral equivalent of a murderer, and punish yourself unfairly for any sloppiness on your own part. Values Clarification exercises will help you to determine whether you are giving mere tastes and preferences the status of moral values.

The Will of Water. Conversely, you'll experience considerable discomfort if you regard moral values like promise-keeping with the same casual attitude you would take when deciding whether to wear green or brown socks. The nature of moral values is that they demand consistent action, regardless of the dictates of expediency. On a practical level, if you don't keep your promises or respect others' rights consistently, few people will trust you or want to associate with you in any serious relationship or enterprise. Also, your self esteem will suffer because you will be lacking any experience of personal integrity.

Double Standards. The flip side of duties is rights. If you have a moral duty to treat others justly, that means that you also have a right to be treated justly yourself. If you insist on your right to be heard, you have a duty to hear others out. Double standards arise when you claim a right without acknowledging your corresponding duty, or when you claim a right for yourself while denying it to others, or when you claim a duty for others without acknowledging it for yourself.

The classic example of a double standard is the idea that it's all right for you to have had premarital sexual relations, but anybody who expects to marry you had better be a virgin. Trying to operate according to a double standard breeds emotional pain because it flies in the face of justice. You are constantly bombarded from within by suspicions of your own hypocrisy and from without by cries of "Foul!"

Exercises

The exercises that follow will give you practice in discovering and clarifying your values. They will help you choose your actions based upon those values, without dictating what those values should be. While doing these exercises, you will become aware of your attitudes about many things. The most common topics that come up in the exercises, and areas to consider if you get stuck or draw a blank, are:

Politics	Religion	Work
Leisure	School	Love, sex
Family	Material possessions	Tastes in art, music, literature
Style in clothes, hair	Friends	Money
Aging, death	Health	Race
War, peace	Rules, authority	Ecology

Prizing and Cherishing

It's not healthy to spend most of your time and energy doing what you don't really like to do. This first exercise will help you explore what you really want out of life.

20 Things I Love To Do

A. List 20 things you love to do. They can be big or little things in your life; things appealing to the senses or more abstract pleasures; things you've always enjoyed or relatively new experiences; things that you do or that others do for you; things done indoors or outdoors, at night or during the day, or in different seasons of the year. Be as specific as you can. Instead of listing "sports," write "watching football on TV" or "playing tennis with Joyce."

This is your list: Put down whatever comes to mind without judging it or wondering what others would think about it. There are no right or wrong answers. You may have a few more or less that 20 items.

	$	A-P	PL	N5	1-5	days
1.						
2.						
3.						
4.						
5.						
6.						
7.						
8.						
9.						
10.						
11.						
12.						
13.						
14.						
15.						
16.						
17.						
18.						
19.						
20.						

B. For each item, if it costs over $5.00 each time you do it, put "$" in the first column.

C. If you like to do it alone, write "A" in the next column; if you do it with others, write "P;" if you like to do it both alone and with others, write "AP."

D. Write "PL" in the next column if it requires planning.

E. Write "N5" if it would not have been on this list five years ago.

F. Pick the five you love most and rank them from 1 to 5 in order of preference.

G. Write approximately how many days it has been since you last engaged in each activity.

Values Checklist

Louis Raths has identified seven distinct steps to the valuing process. Completing this checklist will indicate areas for you to work on in clarifying your own values.

A. In the six spaces provided, jot down brief phrases that will remind you of your position on some general issues that are important to you. For example, if you have strong feelings about pollution, war, and marital fidelity, you might put:

    1. Pollution—everyone's individual responsibility.
    2. War—sanctity of human life.
    3. Fidelity—essential to security in love.

You may have fewer or more than six items. The phrases don't have to make sense to anyone but you.

Item	1 proud	2 affirm	3 alter- natives	4 consider	5 free	6 act	7 repeat

B. After each item, put a check in boxes 1 through 7 if:

    1. You are proud of your position—you prize or cherish it.
    2. You have publicly affirmed your position.
    3. You have chosen your position from alternatives.
    4. You have chosen your position after thoughtful consideration of the pros and cons and consequences.
    5. You have chosen your position freely.
    6. You have acted on or done something about your belief.
    7. You have acted with repetition, pattern, or consistency on the issue.

Notice which steps you consistently omit. Notice where you are inconsistent. Notice if you affirm or act on any positions that you don't really prize. As you go through other exercises, you may want to come back to this one to check out your valuing process in regard to a particular belief.

Affirming Your Values

Publicly affirming your positions or beliefs is one of the most important and rewarding steps in the process of valuing. It is often difficult to determine when circumstances are appropriate. This exercise will help you explore your patterns of self-disclosure in regard to your feelings, opinions, and actions. It will give you the opportunity to find out what you are willing to tell and to whom. It may show you where you are ineffective in your life through being too open or too closed.

The circles below indicate the different "audiences" to which you are willing to reveal things about yourself (The small central circle is dark because there are some things we are not willing to reveal even to ourselves).

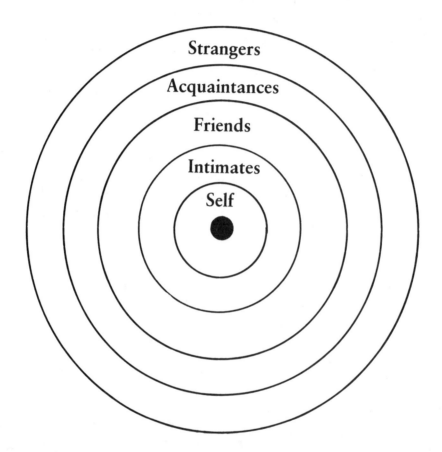

1. In each band, write a key word that will remind you of something you wouldn't mind telling about yourself to the audience represented by that band. For example, if you wouldn't mind telling a stranger what your favorite color is, you might write "color" in the outside band. If there is only one person in the world whom you are willing to tell about your fears regarding sexual inadequacy, you might write "sex" in the "Intimates" band.

2. Write the word "love" in the band representing whom you would be willing to tell the story of your first love affair.

3. Write the word "Money" in the band representing whom you would tell about the money you make and owe.

4. Write "Doubts" in the band representing whom you would discuss religious doubts with.
5. Write "Friend" in the band representing the group with whom you would discuss your best friend's faults.
6. Write "Extra" in the band representing whom you would tell about an extra-marital sexual experience.
7. Pick one of the topics that you would be willing to share with acquaintances or strangers. Some time in the next week, initiate a conversation with an acquaintance or stranger, and let them know clearly what you believe about the topic you have chosen. Notice any resistance to self-disclosure that you experience in yourself. Notice whether you have a sense of taking a risk—if you feel anxious or in danger or exposed to disagreement or dislike. Notice whether you have any difficulty making yourself understood. Notice any reluctance or embarrassment or attempts to change the subject on the part of the person you are talking to.

Choosing From Alternatives

Living from day to day, you are probably not aware of many alternatives. Habits accumulate and offer a convenient way to get through life without pondering over every fork in the road. This accretion of conscious and unconscious habits of choice amount to what is often called your "lifestyle," and it can come to feel like a straightjacket.

To loosen that straightjacket, you can practice the skill of developing and choosing from alternatives. This skill will serve you in all value judgments, from choosing what brand of tire to buy on up to deciding where to go on your vacation or what to do about your spouse's drinking problem.

The rules for developing good alternatives are the same as the rules for successful brainstorming, as described in the chapter on problem solving:

1. **Defer judgment.** At this first stage, don't allow your values to influence or hamper your imagination. You can make judgments later. Anything goes.
2. **Quantity** is more important than quality. Strive for lots of ideas.
3. **Free associate.** Put down anything that comes into your mind, whether it seems to make sense or not. Often the best ideas are sparked by first working through a whole string of apparently silly notions.
4. **Combine ideas.** Increase your pool of alternatives by combining actions and ideas, changing small details, rearranging sequences, objects, or personalities.

With these rules in mind, pick a problem from the following list, or pick a problem that you are currently stuck on in your life that relates to what you value or believe in.

How to save time	Ways to make new friends
What to do at parties when you feel shy	Telling a friend something negative
Where to go on vacation	Ways to save money
Unwanted pregnancy	Personal solutions to pollution
	Settling family arguments

Without a lot of thought beforehand, quickly write ten options or solutions or alternatives to the problem you have selected. Be specific. If you are dealing with unwanted pregnancy, don't just put "abortion," but rather spell out the details, such as "2nd month abortion in out-of-town clinic."

1. _____
2. _____
3. _____
4. _____
5. _____
6. _____
7. _____
8. _____
9. _____
10. _____

If you are dealing with a real life problem of your own, go back over your list of ten alternatives. Next to each one, put a "T" if you are willing to *try* it; put a "C" if your are willing to *consider* it; and put a "W" if you *won't* try it.

There is nothing magic about ten items. In fact, the more the better. This is an exercise you will wish to return to often.

Considering Consequences

Considering consequences is just as important as searching for alternatives. This exercise will help you develop and evaluate the consequences of the alternatives you developed in the previous exercise.

In the spaces provided, put the three best ideas you came up with in the previous exercise. For example, if you were looking for ways to communicate negative criticism to a friend, you might list these alternatives: "1) Write Bill a detailed letter. 2) Tell his wife and let her pass it along. 3) Bring it up casually on the golf course Sunday."

Below each alternative, write descriptions of as many consequences as you can. At this stage, defer judgment about whether the things you list are sensible or right—just get as many down as you can. For example, under "Write Bill a detailed letter," you might put:

> Someone else will see letter and embarrass us both.
> Bill will write me a wonderful letter back.
> Bill will think letter presumptuous, cold, ridiculous, etc.
> Bill will misunderstand letter and never speak to me again.
> Bill will appreciate letter and friendship will improve.
> Bill will never mention letter and relationship will be strained.
> Bill's behavior will improve.
> Bill's behavior will not improve.

Alternative number 1	Alternative number 2	Alternative number 3

Once you have listed the consequences for all three alternatives, consider which alternative looks best now. You may find that you want to change or combine alternatives to maximize beneficial consequences and minimize negative ones. This is what this exercise is all about. Now you have the kind of information you need to make a free choice.

Free Choice

This exercise will examine your patterns of action and reveal how much of what you do is done out of habit or compulsion, rather than out of free choice. Once you become aware of your habitual patterns, you may want to change some of them. Probably you will continue to follow most of them though, because habits are developed as conveniences in getting through the daily routine, and they usually make sense. The difference is that after this exercise, you will change or continue your patterns on a conscious, free-choice basis.

A. Pick several items from the following list that tend to trigger habitual ways of thinking or acting:

dealing with something a little scary
getting up in the morning
how you comb or wear your hair
doing chores around the house
sexual behavior on first dates
giving presents
revealing your age
eating at a restaurant
getting places on time
paying bills
making friends
brushing teeth
making dates
buying clothes
making complaints about service
laundry
grocery shopping
writing letters
dealing with disappointment

getting irritated with
    inconsiderate behavior
seeing mixed racial couples
seeing homosexuals
getting to sleep
daydreaming
thinking about your weight
bathing or showering
bedtime
talking about people who
    aren't present
answering the phone
reading the newspaper
dealing with old clothes
buying secondhand or new items
going to dinner parties
watching TV
reading your mail
dealing with criticism

B. Write what you do about the items you have selected in the left-hand column:

Activity (describe your pattern)	Is it done out of:			like your answers?		
	com-pul-sion	habit	free choice	yes	no	don't know/ doesn't matter

C. Check whether you follow each pattern out of compulsion, habit, or free choice. *Compulsion* means that something outside yourself forces you to do it, for example getting up at a certain time to make it to work on time. *Habit* means an unconscious pattern or inner urge, for example, always parting your hair on the same side. *Free choice* means a conscious choice, for example your decision to brush your teeth three times a day to avoid gum disease.

    Note: Don't allow yourself to become entangled in philosophical considerations of human free will—just check the box that feels right, without a lot of agonizing thought.

D. Check whether you like your answers, don't like them, or don't have any particular feeling about them.

E. Be aware that you can choose freely to continue a pattern, to alter it, or to abandon it entirely. At this point, you may have noticed something you've been wanting to change about yourself or your life. This is a good point at which to go back and consider the alternatives and consequences of such a change. Then you can freely choose to act or not act.

Acting

    The only real test of your values is whether you act on them. This is the step at which many people falter. It's one thing to be willing to take a stand, to cherish it, to affirm it to others, and to consider alternatives and consequences—all that can be easily changed. But once you act, it's hard to "take it back." You're committed. Actions are real in a way that opinions and statements are not. Your actions define your immutable history.

    By now, you should be clear about several of your important values. You feel better when you know and act consistently with your values. This exercise will help you explore and remove any barriers to action that you may be experiencing.

    On the form below, list an action you should take to live in accordance with your values. Then list all the barriers, real or perceived, inside you or outside you, that seem to be keeping you from performing the action. Next, list steps that you could take to remove or reduce each barrier. Finally, arrange these steps into a sequential plan of action for actually removing the barriers and accomplishing what you want to do.

    Note: It may help to put dates next to each step in your action plan. These are the deadlines by which you will accomplish each step.

    The final instruction is the most difficult and important one: Take Action.

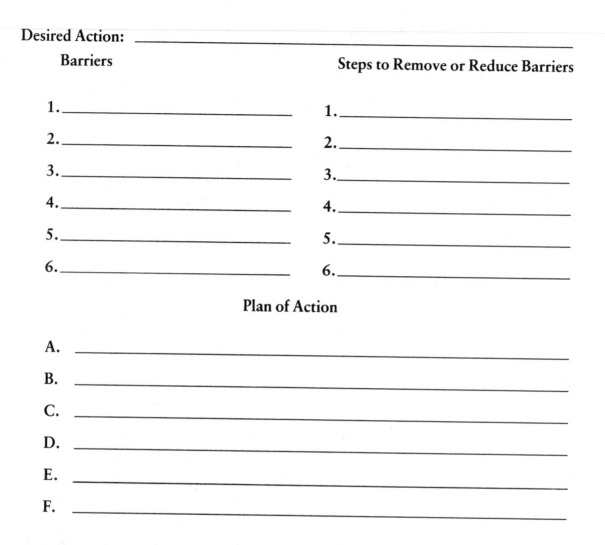

Desired Action: _____

Barriers   Steps to Remove or Reduce Barriers

1._____   1._____

2._____   2._____

3._____   3._____

4._____   4._____

5._____   5._____

6._____   6._____

Plan of Action

A. _____

B. _____

C. _____

D. _____

E. _____

F. _____

Examples

You make hundreds of decisions every day of your life. Most are governed by habit, but some are based on real value judgments. Different values bear on each side of the decision. For example, in the decision of whether to cancel a date, important values may argue for either choice. On one hand, it may be important for you not to disappoint or cause people pain. On the other, you may also value a commitment to "taking care of yourself." What you finally decide to do will be based on your highest value in this situation.

To clarify the values involved in a particular decision, write down each possible action you could take—there may be more than two. Then under each action write the values you hold which tend to push you toward making that choice. The following is from the worksheet of a single parent who was trying to decide whether to keep her daughter in a highly demanding college prep school. The girl was working extremely hard, but suffering poor grades and lowered self-esteem.

A. Stay in college prep school
1. Rise to the challenge, not give up
2. Get a high quality education, know something
3. Prestige of graduating from a good school

B. Leave college prep school
1. Feel good about yourself
2. More time for fun and recreation
3. Live in a non-competitive environment

Six important values were involved in the decision. She examined them carefully to determine which was her highest value in the situation. It turned out that her highest value was "feel good about yourself," and she decided to remove her daughter from the school.

This is the worksheet of a man who was considering separation from his wife:

A. Six-month trial separation
1. Independent growth
2. Possibility of a happy, intimate relationship

B. Not separating
1. Security
2. Avoiding pain of loneliness
3. Not hurting anyone, particularly my wife

When he looked for his highest value, it turned out to be "avoiding the pain of loneliness." He didn't like it, but it was the truth. If he wanted to separate, he was going to have to change his values. Until that time, his choice was necessarily to remain with his wife.

In both examples, the highest value determined the choice of action. Picking your highest value is an intuitive decision—it will feel more powerful, harder to override than the others. The important thing is for the choice to be conscious, made with full awareness.

Consistency

After you are able to put your values into action, the process of valuing becomes one of consistent repetition—but not just repetition of rote *actions*. The goal of values clarification is not to come up with a once-and-for-all list of commandments. The goal is to continue to get satisfaction out of life by continuing the full *process* of valuing: cherishing, affirming, choosing, considering alternatives and consequences, and acting on your beliefs as you continually rediscover and reveal them to yourself and the world.

Special Considerations

Often it is not *value* that is unclear, but a lack of factual knowledge that limits your understanding of a situation and confuses you about what course of action to take. If you're in a dilemma and don't know what to do, stop and see if you have all the facts. You may find that the dilemma clears up after you have asked a question, looked something up, verified details, or consulted an expert.

If you have all the facts and you're still confused, define your terms. Language is very tricky. The same word can have several meanings. For example, "kindness" might describe a non-moral personality trait that is the opposite of rudeness and applies to "nice" people in general. Alternatively, "kindness" may be used to describe an obligatory trait of character reflecting the moral value of not causing harm to others. "Be fair" may apply to a court decision and have moral connotations, or it may come up in a barroom argument about the best linebacker in pro football, and have no moral meaning at all. "Where there's life there's hope" may be a comforting saying to one person, and for another be the key premise in an elaborate statement of his moral stand on capital punishment or abortion. When considering a particular statement of value, it's important to define your terms carefully.

If defining your terms doesn't clear things up, you may not have a third prerequisite for making a moral judgment: good will. Do you sincerely want to do the right thing? If not, you may sabotage your search for it by excessive rationalizations. You may hide the answer from yourself.

Finally, remember that you're a human being and therefore bound to make mistakes. After careful thought you'll do something that you're convinced is right, and later it may be clear that what you did was wrong. Despite your good intentions you may be blamed or even punished for your actions. This is the risk of being human. The only way to eliminate the risk is to never act, which is impossible, or to die, which is hardly a "viable" solution. The only thing to do is to forgive yourself, admit you're human, and learn from the experience.

Further Reading

Frankena, W. K. **Ethics.** Englewood Cliffs, New Jersey: Prentice-Hall, 1963.

Kirschenbaum, H. **Advanced Values Clarification.** La Jolla, California: University Associates, 1977.

Koberg, D. and Bagnall, J. **Values Tech: The Polytechnic School of Values.** Los Altos, California: William Kaufmann, 1976.

Raths, L., Merrill, H. and Sidney, S. **Values and Teaching.** Columbus, Ohio: Charles E. Merrill, 1966.

Simon, S. B., Howe, L. W. and Kirschenbaum, H. **Values Clarification: A Handbook of Practical Strategies for Teachers and Students.** rev. ed. New York: A and W Visual Library, 1978.

Chapter 13

Paradoxical Intention

Paradoxical Intention is one of the fastest, most powerful, and least understood methods of changing behavior. With one series of paradoxical instructions, lifelong stutterers become public speakers, insomniacs sleep like babies, and nail biters and smokers never take another nibble or puff.

Paradoxical Intention is based on the Brief Therapy techniques of psychiatrist Milton H. Erickson and the Logotherapy of Viktor Frankl. Its principles and practice have been elaborated and explored by Jay Haley and by members of the Mental Research Institute in Palo Alto, California.

Because it is based on the paradoxical nature of spontaneous change in people's behavior, Paradoxical Intention can be confusing to understand and even upsetting to experience. If you are attempting to use this treatment technique on yourself, you will probably not succeed. Nevertheless, you are encouraged to try the "Paradox Game" presented later in this chapter, if you wish to have a novel and interesting experience.

Symptom Effectiveness

Paradoxical Intention is most effective in the brief treatment of individual symptoms that are perceived to be involuntary: insomnia, impatience, blushing, bedwetting, fainting spells, obsessions, compulsions, and numerous phobias. It is especially helpful when the symptomatic behavior involves considerable anticipatory anxiety, as is the case with insomnia and speech or performance anxiety.

Many people have anxiety attacks in which they experience escalating fears of "going crazy," heart failure, social embarrassment, loss of control, or increasing dread of the anxiety itself. Some researchers have called this "anxiety phobia" and have treated it with excellent results using Paradoxical Intention.

In dealing with interpersonal problems, Paradoxical Intention can bring about here-and-now behavior changes rapidly, without time consuming considerations of past causes and influences. Family therapists use Paradoxical Intention to break up destructive behavior patterns and to replace them with behavior that is similar in pattern, but positive in its results.

Time for Mastery

As its name implies, Brief Therapy is interested in fast results, and Paradoxical Intention is one of the fastest techniques used by practitioners of Brief Therapy.

If you are using Paradoxical Intention to eliminate a single, well-defined symptom such as compulsively touching things or feeling uneasy in elevators, you should get results in as short a period as a week.

Even when therapists are working with several interrelated, complex symptoms, Paradoxical Intention seldom takes more than ten sessions to be effective. This is in contrast to the years that someone might spend in psychoanalysis in an attempt to "understand" and cure the same set of symptoms.

Instructions

Principles of Paradoxical Intention for Health Professionals

Although this section is primarily intended for health professionals wishing to use Paradoxical Intention with clients, it may also be read by those interested in the technique and wishing to play the "Paradox Game."

The following twelve principles or "rules" of Paradoxical Intention are intended as guidelines only. You may not operate according to all twelve with every client. Different clients will require you to apply some principles more intensely than others, depending on their problems and your relationship. The twelve principles are numbered more for convenience than to indicate an absolutely rigid progression. In fact, several of the steps are usually going on simultaneously in any therapeutic situation. For example, in a single sentence like, "We're agreed that by Christmas you'll be able to pay your mother the compliment of saying 'no' when she offers you money," you may be setting a behavior goal, reinforcing a commitment to change, setting a time limit, and reframing the desired behavior in your client's terms.

1. Forget Understanding

As far as accomplishing behavioral changes is concerned, understanding and insight are often the booby prizes. Much change occurs spontaneously, not as a result of understanding the initial causes or achieving insight into the past.

Paradoxical Intention does not depend on gaining insight into unconscious processes, helping clients understand their interpersonal difficulties, making transference interpretations, exploring motivations, or even seeking to re-condition unfortunate behavior patterns. It is a shortcut that acts directly on behavior, and operates according to a straightforward formula. The only skills you need are a willingness to endure paradox, a modicum of imagination, and the ability to think on your feet.

Once you are clear that Paradoxical Intention doesn't care *why* a problem exists, only *what* the problem is, you can proceed to the second step.

2. Determine the Symptom-Solution Cycle

Having laid the question of *why* to rest, you can concentrate on present behavior. Any change will take place in the here-and-now, and that is where you must examine the symptom. For example, if a woman has fainting spells in department stores, focus on the exact progression of the symptoms of anxiety, dizziness, and collapse. Find out exact times and places and distances, what happened before and what happens afterwards, and what she says to herself as it happens.

It's best to describe the symptom as an action whenever possible. "Falling down in department stores" is better than "Feeling dizzy in department stores." And "Feeling dizzy in department stores" is better than the even more general "Anxiety attacks downtown." Be as specific as the situation allows.

Once you have agreed on the problem in terms of some undesirable present behavior, examine the client's unsuccessful solutions. Some unsuccessful solutions to fainting in the department store would be deciding not to faint, worrying about fainting, expecting fainting, not wanting to faint, feeling helpless about fainting, and so on, up to the point of just never going into department stores at all. The solutions form a vicious circle. All the desperate attempts to solve the problem serve only to perpetuate the problem. In fact, *the solution is the problem.* More active "solutions" like carrying smelling salts and wearing a med-alert bracelet in case she faints are really just more of the same non-solution. The solution to the problem of fainting is to stop worrying about fainting, which is precisely what she can't do—at least on her own, at the level on which she is trying to confront the problem.

(By the way, it is not necessary for the client to fully understand the circularity of his or her dilemma. It is only important that you get it clear in your mind, so that you can devise an accurate paradoxical prescription later in the process.)

Sometimes the symptom-solution cycle is fairly complex, especially when several people are involved in the same problem. For example, a teenager and his parents may come into therapy because the teenager occasionally goes joyriding in stolen cars or defaces school property and lies about it to his parents. The parents' "solution" is to watch the kid like hawks, and to accuse him of wrongdoing whenever they think he is being secretive. This leads to some false accusations, which make the son feel even less inclined to behave, leading to more delinquency, more lies, more surveillance, more accusations, etc. Being able to see the circularity of such a situation is essential for being able to pick the point at which to intervene with a paradoxical instruction.

3. Encourage Resistance

A very strong case could be made for making this the first principle rather than the third, since when practicing Paradoxical Intention you should begin your therapeutic work even in the way you ask for information.

A client's symptoms can often be seen as ways he has learned to affect or circumscribe the behavior of others, including your behavior as the therapist. Even symptoms, and the resistance to changing them, are the client's way of trying to keep control. Clients who sincerely want help will tend to resist the therapeutic process. They will withhold information about themselves at the same time they want to talk about themselves. This is a paradox in itself, and you should handle it paradoxically by encouraging their resistance.

Milton Erickson often tells clients to tell him only what they feel right about telling him—to *hold back* what seems too distressing *until* it seems all right to reveal the distressing information. This gives the client two messages: that it is permissible to withhold, and that a time will come (usually at the second session) when it will feel all right to tell all.

When you instruct a client to resist and he does, he is following your instructions even while he is resisting: you are still in control. He has the experience of following instructions even though he feels unwilling to do so. This makes him more likely to accept positive instructions later on.

A closely related technique of Erickson's is to act very reserved with reserved clients. In this way he gains clients' trust by appearing to be prepared to protect their inhibitions. Then he becomes increasingly open in the subjects he discusses, drawing the clients with him into openness.

4. Define Goal Behavior

You and your client must define a goal in terms of a change in behavior. This must be done in the client's language, in terms that the client can grasp and commit to.

In some cases, the goal will be a simple cessation of an undesirable behavior, such as not wetting the bed or not compulsively counting things. In other cases it will be more subtle, such as feeling relaxed and walking purposefully through crowds or being able to speak up at meetings.

As in the determination of the symptom, it helps here to be as specific as possible. Above all, the goal behavior must stress some kind of action—*doing* or *experiencing* something, not understanding something.

You may want to make an agreement that therapy is to end when the goal behavior is achieved, or that the achievement of the goal behavior will constitute a success, a cure, or the first step on the road to improvement. This will depend on how you are reframing the problem (see principle number nine).

5. Secure a Commitment to Change

Since the success of Paradoxical Intention depends on the client taking action, the burden of motivation must be placed on the client. Sometimes the mere fact that the client has sought help is sufficient indication of a commitment to change. If a bus driver develops an irrational fear of traffic and comes in for help at the first sign of losing her job, the commitment to change is obvious. In that case, you only need to project positive confidence that the change will occur, and get on with it.

Sometimes, the nature of a long-term symptom makes commitment to change difficult, because the symptom is perceived to be entirely involuntary, and therefore not subject to change by an act of will. For example, a lifelong stutterer may need to be asked a series of questions that apparently admit the permanency of the affliction, and yet open the door to the idea of change: "Would you be willing to only stutter on social occasions? At work but not at home? With adults but not with children?"

Making a commitment to change involves taking a risk. When a client's very *symptom* is the unwillingness to take risks, it becomes very difficult to secure a commitment to change. For example, a young man who has the goal of asking girls out and forming a meaningful relationship might be afraid to take the risk of asking someone out. His rule is "carefulness first" and everything else second. More drastic measures are needed to secure his commitment to change. The best tactic is the "Devil's Pact." You tell him that you have a plan that will solve his problem, but that he will not accept it if you present it as just a suggestion. You agree to tell him the plan only if he promises to carry out the instructions exactly, no matter how difficult, unreasonable, inconvenient, or embarrassing they are. Tell him that the plan is not physically dangerous, expensive, or beyond his capabilities, but that he will get no details of it until he commits to it ahead of time.

You might ask for his decision immediately, or suggest that he think it over for a few days, and then decide yes or no. He is forced into making a decision, which is therapeutic in itself. If he decides no, he admits that his problem is not all that important, and the implication is that you will not continue to help him in that case. Hardly anyone ever decides no.

If he decides yes, he is committed. Once he is committed, you can continue with your paradoxical instructions. From this point on, it doesn't matter whether the instructions are actually risky or difficult. The commitment is what you're after.

6. Set a Time Limit

Often this is done as part of describing the goal behavior. You should encourage clients to set their own deadlines or time periods for change. This underscores the general positive tone you want to set, and it shifts consideration away from the possiblility of change to the question of mere timing.

Sometimes setting a time limit is actually part of securing a commitment to change. For example, when you say, "I can help you with your problem by a fast method or a slow method, which would you prefer?" you are only ostensibly talking about length of treatment. By setting up an either-or question about time, you are securing the client's tacit agreement that change will take place—the only real choice is if it will take place sooner or later.

7. Prescribe the Symptom

Tell insomniacs to stay up all night. Order fainters to fall down. Instruct perfectionists to make mistakes.

This is the key to Paradoxical Intention. This is the reason you have so carefully described the symptom behavior and secured a commitment to change. You are now going to have your client perform the symptom behavior under your direction.

To understand why prescribing the symptom works, you must realize that your target for change is *not* the symptom. Your target is the *solution* that your client has been unsuccessfully applying to the symptom. The target in insomnia is not lack of sleep; it is the clients' attempts to force themselves to sleep. The target in fainting is not the loss of consciousness; it is the client's obsessive worrying about fainting. The target in obsessive perfectionism is not making mistakes; it is the client's irrational obsession with making mistakes.

By prescribing the symptom you are directing your client to seek what is habitually avoided, to disclose what is habitually hidden, to choose what is habitually rejected. The prescription seems paradoxical because it operates on the next higher level of abstraction above the problem. It breaks up the vicious circle of symptom-solution-symptom.

Prescribing the symptom changes the situation to one in which the false solution is no longer applicable: If you are following instructions to stay up all night, your habitual worries about whether you will be able to fall asleep are irrelevant. If you are instructed to fall down on purpose, worrying about whether you are going to faint and fall down is pointless. If you are following a plan that directs you to make a mistake every day, it's hard to stay concerned about your perfection.

The false solution *is the problem.* When you remove the false solution from your client's system, the problem also disappears. The insomniac who stops trying so hard to fall asleep is paradoxically able to sleep. The fainter who stops worrying about fainting paradoxically notices that she doesn't feel dizzy any more. The perfectionist who no longer worries about making occasional mistakes paradoxically doesn't make them as often and no longer finds making mistakes devastating.

8. Include a Variation

In prescribing the symptom, it is important to include a variation, however small, on the usual behavior. By controlling the duration, intensity, circumstances, location, sequence, or timing of a symptom, you gain control of the symptom itself. Every time you encourage symptomatic behavior with something changed, added, or taken away, it makes further change possible.

The insomniac who averages two hours of sleep a night is instructed to stay up all night (increasing duration). The fainter who collapses after entering a department store is instructed to collapse on the street outside (changing location). The perfectionist who worries about making unintentional, catastrophic mistakes is told to make calculated, small mistakes (changing intensity).

Often the change takes the form of a more unpleasant alternative or an exaggeration of the most distressing aspect of the symptom. For example, the insomniac who is told to stay up all night may also be given a more unpleasant alternative in the form of a task to perform. This task should be something that the client will dislike, but feels ought to be done—perhaps scrubbing the kitchen floor, meditating on the meaning of life, or balancing the checkbook. In the case of the fainting woman, having her collapse out in the street not only changes the location of the symptom, but also exaggerates its most distressing aspect, the public embarrassment involved.

Sometimes the symptom a client presents is physically dangerous or illegal. In that case, you will introduce a variation that preserves some essential aspect of the symptomatic behavior, but makes it safer, more positive, or legal. In the case of the teenager mentioned earlier in the chapter, it would not be advisable to prescribe the symptom of stealing cars and then lying about it. It would be better to retain the aspect of lying, but vary what is being lied about. For instance, you might instruct the teenager to occasionally do something about which his parents would be proud, and to do his best to keep it from them. The parents in turn would be instructed to continue their symptom of watching their son like hawks. The variation is that now they would be looking for evidence of what he had done right, instead of looking for evidence of transgressions. Thus the overall variation is to change the subject matter of the symptomatic system of acting-lying-watching-accusing-acting.

How you choose and introduce variations on symptomatic behavior will be largely determined by how you apply the next principle, reframing.

9. Reframe in the Client's Language

Reframing is the essence of most psychotherapy. Clients are led to look at themselves and the world in a different light. Reframing goes on at all stages of practicing Paradoxical Intention. It is not really a distinct step at all. However, if there is a single point in the process at which reframing is most important, it is at the point when you are prescribing the symptom and describing the variations the client is to perform. At this point you are essentially telling your client to do what he or she doesn't want to do. Your success will depend on how effective you are at reframing.

At the most mundane level, reframing is simply good sense: speaking in terms your client can understand. It is a basic rule of all therapy and communication. You don't talk to an 80-year-old woman in the same way you talk to a twelve-year-old boy. You match your tone, word choice, sentence length, level of abstraction, enthusiasm, and so on to the age, mood, education, sex, and social background of the person to whom you're talking.

On a more profound level, reframing takes advantage of the way people perceive problems. As you have seen in this chapter and in the problem solving chapter, the problem is rarely the stated problem, but is rather what your clients think about the problem—their opinion of it, way of looking at it, way of talking about it, their point of view, the frame they put around the problem, the language they use to describe the problem.

A religious person who is afraid of making mistakes may talk in terms of sin and punishment. A hard-headed businessman who is afraid of making mistakes may talk about responsibility, profit, and loss. Someone who had an unhappy childhood and is afraid of making mistakes may talk about insecurity, acceptance, and love. They each have a different frame around the same problem, and talk about it in their own unique language.

The language or frame may be described as the client's metaphor. Discovering the central metaphor that clients use to perceive a problem is like breaking a code. It's the key to how they see themselves and the world.   What has appeared disconnected and foreign falls into place, the rules of the system become apparent, and you can understand what before was gibberish.   More important, you can communicate ideas and instructions metaphorically and clients will understand them and accept them, whereas they might reject or misunderstand the same information if presented directly.

Some people's metaphors are fairy tales.   They are Cinderellas waiting to be discovered or they are fighting a wicked witch.   Some people are museums, dedicated to preserving and enshrining the past.   Others experience life like a tide-swept beach, accepting the oil spills, the flotsam and jetsam, anything that washes up. A client may describe a world divided into victims and bullies, or a world like a garden that must be patiently tended.

You can learn about the personal metaphor by observing the style of dress, listening to similes ("They say I'm smart like a fox"), noting favorite movies, songs, heroes, and fairy tales. Find out about important or repeated dreams. Notice unusual or repeated words and phrases.

At this point, it is important to stress that neither you nor your client need be concerned about *why* he or she has framed the problem in a particular way. You as the therapist need only be aware of *what* the frame looks like, what terms are used to describe it, and what rules are operative inside the frame.

It is also important to point out at this time that in the practice of Paradoxical Intention, the purpose of reframing is *not* to supply the client with a more realistic, "better," or "truer" frame. The purpose of reframing in Paradoxical Intention is to break the stranglehold of the old frame and to convince the client to follow your directions. For example, you might tell the religious client that the reason she is so afraid of falling into sin is that she is not conscious enough of her actual sinning. What she should do is to pick out a very minor, venial sin each day, and commit it with great attention to every detail of will, of the act itself, of the additional purgatorial torment it will add to her hereafter.   She should view this sin as an unfortunate but necessary way of achieving good through experiencing evil.

The businessman could be told that running a perfect business is bad business, because in the absence of mistakes there is no barometer to show where the business is weakest. Every day he should deliberately make a small, unimportant, but very real mistake.   Then he should observe what this tells him about the soundness and relative health of that area of his business.

The insecure client who is afraid of making mistakes may have sufficient respect for the therapeutic relationship, or have such a commitment to change, that little elaborate reframing is needed to get her to follow instructions. You might just say,

"I'm going to ask you to make a small mistake every day, and I want you to do it even if you don't see much sense in it right away."

In all three cases, the prescription is the same: make a calculated mistake daily. The difference is in how the clients' perceived problems are reframed in language that they can understand and accept, with the result that they agree to follow the prescription.

Properly constructed, a reframed paradoxical instruction has a certain nutty elegance that attacks a client's problem in two ways: It loosens the tight frame that they had around their behavior, while at the same time it agrees closely enough with their system and its language to make them want to follow instructions. Because the instructions allow clients to do what they have forbidden themselves to do, because the variations seldom make complete sense, and because the reframing language often follows skewed logic, many clients find Paradoxical Intention very humorous. It is common to have clients leave a session in a cloud of giggles, anxious to try what you have suggested, only to return in a week perplexed over their "failure" to follow instructions and their "unexplainable" lack of symptoms.

10. Secure Agreement to Follow Instructions

This is implied in the steps above. Often while you are securing a commitment to change or reframing in the client's language, you are also securing his agreement to follow instructions. However, it is always a good idea to conclude each session with a summary of the desired action and the clear understanding that the client agrees to follow the instructions.

Often clients leave after agreeing to follow instructions and then don't follow instructions. This is fine. Most of the time it doesn't matter at all whether they succeed in doing what you have prescribed. For example, the woman who has promised to fall down on the sidewalk in front of Macy's "forgets" to collapse on her way in the store. Once inside, she reasons that it would be all right with you if she fell down inside, where it's cleaner, or better yet, up on the third floor in the boutique, where they have softer carpeting. Somehow during an anxiety-free two hour shopping trip, she never finds the ideal place to fall down.

Likewise, the insomniac who is supposed to stay up all night meditating on the meaning of life decides that the way to fully concentrate on such matters is to stretch out on top of the bed and close his eyes. He wakes up the next morning after one minute of philosophy and nine hours of refreshing sleep.

The important thing is that clients understand your instructions, agree to follow them, and make a relatively sincere effort to follow them. Whether they actually accomplish the tasks you set is largely irrelevant, as long as the real goal of Paradoxical Intention is achieved: the elimination of the avoidance response.

11. Predict a Relapse

This is really a subset of the principle of encouraging resistance, and the general policy of keeping up a positive tone. It is especially recommended when a client is making fast progress. It recognizes the fact that relapses can happen, and if they do, it makes them part of the treatment.

Like any paradoxical instruction, the prediction should be couched in terms that the client can accept. You might say, "Progress is never a straight line upward. There are plateaus and minor reversals in the natural growth process. Often we have to take a step backwards to get our footing and continue forward. So don't be surprised if you find that your old problem crops up again in the next week or month."

When a client is progressing very rapidly, it is best to actually *prescribe* a relapse. Erickson does this very elegantly by suggesting that the client won't really appreciate his current state of well-being without comparing it with how bad he felt before. Therefore he should try to feel just as awful and confused and unhappy as before, just to notice the difference.

When you prescribe a relapse, you are giving your client the experience of control over his symptoms—if he can bring them back, he can get rid of them again. When you predict a relapse as a possibility, it is an insurance policy—if the client has the relapse, you were right, you're still in control, and treatment is perceived as proceeding according to plan; if the client doesn't have a relapse, it is seen as evidence that he is healthier than you thought.

Conversely, when a client is experiencing very slow progress, you should *advise a slowdown*. This is just another way of encouraging resistance, and often has the paradoxical effect of speeding up change.

12. Demystify and/or Disengage

When the problem behavior has been eliminated, it's time for you or your client to disengage. At this point you may want to demystify the Paradoxical Intention process by explaining what you have been up to. This is advisable if it won't undermine the results, and if the client may be able to apply the techniques independently in the future.

In other cases it may be better to let the process remain mysterious. Since understanding is never the point in Paradoxical Intention anyway, it's often a waste of time to explain the process.

Paradoxical Intention works because it mirrors the way people change spontaneously, without producing or requiring any insight into the change. Often a client will see you once or twice, follow or sincerely try to follow your instructions, and change so quickly that he or she has no idea that you had anything to do with it. That type of client will just break off treatment, and it's best to let him or her drift off under the impression that the problem "just cleared up."

Case Histories

The following case histories exemplify the principles of Paradoxical Intention, and are numbered to correspond to the sections given above.

Speech Anxiety

1. Forget Understanding. A client came to a therapist because he was very nervous when speaking before groups. His throat got dry, his voice cracked, and he stammered so badly that often he had to abandon his speech entirely and sit down in humiliation. His job required that he give oral reports in group meetings, and his speech anxiety was holding him back in his career. The therapist didn't bother going into the history of his public speaking, and didn't attempt to explore or help the client understand the underlying causes of his nervousness before groups.

2. Determine the Symptom-Solution Cycle. The therapist spent thirty minutes having the client describe exactly what he did before a speech: memorizing key phrases and quotes, practicing in front of a mirror, picking his suit up at the cleaners, making sure he had a fresh haircut and clean shave on the morning of the speech, chatting casually with fellow workers before the meeting started, taking a breath mint and a small drink of water, running over his opening sentence in his mind, approaching the podium, smiling at the audience, feeling the rush of anxiety and trying not to show it, beginning the speech, fighting to keep his voice under control and to appear calm, feeling the dry throat and hearing his voice crack, feeling obviously in panic, and finally succumbing to the nervousness and completely losing track of the speech. The therapist determined the problem to be speech anxiety, and the client's unsuccessful solution to be his attempts to cover up all signs of anxiety, which only made him more anxious, which made him still more desperate to cover up, and so on to collapse.

3. Encourage Resistance. Since the client was capable of talking freely about his problem, the therapist didn't encourage resistance at this point.

4. Define Goal Behavior. They agreed that the goal was for the client to get all the way through his next presentation on his feet. The therapist rejected the client's goal of "being able to figure out once and for all why I get so uptight." Nor did he include in the goal any mention of the client not feeling nervous, or the audience not noticing the nervousness.

5. Secure a Commitment to Change. Since the client was very afraid of appearing foolish or letting an audience know about his nervousness, and because the therapist had in mind an instruction likely to be resisted strongly, he chose to use the Devil's Pact. "I know one simple strategy you could adopt," he said, "that would solve your problem once and for all, but I'm not going to tell you what it is right off. If I told you right off, you might think it was just a funny idea that you might try one of these days. That kind of attitude won't work. The only way I'll tell you this strategy is after you promise me that you will put it into effect, no matter how crazy it sounds and no matter how much you don't want to do it." The client was intrigued, and after being assured that he would have to do nothing dangerous or beyond his capabilities, he agreed.

6. Set a Time Limit. This was done as part of the goal behavior, since the spring sales meeting was only two weeks away, and the client had to give a talk then. The time limit was reinforced by the establishment of a Devil's Pact, since the therapist stressed that there was only one treatment that would give such fast results.

7. Prescribe the Symptom. "First of all," the therapist said, "I want you to go ahead and be nervous as you walk up to the podium. As you turn to face the audience, notice how dry your throat is, how hard your heart is pounding."

8. Include a Variation. "Then," he continued, "instead of the opening sentence of your prepared speech, say: 'I'm so nervous I'll probably blow this whole talk. I doubt I can get through it, but here goes.' Then you can go into your speech."

9. Reframe in the Client's Language. The therapist reframed this instruction in the client's terms by saying, "When you hide your nervousness from the audience, you are lying to them. Then you punish yourself for lying by getting even more nervous, making the lie bigger. By telling them up front that you are nervous, you make an act of confession. Then you will be able to continue with a bearable level of anxiety that will tend to decrease rather than increase." The therapist chose this language because the client placed great stress on honesty and truthfulness, and because it played along with the client's tendency to be very concerned with the audience's reaction.

10. Secure Agreement to Follow Instructions. Since he had established a Devil's Pact, the therapist had laid good groundwork for this step. He reminded the client of his commitment, got him to state that he would follow instructions, and reinforced the desired behavior by having the client rehearse the opening statement several times in his presence.

11. Predict a Relapse. The day after the client delivered his talk he called the therapist to report that he had felt like "a damn fool" getting up in front of the meeting and saying he was nervous. However, he did manage to make the opening announcement, and then "breezed right through" the rest of the speech. The therapist told him to use the same statement to start future speeches. He warned him that a relapse was possible, and not to worry if he didn't breeze through every moment of every speech. "In fact," he said, "if you give the next three speeches perfectly, I want you to deliberately stammer and squeak in the next one. If you don't occasionally show your nervousness, your opening statement won't be taken as true, and you'll be telling another kind of lie—so make a point to show nervousness in the fourth speech, just to keep in touch with how it feels."

12. Demystify and/or Disengage. In this case the therapist didn't hear from his client for months—the disengagement was effected by the client. Nearly a year later, the client was still giving successful speeches, and called merely to ask if his treatment costs were tax deductible.

Insomnia

1. Forget Understanding. A middle-aged woman came to a therapist complaining that she only slept two hours a night. She was nervous, tired, and afraid of losing her job because she was too jittery and upset about not sleeping. The therapist didn't go into her sleep history, didn't pin down when she first started having problems, and didn't focus on her family life. He questioned her about exactly how she handled not sleeping.

2. Determine the Symptom-Solution Cycle. The woman would go to bed at about the same time each night, and lie awake worrying about her life—what she had to do the next day, and how she wouldn't be able to do it if she didn't get enough sleep. She tried relaxation exercises and listening to soothing tapes of sea sounds, but all through these remedies she kept worrying and stayed awake. She would finally drop off to sleep for two hours and wake exhausted. Whatever happened, she stayed in bed all night.

3. Encourage Resistance. The woman was desperate and quite willing to talk about her problem, so this was not necessary. In talking about herself, she did indicate that what she hated to do most was to think seriously about her life and what she had to do with it.

4. Define Goal Behavior. The woman and the therapist agreed that her goal would be to sleep eight hours a night.

5. Secure a Commitment to Change. Not sleeping gave the woman a perfect excuse to fail at her job and to avoid looking at other concerns in her life. The therapist decided to use the Devil's Pact to assure that her commitment to change would be strong enough to stand up to the loss of this secondary gain. He got her to agree to his plan before he told her what it was.

6. Set a Time Limit. This was not necessary, since the symptom was fairly recent, and since by its very nature it would have to be relieved quickly.

7. Prescribe the Symptom. The therapist told the woman that if she went to bed and noticed that she wasn't sleeping, she should make a conscious decision to stay up all night worrying about her life.

8. Include a Variation. The difference was that she was not to stay in bed until she dropped off to sleep toward dawn. She was to get up and sit at the kitchen table all night. The place and duration of the symptom were thus changed, and changed for the worse. A further worse feature was that while sitting at the kitchen table she was to purposefully review her life and think about all her failures and obligations.

9. Reframe in the Client's Language. The therapist said that by staying in bed all night she was not doing either thing right: She was neither staying awake nor obsessing about her life properly. He wanted her to do things properly by putting herself in a position where she couldn't sleep, and where she could concentrate on her life without the distractions of trying to sleep, listening to tapes, and doing relaxation exercises. The fact that she hated to think about her life was shown to be evidence that that was exactly what she needed to do.

10. Secure Agreement to Follow Instructions. The woman thought that the instructions were incredibly funny, but she was willing to try anything and had already agreed to the Devil's Pact.

11. Predict a Relapse. The first night after this session, the woman went to bed, couldn't sleep, and got up and sat at the kitchen table thinking about her life. She dropped off to sleep sitting up and slept for about four hours. The second night she went to bed and slept for eight hours. A week later she was averaging eight hours of sleep a night. She went in for her second session and was defiant about not following the instructions. The therapist forgave her and pointed out that she would probably have sleep problems once or twice in the future. If she had trouble sleeping two nights in a row, she was to repeat the instructions for getting up and sitting at the table.

12. Demystify and/or Disengage. The therapist explained that her old solution of staying in bed and worrying about sleep was her real problem, and that following the paradoxical instructions for one night had broken a vicious circle. He informed her that since she now knew the instructions, she could break the circle any time it was reestablished.

Social Anxiety and Fear of Going Crazy

1. Forget Understanding. A woman in her thirties came to a therapist and told her that she was very nervous around certain people at work. She had been to a staff party at which everything she did drew some form of implied criticism, and she got so uncomfortable that she had to leave. When asked what the exact problem was, she appeared confused and irritated at the therapist's interruption.

2. Determine the Symptom-Solution Cycle. The therapist found that she was making no progress toward uncovering the actual symptom, except that in general it had to do with anxiety and other people.

3. Encourage Resistance. The therapist said, "I'm glad to see that you are taking your time in telling me about your problem. It's important when you are just starting to talk to someone like me to go slowly. In fact, you probably won't get to what you're really worried about until our second session, and that's fine." the client immediately began to reveal what was really worrying her, without waiting until the second session. She was afraid she was going crazy. Every novel experience—smoking marijuana, meeting someone new, an unaccustomed twinge of dizziness, the sight of her tired face in a mirror—she took as evidence that she was going crazy. She constantly watched her own internal state for any sign of anxiety. When she found any, she worried about it, increasing the anxiety, increasing her conviction that she was going crazy, increasing her anxiety, and so on in a vicious circle. A few months before, her brother had been committed to an asylum after becoming increasingly anxious and withdrawn. She was afraid the same thing would happen to her, that her anxiety would increase to the point that she could not handle normal social contacts.

4. Define Goal Behavior. The client wanted to "stop worrying." The therapist privately expanded this to include the ability to tolerate novelty without undue anxiety, and the ability to see a social engagement through to its conclusion.

5. Secure a Commitment to Change. The client readily agreed that she would try anything that would help her stop worrying.

6. Set a Time Limit. They agreed that the treatment would take no more than 12 weekly sessions.

7. Prescribe the Symptom. At first the therapist told her to spend ten minutes each day staring at herself in the mirror, trying to look as crazy as possible. She was to keep this up for ten minutes, no matter how painful or boring it became. The therapist's reasoning was that this instruction was symptomatic in that it allowed the client to think about craziness. It included a variation by changing her fear of seeing craziness in the mirror to an expectation of seeing craziness.

At the second session, the woman reported that she had tried the instruction once, but that it was too frightening. It became clear that so much of her anxiety centered around looking crazy in the mirror that the prescription was just too confronting for her to carry out. Also, the therapist realized that the instruction was too emotionally loaded. She began to look for an instruction that would involve more overt action and occur in a social context.

The second, successful instruction was for the woman to arrive late at an upcoming luncheon date with a close friend. She was to allow herself to feel increasingly nervous as the lunch progressed. She was to show her nervousness by dropping her fork, answering questions as briefly as possible, and by finally cutting the lunch short with a quick statement that she didn't feel well. She was to get up and exit immediately, leaving her friend to pay the check.

8. Include a Variation. This instruction prescribed the symptom of social anxiety, worsening it to the point at which her greatest fear came true: appearing so anxious that she had to break off a social engagement. The main variation was that she was to reveal the anxiety that she normally kept covered up.

9. Reframe in the Client's Language. The therapist induced her client to perform this little act by pointing out that only really secure and sane people didn't have to hide it when they felt disturbed. She was to see how nutty she could be on a one-shot basis. The therapist openly challenged her by saying she didn't think she could act really outrageously.

10. Secure Agreement to Follow Instructions. The client, who was actually quite good at keeping up a show of appearances, rose to the challenge and agreed to be outrageous. She rehearsed mumbling an apology, getting up from a table, and leaving abruptly. The next week the client came back and said she had had a hard time appearing nervous at the lunch. She kept "forgetting" to be anxious. She found herself chattering on and on instead of answering questions with curt replies. The only thing she found easy was dropping her fork, which she did three times. Finally she had to drag herself away during dessert, and she finished up by leaving a twenty dollar bill with the maitre d' on the way out instead of stiffing her friend for the tab.

In the next eight weeks, similar scenarios were followed at home, at work, with grocery store clerks, school principals, and even the postman.

11. Predict a Relapse. Over the weeks, the client had several predicted relapses, until her general level of anxiety was low enough so that she could tolerate new experiences and see social situations through to their satisfactory conclusions. She learned that if she became anxious in the future, all she had to do was to pick a situation in which it would be all right to act a little strange, and the intense fear of acting strange would fade away.

12. Demystify and/or Disengage. The therapist continued to talk to the client by phone about once a month for six months. The client was satisfied with the explanation that the key to staying sane was to act a little crazy once in a while. The actual details of Paradoxical Intention were never explained.

The Paradox Game

Paradoxical Intention is one of the few therapeutic techniques that can be fun, but usually isn't. Although the instructions are often not easy, they do lend themselves to a game approach.

In this game, you will choose a problem to work on, describe the solution to the problem in terms of goal behavior, devise a plan to follow to achieve the goal, and evaluate your results.

You will probably not succeed in stopping any of your symptoms with the paradox game. Paradoxical Intention is usually effective in the hands of therapists, but is very difficult to use by yourself. You can try, and you may have an interesting experience, but you probably should not expect results. Don't be surprised if you decide to give up very quickly, concluding that the whole process is ridiculous.

This game often has curious side effects. As you move through each section, you may find yourself becoming bored, amused, irritated, confused, or nervous. This is normal. If side effects develop, don't fight them or try to change them. Simply notice them and continue on with the step you are doing. If they bother you a lot, you should probably stop playing the game.

The game takes about 20 minutes to complete. Sometime when you have at least that much time to devote to yourself, sit down in a comfortable, well lit place with a pen or pencil you like, and play your way through the Paradox Game:

The Problem

What is the one thing in life that you are afraid of experiencing, that you most want to avoid or stop doing? The thought that just ran through your mind is probably the answer. Write it down here in just one word:

_____

Take a look at the word you wrote. If it's an abstraction like anger, jealousy, or depression, change it to a word that describes something you do—an action or pattern of behavior. For example, instead of "anger" you might put "screaming" as a shorthand for "screaming at the kids to be quiet." For "jealousy" you might put "nagging," referring to how you nag your mate about where he or she has been. Don't go on until you have a single action word and you know the exact behavior it describes.

When does this behavior occur? _____
    (day or night, weekdays, after eating, etc.)

Where does this behavior occur? _____
    (at home, at parties, in bed, everywhere, etc.)

How long does it last? _____
    (seconds, a few minutes, two hours, days, etc.)

Who is around when it occurs? _____
    (wife, husband, no one, kids, doctors, strangers, etc.)

What exactly do you *do*? _____

_____

_____

(Go into great detail—your every action, experience, physical sensation, etc. Follow the exact sequence of events. Concentrate on physical actions and sensations only at this point.)

What exactly do you say to yourself? _____

_____

(Explore the brief thoughts that flash across your mind as the problem behavior is going on. Watch what you do and what you think as if it were a movie. You may be saying, "This is crazy...people will laugh...this is wrong...I'll get hurt," or there might be a single word that pops up and goes away so fast you can hardly catch it: "No!...Help!...Failed.")

What reasons do you give for this behavior? _____

_____

(Put down everything you think causes this behavior. If you have no theories about it, you may leave this space blank.)

How do you feel when you see yourself doing this behavior? _____

_____

(Nervous, afraid, ashamed, sad, angry, confused, worried, depressed, etc.)

Do you want this behavior to change?   ☐ **yes**   ☐ **no**

If you wrote "no," congratulations on being honest. You can go right on to the next section. If you checked "yes," you are probably ignoring reasons why you should keep behaving this way. Go on with a great deal of caution.

The Goal

Check at least five ways in which you would be willing to have your problem behavior change:

☐ It would happen less often.
☐ It would be only half as intense.
☐ I'd never do it again.
☐ It would only happen when convenient.
☐ It would last a shorter time.
☐ I could learn to enjoy it.
☐ It would only happen on weekends.
☐ I'd only do it during the day.
☐ It would happen but not bother others.

☐ I could decide when it would happen.
☐ It would happen but not bother me.
☐ I would be able to do the opposite.
☐ It would only happen on week days.
☐ I'd do it when people were around.
☐ I'd do it only once a month.
☐ I could do something else instead.
☐ I'd do it only at night.
☐ I'd do it only alone.

Now that you see some of the ways behavior can change, describe exactly how you would like your problem behavior to change. Describe the change in terms of a positive behavior or action. For example, if your problem is insomnia, the goal should be something like "get a minimum of 7½ hours refreshing sleep per night," not merely "be able to sleep." If you are afraid of open spaces, pick a goal such as "stand in the middle of the football field for five minutes without getting dizzy," instead of the negative phrasing "not be afraid of open spaces." Write your positive behavior here:

_____

(If you have trouble being specific about your goal behavior, ask yourself: When will this behavior occur? Where will it occur? How long will it last? Who will it affect? Will I do it alone or with others? What will the sequence of events be? What thoughts will I have while doing it?)

The Commitment

It's time to commit yourself to finishing the Paradox Game. Read the statement below and sign it. *Do not look ahead* until you have signed.

I _____ will play through to the end of the Paradox Game.
     your signature

I understand that I won't have to do anything physically dangerous or expensive. I further understand that I am not necessarily expected to change.

(Note: if you don't sign this statement, you may continue playing the game with the understanding that you definitely won't change.)

The Plan

This is the hardest part of the game, and the least interesting. You are about to decide to do exactly what you want to stop doing, to give yourself permission to do what you think you shouldn't, to indulge yourself in what you have been denying yourself. This is the part that doesn't make logical sense. This is where the side effects of boredom, irritation, amusement, and anxiety may come up. Just remember that such distractions are side effects, and that they will probably persist to the end of the game.

A. The Symptom

Refer to the first part of this game, and use your description of your problem to fill in this paradoxical prescription, as if you were ordering yourself to do exactly what you do:

I will _____ ,

(brief action phrase using the one word that sums up your problem behavior)

_____ ,

(when you usually do it)

_____ ,

(where you usually do it)

_____ ,

(for how long you usually do it)

_____ ,

(with whom you usually do it)

_____ ,

(in the usual sequence)

_____ ,

_____ ,

_____ ,

_____ .

(Add as many phrases or sentences as it takes to get an accurate set of instructions telling yourself to behave exactly as you behave.)

B. The Variation

Proceed here with caution. This part is extremely difficult and is beyond many people's capabilities. This step is included for the sake of completeness, so that you can see how to create an effective paradoxical instruction.

Go back and change at least one, but no more than two, elements in your paradoxical prescription. Change may involve adding something, taking something away, or varying something already present. Here are some examples of change:

Adding something:

Add a person to something you usually do alone.
Do it twice in a row, or more often.
Add an unpleasant but beneficial task.
Do it for a longer time.
Say something about it if you usually don't say anything.
Advertise what you usually hide.

Taking something away:

Do alone what you usually do with others.
Do it only once, or less often.
Remove one step in the usual sequence.
Do it without an associated action.
Do it for a shorter time.
Don't say something you usually say.
Hide what you usually reveal.

Varying something:

Do it with someone different.
Do it in a different place.
Do it at a different time.
Rearrange the sequence.
Say the opposite of what you usually say.
Do it slower or faster.
Do it harder or easier.
Exaggerate or minimize usual actions.

An important consideration is to pick a change that is possible for you to act on, but not too easy. For example, if you are subject to dizziness when you climb a stepladder, changing the place where dizziness occurs to a 100-foot high tightrope would be an impossible change for you. On the other hand, deciding to experience dizziness when changing from one-inch to two-inch heels would be too easy a change for you.

Invent Reasons

If you have followed instructions well so far, you have devised an instruction for yourself that seems absolutely crazy to you and will seem crazy to others. The less sense it makes, the better it probably is.

At this point you may be anxious to try your paradoxical prescription, and the mere fact that you have taken the trouble to devise it is reason enough to go ahead and do it. Fine. Skip this section.

However, you may be asking the question, "Why on earth would anybody do this?" You need a reason to do it and to justify your doing it to others. This is where the process of inventing reasons comes in.

Imagine that you are watching a movie of your life. You have come in after the start of the show, and you don't know the plot so far. You see yourself on the screen performing your paradoxical prescription. Fill in some plausible reasons why anyone would do that:

_____

(a therapeutic reason)

_____

(a religious reason)

_____

(a practical reason)

_____

(a financial reason)

_____

(a ridiculous reason)

_____

(a humorous reason)

_____

(a philosophical reason)

_____

(an emotional reason)

_____

(a devious reason)

_____

_____

When you have thought up as many reasons as you can, even impossible or fanciful ones, pick the reasons that make the most sense. Use them to complete this statement:

I am going to follow my paradoxical prescription because _____

_____

_____.

Do It

You now have an exact prescription to perform your symptom with certain variations. And you still have your problem. The sensible solutions you've tried so far haven't worked. Putting your paradoxical instruction into action could change your life. But without a therapist, most people find it too difficult to follow the prescription.

You may be the exception.

Results

If you follow your prescription, something will definitely change. Note your results:

First Trial Results: _____

_____

Second Trial Results: _____

_____

Third Trial Results: _____

_____

Don't be surprised or discouraged if your problem behavior flares up after a period of success in eliminating it. Change does not occur absolutely or overnight. In fact, if you progress too rapidly, you should plan on relapsing into your old pattern of behavior at least once. This will allow you to compare the feelings surrounding your old symptoms with the feelings brought up by your goal behavior. It will act as a barometer to measure where you are, how far you have progressed, and how much better you want to get.

Special Considerations

There are three common reasons why Paradoxical Intention techniques may fail:

1. **Unrealistic or inappropriate goals.** If your goal is to never experience grief or sorrow, or to love everyone equally, to to always feel confident regardless of circumstances, then Paradoxical Intention will probably not work for you, since such general, absolute goals are unattainable. You should go back and concentrate on a goal that can be expressed in a certain, concrete, specific behavior.

2. **Faulty instruction.** If you are unclear about what the undesirable behavior is, you may prescribe the wrong symptom, or add variables to it that are self-defeating. Go back, take a fresh look, and start over.

3. **Unwillingness to follow instructions.** If you find that you just didn't get around to following your paradoxical prescription, or that on second thought it just seemed silly or unworkable, then there is something wrong with the reasons you are using. Go back and discover a reason compelling enough to motivate you to follow the prescription.

Further Reading

Frankl, V. "Psychotherapy and Existentialism." **Selected Papers on Logotherapy.** New York: Simon and Schuster, 1967.

Haley, J. **Uncommon Therapy: The Psychiatric Techniques of Milton H. Erickson, M.D.** New York: W. W. Norton, 1973.

Watzlawick, P., Weakland, J. and Fisch, R. **Change.** New York: W. W. Norton, 1974.

Chapter 14

Orgasmic Reconditioning

Orgasmic Reconditioning uses directed masturbation fantasies to alter your sexual responses. With this technique you can increase your sexual arousal for someone you would like to respond to but have lost interest in. You can also learn to be aroused by someone you were not previously attracted to. Simultaneously, you can decrease your interest in inappropriate or unwanted sexual fantasies and partners.

In brief, Orgasmic Reconditioning directs you to masturbate almost to orgasm, using any fantasy that arouses you. When orgasm is inevitable, you shift your fantasy to the person by whom you wish to feel sexually aroused.

In this process, your chosen fantasy is substituted for your old, unwanted fantasy just prior to and during orgasm. Through reinforcement your new fantasy grows in its power to evoke sexual arousal and orgasm. Later, through the process of stimulus generalization, your new and appropriate fantasy helps generate sexual arousal with your chosen sexual partner in real life.

Orgasmic Reconditioning assumes that inappropriate or unwanted sexual fantasies and behavior are the result of learning, stemming from simple, mechanical conditioning which is often accidental or capricious in origin. Unwanted or socially unacceptable thoughts and behavior are not seen as defects in your character. They are seen instead as learned responses that you can choose to unlearn and replace with new sexual patterns that you feel are appropriate for your life.

In the process of connecting your sexual arousal to an appropriate partner, Orgasmic Reconditioning also presents you with an opportunity to rehearse in your mind your sexual behavior in response to your partner. This practice can serve as a blueprint for building a new and successful sexual pattern.

For example, Orgasmic Reconditioning can help you to overcome performance anxiety with your chosen partner. It desensitizes you to your anxiety by pairing it with sexual arousal and orgasm.

Orgasmic Reconditioning also helps you let go of unwanted sexual partners, objects, and fantasies. It turns off your sexual excitement for these at first by preventing them from being paired with orgasm, and eventually by blocking the connection between them and the earlier stages of sexual arousal.

Three factors make Orgasmic Reconditioning particularly effective. First, orgasm and sexual arousal are powerful reinforcements for behavioral change. Second, the technique allows you guilt-free pleasure as a prescribed effect of its strategy. Third, expecting and getting rapid improvement to a distressing problem provides an important incentive to maintain your commitment to change.

Symptom Effectiveness

Orgasmic Reconditioning has been found to be a useful technique to decrease sexual arousal in response to inappropriate partners, objects, and fantasies while simultaneously increasing sexual arousal toward a chosen sexual partner. It has also been proven effective in increasing sexual excitement toward a sexual partner who had previously been associated with anxiety or dulled sexual interest.

Orgasmic Reconditioning does not work for everyone. It is not a substitute for good communication skills. Sometimes Orgasmic Reconditioning effectively increases sexual arousal toward the appropriate partner but fails to sufficiently eliminate sexual interest in the old, inappropriate partner, object, or fantasy. Some people, particularly some women, have reservations about masturbation that may initially inhibit their use of this technique. If this is the case with you, consider reading Lori Barback's *For Yourself*. Also, the "Special Considerations" at the end of this chapter include some interventions that you may want to pursue in addition to or instead of Orgasmic Reconditioning.

Time for Mastery

Orgasmic Reconditioning generates positive results in one week to one month of once-a-day practice. The technique can be reapplied if sexual interest in the appropriate partner flags or sexual interest in the inappropriate partner, object, or fantasy resurfaces.

Instructions

1. List Arousing Stimuli

First, write a list of what currently turns you on. Be very specific, as in these examples:

> My neighbor's wife when she comes out to get the morning paper in her baby doll nightie
> Big penises

Big breasts
Having my genitals stimulated by a stranger
Members of my own sex
My boss/employee, especially when we are alone together or accidentally
    touch
Fur, silk, leather, rubber, etc.
Playboy centerfolds
Young girls or boys
Sadomasochistic behavior
Black garters and nylons

Next, what turns you off that you wish turned you on?   Again, be specific, as in these examples:

My spouse or lover
Someone of the opposite sex
Janet, who is twenty pounds overweight
Too small a penis
Small breasts
Ann, who is a "good woman"
Gary, who is very passive sexually
The woman I am dating who refuses to wear the clothes that turn me on
A physically unremarkable but nice person I recently met at a party
A remarkably good lover whom I don't want to lose because of my inconsistent
    sexual performance
Anyone interested in a serious relationship

2. Select and Describe Appropriate Fantasy

From the list of items that turn you on, select a sexual fantasy which will arouse you and move you to orgasm while masturbating. From the list of items that you *wish* turned you on, select the appropriate person you most want to be attracted to sexually. Clearly describe to yourself an appropriate sexual fantasy. Note as many details as possible. Initially your fantasy may be as simple as envisioning your chosen partner's face. As you practice Orgasmic Reconditioning, you will find that your appropriate sexual fantasy will expand.

If you are currently unattached you will probably want to have several variations on the appropriate fantasy, so that you do not become overly focused on just one set of physical attributes. You must decide what is appropriate for you, given your particular situation and goals. Unless you yourself look like a movie star, selecting a starlet to feature in your appropriate fantasy will defeat the purpose of the technique and probably lead to your disappointment.

3. Relax

Lie down and take time to relax before masturbating. It is particularly important to relax first if you have some reservations about masturbation or sexual fantasizing. You can use deep breathing, Progressive Relaxation, meditation, soothing music, or a warm bath to achieve a quiet, relaxed mind and body, ready for enjoyment.

If you take the time to relax after an Orgasmic Reconditioning exercise, it will help reduce any anxiety or guilt you may have regarding masturbation or fantasizing.

4. Masturbate

Use the sexually arousing fantasy you have selected. Continue this fantasy to the point where you feel orgasm is inevitable. Then switch to your appropriate fantasy.

Masters and Johnson found in 1966 that the onset of orgasm can be anticipated by two to four seconds. In women, an initial isolated contraction of the orgasmic platform occurs two to four seconds prior to the beginning of the rhythmic contractions of orgasm. In men, the prostate and perhaps the seminal vesicles contract once about four seconds before ejaculation. The feeling of the inevitability of orgasm reported by their experimental subjects corresponded exactly with these physiological events.

You may find making the switch in fantasy difficult at first, but you won't lose your sexual arousal if you wait long enough and make the switch at the point of orgasmic inevitability.

5. Gradually Stress Appropriate Fantasy

When you have successfully made this shift in fantasy four or five times, gradually move the switch to your appropriate fantasy toward the beginning of masturbation. If you experience a decrease in sexual arousal upon switching fantasies, you have switched too soon—go back to the original fantasy and switch at a higher level of sexual excitement. Eventually, you will be able to go through an entire masturbatory session using only your appropriate fantasy.

6. Discard Inappropriate Fantasy

As soon as you can, stop picturing the inappropriate fantasy both in masturbation and sex with a partner. This will gradually decrease and eventually end the inappropriate fantasy's power to arouse you. Through stimulus generalization it will also tend to reduce and eliminate your sexual interest for the actual partner or object involved in the inappropriate fantasy.

7. Enhance Interest in Appropriate Partner

Whenever you encounter or fantasize someone who turns you on, pair that person in your mind with the person to whom you want to be attracted. Shuttle back and forth in your imagination between the "turn-on" and your appropriate partner. In this way, your thoughts about your partner will occur in a context of arousal, enhancing your sexual interest in that partner.

Take care that this pairing procedure goes in the right direction—that you get more turned on to your appropriate partner. If the reverse happens, stop this pairing procedure.

Examples

Jane was married to Howard, an emotionally aloof and passive man. After eight years of marriage and two children, Jane had lost all sexual interest in him and left him. After four months of separation she realized that she still loved him and wanted the family to be together, but she felt depressed at the thought of a lifetime of uninteresting sex.

Jane's parents had instilled in her a strong taboo against masturbation. She had previously only masturbated twice, each time with strong feelings of guilt and anxiety. To prepare herself for Orgasmic Reconditioning, she read *For Yourself* and practiced some of the exercises recommended in the book, using relaxation exercises before and after masturbation to further reduce her tension. In a few weeks she had begun to overcome her old taboos and felt sufficiently comfortable with masturbation to proceed with Orgasmic Reconditioning.

Her first step was to list the fantasies which turned her on. These included sexual intercourse with her first lover, intercourse with a strange man who dominated her, and intercourse with a strange man whom she dominated. She found that she could easily imagine each of these fantasies.

She listed "making love with my husband" as her appropriate fantasy and filled in the details in her imagination.

Jane began masturbating once a day, using a lubricant to enhance the physical stimulation, as recommended in the book she had read. At first she found it difficult at the point of orgasmic inevitability to get a clear image of even her husband's face. But by the fifth day she was able to imagine him with ease. Then she began gradually ending her favorite fantasy earlier in the course of masturbating, spending more and more time fantasizing about making love with her husband.

At one point, Jane had a fight with Howard and returned to her old fantasies, excluding him. A couple of days later, however, she returned to Orgasmic Reconditioning. The first few days she found that she had to use her old fantasies up to the point of orgasm, but that she was able to push back the favorite fantasies and replace them with one of her husband much more quickly than the first time she used the technique.

To further increase her attraction to her husband, she would visualize him whenever she saw someone who turned her on during the day, or whenever she had a sexually exciting daydream. She would go back and forth between the "turn-on" and images of her husband.

Jane continued Orgasmic Reconditioning for four weeks before she was able to become aroused and have an orgasm by fantasizing solely of making love with her husband. During this time she also had sexual intercourse with her husband, making certain that she did not allow her favorite fantasies to continue through orgasm. As she did when masturbating, she gradually replaced her favorite fantasies with images of making love with her husband. She noted a small increase of sexual interest in her husband by the end of the first week, and by the end of the third week she was actively plotting ways of seducing him.

Following Orgasmic Reconditioning, her old fantasies would occasionally reemerge. She did not find them threatening because she continued to have a satisfying sexual relationship with her husband. However, she did routinely fantasize her husband at the point of orgasmic inevitability as a way of enhancing her sexual attachment to him and to guard against inappropriate fantasies once again dominating her thoughts.

Jane and her husband both took an assertiveness training class which enabled them to begin to reverse their passive and aggressive patterns of behavior toward each other.

Bob was a 28-year-old businessman who had masturbated with fantasies about "molesting" little girls since adolescence. He had never thought of acting out his fantasies with children, but he had once told his wife about his fantasies in hopes of persuading her to shave her pubic hair and dress as a little girl. She was horrified and he was shamed by her response. Their marriage deteriorated to the point that they were considering separation.

Bob had no qualms about masturbating. He was able to list and imagine clearly his fantasies of little girls as well as appropriate sexual fantasies about making love to his wife. He ceased masturbating more than once daily to increase his sexual drive. Within four days he was fantasizing about his wife at the point of orgasmic inevitability while masturbating and while having intercourse. He started rolling back the undesired fantasies of little girls and replacing them sooner and sooner with fantasies of his wife.

Whenever Bob saw or fantasized about a little girl and felt aroused, he would shift to fantasizing about his wife. He moved back and forth in his mind between the two, so that he experienced the thoughts of his wife while in a state of arousal. He was careful to make certain that pairing the two stimuli actually increased his attraction to his wife.

He had difficulty completely extinguishing his old fantasies using Orgasmic Reconditioning. At the end of four weeks he began Covert Sensitization as an additional intervention to eliminate his inappropriate fantasies. Within another two weeks the unwanted fantasies no longer intruded and he was able to masturbate and have sexual intercourse while thinking only of his wife. He felt better about himself and his marriage gradually improved.

Gary was a 19-year-old college student who had always masturbated, fantasizing *Playboy* centerfolds. He was a homely guy who was painfully shy around women, especially around the beautiful coeds to whom he was attracted.

Fearful of rejection, he played the clown. While his behavior got a lot of laughs and attention, it did not get him any dates.

He joined a social skills group at his college student health service. In this group he became desensitized to criticism and rejection, practiced being assertive with women, and learned how to behave on a date.

During the same period he practiced Orgasmic Reconditioning on his own, after reading an article describing it. He decided that he was unrealistic in going after *Playboy's* image of beauty and came up with fantasies involving several more appropriate women whom he liked. In addition to practicing the masturbation sessions, he would fantasize about one of his sexually appropriate partners whenever he saw or thought about a sexually exciting *Playboy*-type woman. He would shift back and forth between the sexually arousing image and the sexually appropriate one. In about three weeks he found he was becoming genuinely interested in the women about whom he had been fantasizing.

Bob began practicing the social skills he was learning in the health service group. In two more weeks he was dating two of the women he was fantasizing about, with growing sexual interest. A month later he was having satisfying sexual relations with one of the women.

Jean was a 23-year-old airline service representative who considered herself lesbian after six years of off-and-on involvement in homosexual relationships. She was an attractive, outgoing woman with many friends and interests. During the last year she had had an affair with a married man, which ended when his wife found out. Since that time she had met three interesting men whom she thought of dating, but felt no attraction to them. She continued to have occasional, brief affairs with other women. She entered therapy in hopes of learning to be attracted to men so that she might eventually marry and have a family.

Jean listed her most frequent sexual fantasies involving women as well as some that included her old married lover. She devised several sexual fantasies of young, single men she had talked to through her work who she thought were good-looking and friendly.

She began Orgasmic Reconditioning by using fantasies involving women or her male ex-lover up to the point of orgasm, then shifting to fantasies of the new men. After the second week she was able to masturbate while fantasizing only about the new men. Even when she had sex with a woman during this period, she was careful to fantasize about men from the point of orgasmic inevitability onward.

Within a month Jean found that she was becoming increasingly attracted to the appropriate men around her. To further enhance sexual arousal for these men she would during her workday intersperse her fantasies about her old male lover with thoughts of the new men. She eventually developed a sexual relationship with one of these men, and started using Orgasmic Reconditioning to increase her sexual excitement for him specifically.

Special Considerations

Lack of or misdirected sexual arousal can be caused by many factors. These factors may require therapeutic interventions beyond the scope of Orgasmic Reconditioning. Consider your own situation carefully. The following questions are directed at some of the more typical reasons for losing interest in a sexual partner or not developing a sexual relationship with someone who is sexually appropriate:

Do you have a good understanding of sex? If you have not recently read a book on the subject, consider the "Further Reading" section at the end of this chapter.

Do you have the social skills necessary to make contact with appropriate sexual partners? If not, refer to the "Further Reading." Consider joining a class or psychotherapy group to increase your social skills. Numerous singles organizations provide a wide variety of opportunities to practice your social skills on your own.

You can also create situations to desensitize yourself to social anxiety. For example, a shy socially awkward doctor desensitized himself to talking to attractive women by going up to them, introducing himself, and engaging them in small talk. He made a point of attempting at least three gambits before he would accept a rebuff. Often he was not rejected. He was soon asking women to go on low-risk dates, such as going to the hospital cafeteria for a cup of coffee.

Are you afraid of being dominated by your sexual partner? This is a common fear that often prevents people from developing satisfying intimacy. As one woman put it, "Every time I become sexually involved with a man, my usual independent spirit seems to dissolve and I feel as much a slave to him as my mother was to my father." A course in assertiveness training may help to break this cycle.

Are you so preoccupied with performance anxiety that the joy of sex is lost? The premium placed on a man's ability to produce and maintain an erection and on a woman's capacity to have orgasms often casts shadows over a sexual relationship. Again, see the "Further Reading."

Do you spend as much intimate time together with your sexual partner as you did when you were courting? One-tenth as much time? Sexual excitement does not flower in a vacuum—it requires some intimacy to sustain itself. Schedule some intimate time alone with your mate each week.

If you find yourselves not scheduling time together due to "other priorities," consider the possibility that you are avoiding each other. If your time alone together is filled with silence, fighting, and talking about others rather than intimate sharing, you are probably in need of some communication and conflict-resolution skills. Consider the "Further Reading" section, a couple's communication workshop, or couple's therapy.

Do you masturbate to orgasm? Do you feel comfortable doing this? If your answer is "no" to either question, see the "Further Reading."

Are you sexually aroused only by people or objects you find inappropriate, even after learning to be attracted to an appropriate partner? Consider Covert Sensitization or Aversive Conditioning.

Further Reading

Barback, L. G. **For Yourself: The Fulfillment of Female Sexuality.** New York: Anchor Press, 1975. (Learning to have orgasms and improve orgasms)

Campbell, S. M. **The Couple's Journey: Intimacy as a Path to Wholeness.** San Luis Obispo, California: Impact Publishers, 1980.

Friday, N. **My Secret Garden: Women's Sexual Fantasies.** New York: Pocket Books, 1973.

Fuchs, E. **The Second Season: Life, Love and Sex for Women in the Middle Years.** Garden City, New York: Anchor Press/Doubleday, 1978.

Hite, S. **The Hite Report.** New York: Dell, 1976. (Women's sexuality)

James, M. **Marriage is for Loving.** Reading, Massachusetts: Addison-Wesley, 1979. (Communication, problem solving, assessing relationship)

Jourard, S. M. **The Transparent Self.** New York: Van Nostrand Reinhold, 1971. (Communication)

Marquis, J. N. "Orgasmic Reconditioning: Changing Sexual Object Choice Through Controlling Masturbation Fantasies." In **Handbook of Behavior Therapy with Sexual Problems** by Fifcher, J. and Gochros, H. L. New York: Pergamon, 1977.

Masters, W. J. and Johnson, V. E. **Human Sexual Inadequacy.** Boston: Little, Brown, 1966. (Classic on sexual problems and what to do about them)

Satir, V. **People Making.** Palo Alto, California: Science and Behavior Books, 1975. (Communication)

Smith, M. **When I Say No, I Feel Guilty.** New York: Deal Press, 1975. (Assertiveness and dealing with criticism)

Zimbardo, P. G. **Shyness.** New York: Addison-Wesley, 1977.

Chapter 15

When It Doesn't Come Easy

The purpose of this book is to help you form a new attitude toward the stress syndrome. You are continually reacting to events that occur outside and inside your body, but what happens out in the world or inside your body cannot cause emotional pain until you interpret it as dangerous or bad. In the simplest terms, the pain depends on what you think.

Each of the techniques covered in this book are designed to change the way you react to things. But your old way of reacting has been with you a long time. It's habitual and familiar. This chapter takes a look at why old habits are hard to part with, even when they are clearly contributing to your pain.

If you find yourself skipping an exercise session or become aware that you are just going through the motions of the exercises, ask yourself some of the following questions:

Why am I doing these exercises?
Are these reasons really important to me?
What am I doing or would I like to be doing instead of these exercises?
Is this alternative activity more important to me than doing the exercise?
Can I schedule my life so that I can do both the exercises and this alternative
    activity?
If I do not do the exercises now, exactly when and where will I do them next?
What would I have to give up if I succeeded with my exercises?
What would I have to confront if I succeeded with my exercises?

Common Difficulties With the Exercises

The most common roadblock to Cognitive Stress Intervention is failure to fully utilize the imagination. To improve your ability to imagine, you can:

1. Focus on sensory modalities other than the visual, such as touch, taste, sound and smell. For instance, if you are trying to imagine your kitchen, the visual impressions may be very hazy to you. But you can focus your imagination on the smells of food cooking, the taste of a cold beer, the temperature of the room, and the texture of the wooden table top your fingertips glide across. Notice the predominant color in the room. Be aware of any movement. Pick out the major objects in the room.

2. Tape record a detailed description of the scene you want to practice imagining.

3. Draw a picture of the original scene you want to practice imagining as a way of tuning into the visual details. Notice which objects and details give the scene its unique identity.

Another major obstacle is simply not believing that a technique or exercise will work. Failure to believe is a cognitive problem. You repeat to yourself such discouraging statements as, "I'll never get better. . .it won't work. . .these sorts of things don't help me. . .I'm too stupid. . .somebody has to show me how." One of the basic tenets of this book is that you believe what you repeat to yourself. If you say any negative statement often enough, you will act in such a way as to make it true for you. This book will be of little or no value until you overcome the belief that it cannot help you. Refer to the chapter on Covert Assertion to learn how to block pessimistic automatic thoughts and create constructive alternative thoughts.

Boredom is a frequently mentioned barrier to success with Cognitive Stress Intervention. Many or these exercises *are* boring! But they work. Practicing them becomes a trade-off: a few weeks of occasional boredom in exchange for years of an unwanted symptom. This is the choice you may have to make every day when you do these exercises.

Another difficulty, often overlooked, is too rapid success. When you recover from a symptom too quickly, you should expect a setback. The danger is that you may say to yourself, "That was a snap to get over—maybe it wasn't a problem after all. I don't have to worry about *that* anymore." By minimizing a symptom's significance like this, you are laying the groundwork for its reoccurrence. It may gradually reemerge in your patterns of behavior, perhaps without your immediate awareness, and then you are stuck with it again. To avoid reoccurrence, continue Cognitive Stress Intervention techniques for a time after you are free of symptoms. If symptoms should reoccur, immediately resume the technique for a few "booster" sessions.

Fear of novelty is a well-documented obstacle to treatment success. Just following new directions may be anxiety-provoking for you. The directions may not quite fit your unique needs. They may be too detailed, cumbersome, or rigid. They may not be detailed enough and leave you floundering without sufficient guidance. It is important to remember that the directions are intended to provide a general outline, which you must adjust to fit your individual situation.

Recognizing that you have the power to change how you think and therefore how you feel forces a change in world view. You are no longer a helpless victim of good and bad fortune, but an active creator of your own experience. When you give up a symptom, your life changes. Many people prefer to hold onto a familiar though painful symptom rather than learn to cope with their new life without it.

Poor time management is a major roadblock to success. People who give up after half-learning a technique often explain that they were overscheduled and didn't have time for doing exercises. The real problem is one of priorities. Everything else had a higher priority than mental and physical health. The after-work drinks came first, the errands came first, the long phone calls came first, the television came first. You need to schedule your exercises just as you do other important parts of your day. Write down the time and place, and keep the commitment just as you would an appointment with a friend.

What's Your Excuse?

When you miss an exercise, find out how you justify it to yourself. Typical reasons are "I'm too busy today...I'm too tired...missing once won't hurt...I'm too bored...I feel OK today, so I don't need to do the exercise...I feel too awful today to do any exercise...my family needs my help...this isn't going to work anyway." Many of these excuses are partially true—you do in fact feel busier or tired, somebody may want your help, and missing a single session probably won't hurt. The part that isn't true is the implication that being rushed or tired or feeling the weight of obligations necessarily prevents you from doing the exercise sessions. The complete truth would be "I'm tired, I could do the exercises, but I choose not to," or "I could do my exercises, but I choose to focus on the needs of my family today."

The important point is that you take responsibility for your decision to choose one activity over another, rather than pretend that you are the passive victim of circumstance. You need to honestly assess your priorities. If your psychological health is not very high on your list, then you are not likely to make sufficient time to master any of these techniques.

Most people fall back on a favorite theme for avoiding the exercises. A common theme is, "I'm indispensable. Things will fall apart without me." An insurance executive had difficulty delegating responsibility. Her desk was piled with a dozen half-finished tasks and projects. She was nagged by the belief that any time taken for her exercises would make her fall hopelessly behind. After years of compulsive attention to detail and chronic fear of failure, she had become increasingly phobic. She was afraid of driving more than 20 miles from home, and had the sweats whenever she deviated from her normal routine. She was a victim of her irrational belief that she could never take the time to take care of her psychological needs. This belief had exhausted her and prevented her from attempting a solution.

The excuses you give yourself for not taking time to master a technique are likely to be the same ones you have used for years to perpetuate old habits. These excuses are based on faulty premises. The executive believed that only she could do the job right, and that the slightest mistake would bring her downfall. Her priorities were "successful business person first, healthy human being second."

Making a Contract

Often it is not enough to make agreements with yourself to master a particular technique. After a time you slack off and return to old patterns. Your commitment to yourself doesn't have the same power as commitments you make to other people. Nobody else feels disappointed or concerned when you fail yourself. Nobody knows about it. If you have a tendency to start and not finish things, make a contract with someone who knows and cares about you to really master a particular technique. Make sure you select someone whose good opinion you value, someone you will be afraid to let down. Use the contract form that follows, or a similar document to formalize the agreement. Both of you should sign it and keep copies.

Official Contract

I have decided to deal with my problem of _____

by using _____ technique(s).

I am committing myself to _____ to undertake
(person's name)

the following: practice the _____ technique

_____ times per day/week for _____ days/weeks. I will evaluate

my improvement only at the end of this period. I will immediately notify the above

mentioned person of any failure to uphold this commitment.

_____   _____
(date)   (signature)

I commit myself to taking this work seriously, and I will periodically check with

_____ as a reminder that your progress is
(your name)

important to me.

_____   _____
(date)   (person's signature)

If failing a friend isn't a sufficient motivator, write a penalty clause into the contract. Failure to keep your commitment might obligate you, for example, to donate $20 to the candidate or cause you hate most. Failure might obligate you to clean out the weeds in your backyard or to put off buying your new television set. If your penalty clause includes a donation, have your friend hold the check in a stamped, addressed envelope, to be mailed upon notification of your failure.

When Symptoms Persist

Occasionally you will be unable to rid yourself of an unwanted symptom, even though you have been conscientious and have practiced regularly. There are several reasons why this may occur.

Oddly enough, many people are attached to their symptoms. These symptoms may serve an important function in their lives. For example, your fears may relieve you of social obligations you find unpleasant, in a way that lets you avoid taking responsibility for disappointing others. A simple way to determine if your symptoms rescue you from unwanted experience is to keep a log of when your symptoms occur and what activities (or would-be activities) surround them. You might find out, for instance, that you thought you were nervous in all social settings, but are actually nervous only when people are flirtatious with you, and that you have been saying "no" by being nervous.

What needs are being met by your problems? How do your problems modify the way other people have to relate to you? Although you usually see your problems as inhibiting you, you may find from an examination of your log that they enhance your life. Also consider that your symptoms may be signals that you are not dealing effectively with some important conflict, and that you are repressing strong feelings. For example, you may be angry with your daughter for her many demands on you, but you say nothing because of your belief that all good parents are loving and giving.

If your symptoms do provide some secondary gain, it is important to find more direct ways of meeting your needs. Alternatives may include setting limits, learning to say "no," getting in touch with your feelings, and directly expressing what you want from others.

Often symptoms date back to a specific event or situation. Ask yourself when your symptoms first began. They may have been an appropriate and adaptive response to a stressful situation. How did you learn your symptom? For example, a young teacher was anxious when being driven in a car. She had experienced the symptom since childhood. In those early days she was frequently driven by an intoxicated father. If she became sufficiently frightened and noisy, her father would quickly bring her home.

At times you may share a symptom with an important person in your life as part of your identification with them. For example, you may share with your father a belief that people are victims of circumstances, accompanied by a feeling of depression and helplessness. As a result, any new challenge you encounter includes the expectation of failure and the opportunity to reinforce your world view. Ask yourself who in your family shares your symptoms. Examine their belief system and compare it with your own. The easily seen speck in someone else's eye may help you begin to notice the beam in your own.

Should symptoms persist, consult a professional therapist or counselor. The old patterns and beliefs which produce symptoms are difficult to identify. A professional may uncover your psychological culprits. Even when you know that certain patterns and beliefs are maladaptive, it is hard to give them up because they are so familiar. After all, change could make things worse. A professional can help you outline and implement a treatment program and provide support when the going gets tough. Your medical doctor, company health plan, or community health organization are good places to start looking for professional help.

Persistence Pays

Persist. Don't give up. Your ability to learn to handle stress syndromes and heal yourself is a tremendous power. You *can* control what you think, and therefore what you feel. You can change the structure of your life by altering the structures of your mind. You can take away your pain.

"It's supposed to be a professional secret," Albert Schweitzer said, "but I'll tell you anyway. We doctors do nothing. We only help and encourage the doctor within."

To order additional copies of this book, send your check for the cover price, plus sales tax if you are a California resident, to:

New Harbinger Publications
Department B
5674 Shattuck Ave.
Oakland, CA 94609